PSYCHOLOGICAL
REPORT
WRITING

PSYCHOLOGICAL

REPORT

WRITING

NORMAN TALLENT

PRENTICE-HALL, INC., ENGLEWOOD CLIFFS, NEW JERSEY

Library of Congress Cataloging in Publication Data

Tallent, Norman,   (date)
  Psychological report writing.

  Bibliography: p. 245
  Includes index.
  1. Psychology–Authorship. 2. Report writing.
I. Title. [DNLM: 1. Psychology. 2. Writing.
WZ345 T147p]
BF76.8.T33   808'.066'15   75-33309
ISBN 0-13-732503-7

This book is lovingly dedicated to Shirley,
who suggested that I write it

©1976 by Prentice-Hall Inc., Englewood Cliffs, New Jersey

PRINTED IN THE UNITED STATES OF AMERICA

10 9 8 7 6 5 4 3 2

Prentice-Hall International, Inc., *London*
Prentice-Hall of Australia, Pty., Ltd., *Sydney*
Prentice-Hall of Canada, Ltd., *Toronto*
Prentice-Hall of India Private Limited, *New Delhi*
Prentice-Hall of Japan, Inc., *Tokyo*
Prentice-Hall of Southeast Asia (Pte.) Ltd., *Singapore*

Contents

Preface, ix

Part One PERENNIAL CONSIDERATIONS

IN PSYCHOLOGICAL REPORT WRITING

chapter one

The Psychological Report: Purpose and Context 3

Mission, 3
Initiation of Psychological Evaluation, 6
The Psychological Report, 9
The Team, 11
Role of the Psychologist, 13
Personal and Interpersonal Dynamics of the Staff, 14
Continuity, Change, and Evolution in the Psychological Report, 16

chapter two

Pitfalls in Reporting 27

The Persistence of Pitfalls, 30
Pitfalls by Category, 32

chapter three

Responsibility and Effectiveness 50

The Client Is an Individual, 52
Points of View on Interpretation of Psychological Data, 56
The Flavor of the Report, 60
Orientation of the Report, 63
The Manner of Presenting Conclusions, 64
Primary Presentation of the Report, 66
Terminology in the Report, 66
Unfamiliar Concepts in the Report, 71
The Length of Reports, 72

chapter four

Content of the Psychological Report 74

The Multiple Purpose of Report Content, 75
Definition and Classification of Content, 76
Sources of Content, 78
Selection of Content in Terms of Relevance, 82
An Evaluation of Common Content Categories in
"Traditional" Psychological Reports, 84
Frequently Appropriate Content, 93
Inappropriate Content, 101
The Appropriate Emphasis of Content, 101

chapter five

Conceptualizing the Psychological Report 104

The Rationale for Flexibility, 104
How to Organize Reports: An Old Problem, 106
The Basic Scheme of Psychological Consultation, 106
Some Basic Considerations in Organizing the Report, 108
Theoretical Constructs and the Report, 112
The Client's Needs and the Report, 113
The Process of Conceptualization, 118
Exemplification: Conceptualizing a Psychological Report, 129

Part Two PSYCHOLOGICAL REPORT WRITING
PRACTICUM

chapter six

A Workshop on Psychological Reports 147

Cases and Comments, 148
Some General Conclusions from the Workshop, 179

chapter seven

Some Case-Focused Reports:

Exemplification of An Approach   181

Cases and Comments, 182

chapter eight

Some New Departures in Psychological Report Writing   213

Behavioral Reports, 214
Humanistic Reports, 219
Enter the Computer, 225
Quickie Reports, 236
Psychological Reports as a Group Psychotherapy Tool, 240
Psychological Reports in Journal Articles, 242

References, 245

Author Index, 253

Subject Index, 257

Preface

PURPOSE, SCOPE, AND SOME POINTS OF VIEW OF THIS BOOK

The psychological report is the end result of the psychological evaluation process. The best psychological instruments in the hands of an otherwise knowledgeable psychologist are to little avail if that psychologist cannot generate with their use, and effectively present, statements that likely will be pertinent to his clients' needs. Properly speaking, we do not validate tests, but rather the statements that are made with the aid of tests. Generally this means validating individual psychologists.

In this book we attempt to examine all pertinent aspects of the psychological report, from its rationale, to its formulation, to its effective use. The roles and intereactions of all those personnel who contribute to and utilize the report receive appropriate attention. So also do we recognize the specific requirements of the setting in which the report originates as exerting a strong influence on its form and content. Schools, various kinds of clinics, hospitals, prisons, courts, and social agencies share common needs for psychological information, but each makes its own peculiar demands on the report.

The theme runs throughout the book that the psychologist, rather than presenting "results" of his tests, interacts with his data and generates conclusions that might be useful in meeting perceived needs of the client in

his personal uniqueness and the uniqueness of his situation. The generation
of such situational conclusions *is* interpretation. *A* (test data) means
B (conclusions) *only* for a given client, with given needs, in a given situation.

The orientation is broadly *clinical,* in the original sense of the Greek *kline*
(bed). The bed symbolizes our attempts to deal with or rectify, broadly speaking,
problems of human illness. Thus, school problems, delinquency, or absence of
occupational goals are no less clinical matters than schizophrenia or
brain syndrome.

The psychological report is seen as an evolving instrument. How well the report
is written is of great importance, but, in contrast to past approaches to report
formulation, tips on rhetoric are not the central feature of this book. Nor do we
regard the psychological report writer, as has often been prevalent, as a "tester,"
whose function is "to pass along test results" to a "referral source" or to a
passive "consumer" of his efforts.

The psychologist relates to his tests, of course, but he is not "test-oriented."
He relates also to the client (patient, student, defendant or whatever), to his
associates, to the setting in which he works, to his methods and to the theories he
holds. To produce a good report he must also understand himself and be tuned
in to the interpersonal dynamics of the team.

It is against this background that various new departures and new roles for the
psychological report must be examined. A host of questions present themselves.
What contribution can the report make to the recently introduced Problem-
Oriented Medical Record? Can it prove a useful tool in behavior therapy, or in
the humanistic and existential therapies? Will it continue to be a viable instrument
for the therapies of the future?—Or will it perhaps be partially supplanted by
computer printout reports? Does the new team-generated report we have
described have wide applicability? Can reports be produced much more quickly,
efficiently, and economically?

For whom is this book written? For all psychologists (and student
psychologists, of course) who write reports, to be sure, but also for their colleagues.
Teachers, administrators, psychiatrists, social workers, counselors, and therapists
should not be passive recipients of the psychologist's efforts. They *should*
understand the basic rationale of the report and how they can actively contribute
to it. They *should* be in a position not only to make the most of the report, but
also to judge its quality, and, for better or worse, its writer.

I want to thank Professor Virginia Bennett of Rutgers University for her
helpful comments during the preparation of the manuscript.

N.T.

part one

PERENNIAL CONSIDERATIONS IN PSYCHOLOGICAL REPORT WRITING

CHAPTER ONE

The Psychological Report: Purpose and Context

The psychological report may be likened to an individual. It too reveals a continuity with the past, an ongoing process of change, and an evolution toward the future. Neither has the role of the psychologist remained static. In the early days psychologists were merely "testers" or technicians. Now they are professionals, and many function as members of a team whose needs they service. Thus there is need for efficient interaction of the psychologist with team associates, a process that requires mutual understanding. The psychological report can be instrumental in this process.

Psychological reports are prepared in many settings as a contribution to dealing with many questions. They have in common a concern with the individual, his problems, and, in many instances, the shared goals of the individual and those who seek to help him professionally. How effective a particular report is may be of great consequence for the individual about whom it is written.

MISSION

Each institution requiring the services of a psychologist has a general mission. The purpose of the schools is to educate and to enhance the quality of life of their students. Hospitals and clinics deal broadly with problems of health, physical and/or mental, or emotional. Juvenile training schools are charged with rehabilitating youthful offenders. Courts are concerned with dispensing justice.

Subsumed under such general missions are the specific missions a psychologist must deal with in his daily work. Each mission generally involves an individual, though groups and the interaction of individuals may also be proper topics of concern. Whatever the problem, the psychologist brings to bear the resources available to him and delivers needed information in the form of a psychological report, written, oral, or a combination of the two.

The question the psychologist is asked to deal with may necessarily be quite general. What is wrong? A child is doing poorly in school. Why? Is there an intellectual problem? Brain damage? A personality disorder? Autism? Excessive anxiety? Lack of goals or interests? A problem with authority figures? Situational stress in the home? An abnormally high intellect to which the curriculum does not cater? And so on. Or he may be asked to deal with an employee who is in frequent conflict with his superiors, performs his duties poorly, and is prone to absenteeism. What is the problem? Can the man be salvaged? How?

A commonly occurring problem is the diagnosis of a patient newly admitted to a mental hospital. The general problem area must be identified: Does the patient suffer from an anxiety neurosis or from schizophrenia? Or perhaps the problem is sufficiently vague to render an early differential diagnosis impossible. Beyond general definition of the problem, as required by a formal diagnosis, much specific information is needed. Answers may be sought to such questions as a person's problems in living, his inner conflicts, his major defenses and how well they serve him, the extent to which depression may be present, the possible existence of acting-out tendencies, and whatever else would appear to be of practical significance.

As the individual is better understood, increasingly specific questions may arise. Thus, "There is reason to suspect that this student's intellectual level as established by group testing is not representative. Please evaluate individually." "From what sort of psychotherapy is this person most likely to benefit?" "The patient's family indicates that a suicidal threat was made prior to admission. Are there any further indications that he might be potentially suicidal?" "Six months ago the psychological examination showed disturbances of the formal thought processes. The patient has since improved considerably. Are the thinking disturbances noted still present?"

Beyond generating descriptive material on an individual, the possible decision implications of the data must always be kept in mind and may be transmitted in the form of recommendations. These may be entirely implicit, as for example when the psychologist reports to a physician on the presence of an anxiety neurosis, neurotic depression, or hypomania. The accepted *medical* options for treating each of these conditions are limited, and the competent physician will prescribe accordingly. On the other hand, where psychotherapy is available, the psychologist may judge a person a suitable candidate for such therapy, and it is important to spell out from what sort of therapy he is most likely to profit. Will he, for example, most probably do best in group or in individual therapy, or should he have both? Should he have behavior therapy (and what kind), a structured ward program, insight therapy, or should this be avoided if possible; should efforts be primarily supportive, or is the essential need of the person practical guidance? How should staff react to the individual? To what extent, for example, should a student be coached, or to what extent should he be encouraged to remedy educational deficiencies on his own initiative? Should staff listen one-sidedly to a person's martial difficulties? Might this reinforce some unconstructive viewpoints and help him to rationalize self-defeating behaviors? Might this approach keep him from seeking competent marriage counseling with his spouse?

A variation of mission exists in the case of screening or routine evaluation. Here the report may be based on impressions gained from group testing, individual testing, or both. The goal is to generate a data base and to identify salient features such as problem areas, intelligence level, insight, and motivation for change. These data may then suggest the need for further evaluation. Subsequent events may also give rise to specific questions that require answers.

Innovation exists in the case of the behavior therapies and some of the humanistic approaches. The behavior therapist may approach his task by listing target symptoms or other behaviors to be changed and the treatment strategy to be followed. A bioenergetic therapist may take a similar tack. A humanistic-existential approach may include a report to be shared with the client as a vehicle of interaction between therapist and client. Examples of these several approaches are presented in Chapter 8.

Another recent variation of mission has followed the introduction of community psychology, the "community mental health movement." Here naturalistic observation takes on increased importance. Concern is likely to center about environmental rather than intrapsychic forces, since a community model of psychopathology stresses etiological factors that are "outside" rather than "inside" the individual. Although testing may not be central to a mission— it may in fact be eliminated or minimized, especially when the psychologist's interpersonal assessment skills are high—psychological instruments are typically a valuable resource. The competent psychologist, of course, can never overlook social and cultural factors, and he must be wary that what he derives from his instruments does not influence him to neglect the individual's unique situation.

Not to be overlooked is the teaching value of the psychological report. With every report the psychologist writes he should add to his own skill and knowledge. A well-written, well-conceptualized report, depicting a person in his individuality, similarly enriches the serious reader of the report.

When psychological reports are prepared for a case conference, and especially for a training seminar, the teaching mission of the report is uppermost.

INITIATION OF PSYCHOLOGICAL EVALUATION

Individuals become involved in psychological evaluation in various ways. As we have seen, many settings begin with some sort of routine initial evaluation. In a school it is often a teacher, counselor, or principal who feels the need for psychological information. In institutional settings it may be a nurse, a social worker, or a therapist. Where a psychologist functions as a hospital ward administrator, it is his decision which patients are to be evaluated. In highly traditional psychiatric settings, psychological evaluation (probably called "psychological testing") typically has been initiated at the request of a psychiatrist.

In some cases the psychologist initiates his own evaluation, as in routine screening or in the practice of behavior therapy. Where he does not, the mechanics of referral, the manner in which requests for evaluation are made, may have much bearing on the usefulness of the psychological report. The request for evaluation is the means, or should be the means, by which the psychologist is charged with a mission. When the psychologist understands the problem to be dealt with and can choose the most relevant and economical battery, the person who makes the referral and indicates the nature of the problem will be more likely to benefit from the psychologist's efforts. It is apparent that when referral is made with good knowledge of the psychologist's function and the kinds of information he is capable of eliciting, the assignment is likely to be a meaningful one.

Often the request for psychological evaluation comes in general terms when the raising of specific questions would be more appropriate. The overly general referral may come from less well-trained personnel who have difficulty pinpointing the individual's problems and possess inadequate knowledge of the psychologist's skills and procedures. Such a referral may read "psychological examination," "for psychological testing," "psychological survey," "Have the psychologist test this patient," or "Give this patient a Rorschach and see what you get." On the other hand, the psychologist is likely to be displeased with certain requests for specific information. He may not welcome requests for a formal diagnosis to be used largely for administrative record keeping rather than as a basis for treatment; equally unwelcome, in a psychiatric setting, are requests for an IQ, particularly when such information is asked for on a recurring basis or is the only sort of information requested.

When the psychologist receives a request for evaluation in terms that are inappropriately general, he has several options. He may simply ask the person seeking his services for more specific information on the problem. He may try to guess what is needed or wanted, with unpredictable results. Some psychologists prepare a general report that is likely to be both stereotyped and overinclusive, hoping somehow that one or more of the statements will hit the mark. Such documents commonly are referred to as "shotgun reports," with pejorative meaning intended.

In sharp contrast to such reports, we advocate *case-focused* reports. Case-focused reports attempt to reveal the unique aspects of persons, hence the psychologist tries to avoid stereotypes, theory-linked and test-linked statements. An attempt is made to interrelate statements, just as personality features in an individual are interrelated. Uppermost, the focus is on the mission; the client's problem(s) and the helping measures that should be taken are spelled out as recommendations or are clearly implied. In most situations recommendations should be explicit. The advice for which the psychologist in a school setting, for example, is consulted is far more important than general statements about the child. In a psychiatric situation, however, where psychologist and psychiatrist are in close working relationship and there is good mutual understanding and frequent contact, specific statements of recommendation can often be redundant. The options for treatment are broadly implicit.

Case-focused reports are further discussed on **pp. 114-118**. Numerous examples are presented in Chapter 7.

The psychologist should encourage the making of specific referrals, when these are appropriate, and discourage those that do not seem to charge him with a mission, especially those which simply request that a given test or tests be administered. If a request is made, the reason should be stated. A general request may simply be an example of poor communication; that is, the writer fails to express his underlying thoughts. Several surveys (Tallent & Reiss, 1959 a, b; Tallent & Rafi, 1965; Lacey & Ross, 1964) indicate that many psychiatrists and social workers in a psychiatric setting have definite ideas as to what sort of information they wish to receive through psychological evaluation. Perhaps they assume psychologists know how they can best render services to their associates.

Although we stress the value of the specific referral, cases definitely exist where a referral cannot be based on a circumscribed problem. Sometimes not enough is known about a person to raise specific questions. Or, circumstances may reveal an *apparently* clear-cut problem. "Is this patient homicidal, suicidal, depressed, likely to act out antisocially?" "Is his conduct attributable to mental deficiency; to brain damage?" "Is he ready for discharge from a hospital or clinic or from office treatment?" "Can he be rehabilitated, and to what extent?" "Will he profit from psychotherapy; if so, from what approach?" But often the problem is not so specific.

An example of a nonspecific problem is a patient who appears anxious, depressed, or schizophrenic. He evidences certain deviant behavior. It is too early to crystallize out definite problem areas. Is it not legitimate in such a case to refer the patient for psychological evaluation? Implicit are a number of specific questions about the patient concerning the dynamics of the situation, his defenses, ego strengths, reality perception, thought organization, severity of his condition, impulse control, central conflicts, goals, fantasies, interpersonal relationships, the psychoeconomic value of his symptoms, probable outcome, and indications for various sorts of intervention. If the psychologist is personally aware that the psychiatrist has such questions in mind, he has a broad, but definite mission. Such an assignment will be more of a challenge to him than a general referral he thinks represents a lack of reflection or acumen.

Daigle (see reference to Vernon, 1955) suggests that the emphasis should be away from *what* is to be known about a person and in the direction of *why* certain information is important. He refers to the first as charging the psychologist with "testing for areas," the second with "testing for alternative means of management." The suggestion appears to have merit. It is important that the psychologist know the alternative procedures that might stem from his evaluation so that the pertinent information can be specifically sought and the conclusions be presented so as to be most meaningful practically. Of course, this does not mean that "testing for areas" should or can be abandoned. The point Daigle makes has to do with emphasis. Often the test battery may be modified only partly, or not at all, because of an awareness of why certain information is needed. Daigle's recommendation applies partly to how the request for referral should be made and partly to how the psychologist should present his findings.

Request for psychological evaluation may be made with various degrees of formality. In private practice and in many institutions, a phone call or direct personal contact is often most expeditious. The important thing is that the needs of the referring person be set forth clearly. This objective can best be accomplished when there is a close working relationship between the person referring the case and the psychologist, whether referral is in writing or transmitted orally. Ideally, all cases should be discussed prior to evaluation. In this way the points to be explored can be jointly developed and differences in understanding the nature of the problem(s) resolved.

A written referral form may be most appropriate in a large setting or when there is a legalistic aspect (as in a court of law). In many institutions requests for specialized evaluations, medical or psychological, for example, are by regulation printed on standard consultation forms on which the report may be typed. Many such forms are extant. A sample form (from a medical setting) on which psychological evaluation may be requested, is presented on page 9. No particular claim is made for its merit: changes would perhaps have to be made in terms of the mission of any particular setting. But the main consideration for a referral form is the conscientiousness with which it is used. Most important is the detail and explicitness with which the nature of the problem is stated.

THE PSYCHOLOGICAL REPORT

At one time it was easy to define a psychological report. It was simply recording a child's IQ. Soon after the introduction of the Binet, however, it

Request for Psychological Evaluation

To:
Name of Patient:
Age: Sex:
Provisional or Established Diagnosis:
Nature of Problem:
(Reason for Referral)

Special Characteristics:

Psychological

Untestable _____
Poor Cooperation _____
Assaultive _____
Unduly Suspicious _____
Mute _____
Aphasic _____
Poor Understanding of
Language _____
(Why?)
Other _____

Physical

Limitation of Movement Which
Might Hinder Testing _____
(Specify)
Hearing Loss _____
(How Serious?)
Poor Vision _____
(How Serious?)
Is Visual Defect Properly
Compensated? _____
Speech Impediment _____
(Specify)
Other _____
Patient is: Ambulatory _____
             In a Wheel Chair _____
             Confined to Bed _____

became a matter of interest which subtests or items were passed and failed and
their year levels. Psychologists also began to determine whether the IQ
was representative or optimal and gave reasons for making such judgements
based upon the cooperativeness and motivation of the child or upon such
detracting factors as poor hearing or faulty vision. These "results" were directly
useful for understanding the child in a school situation.

There appeared to be some slippage of rationale when psychologists became
IQ testers in mental hospitals, since there was little correlation between a
patient's IQ and the treatment prescribed for him. The same may be said of the
psychologist's diagnoses and dynamics, probably following a Freudian
orientation. (This writer's early reports "outfreuded" Freud, and the reader
would be in line for laughs as well as instruction if any could be located.)
But many fine dynamic reports were produced to no particular purpose.
"They all get shock anyway" was the cynical but accurate observation.

Dynamics, an understanding of the individual, became increasingly important
(in the opinion of many) as psychotherapies multiplied and psychotherapy
became widely practiced. But whether to test or not to test depended, and still
does, on the orientation of the therapist or his "school." There is similar
disagreement on the matter of diagnosis. We are among those who insist
that diagnosis often does make a difference. It makes a difference to know if a
child's school deportment is related to a brain dysfunction or to something

else. It makes a difference to know whether a person is suffering from schizophrenia or others are suffering because of his hysterical personality. Misdiagnosed people are likely to receive faulty treatment. Diagnosis in the broad sense of making descriptive statements about a person routinely enters decisions made about a person, for him, or with him. Most psychological reports today consist largely of such descriptive statements.

In recent years psychological reports increasingly reflect a rationale. Many reports now are sharply focused and highly prescriptive. What is the problem and what can we do about it? In this tradition the behavior-oriented report is strictly a no-nonsense, business-like approach.

It is because the need for a guiding rationale for psychological reports is widely recognized that psychological reports now are seen in protean form, and properly so. Their content and organization obviously reflect the orientation of the writer and the use to which the report will be put. Thus a behavioral report would be quite beside the point for a psychoanalyst and an analytically oriented report would probably not be acceptable to a humanistic therapist. Early Binet and psychoanalytically oriented reports were about the individual— what is "inside" him, so to speak. Current reports may heavily emphasize social and cultural factors in a person's life, and his circumstances.

Reports also vary in the degree to which they are "traditional," i.e., built on early school and mental hospital models that stressed matters of the intellect and/or dynamics and pathology. The case-focused report may be regarded as a refinement of the traditional report based on explicit rationale. Behavioral reports generally differ from the traditional report according to the specific understanding of the therapeutic approach. Humanistically oriented reports may also depart from tradition for different but equally valid reasons. But because narrative, case-focused reports are highly flexible, they can accommodate both behavioral and humanistic orientations. These thoughts are developed and illustrated in subsequent chapters.

In general the psychological report may be defined as a document written as a means of understanding certain features about a person and his circumstances in order to make decisions about, for, or with him, and to intervene positively in his life. But the report need not necessarily be written. Commonly it is prepared by a psychologist for others, such as a teacher, a psychiatrist, or a court. But a psychologist—a behavior therapist, for example—might prepare a report for himself to outline a treatment approach. Subsequently, for the same client, he may note changes in the person and in his approach. His reports are in the nature of progress notes.

Originally the psychological report was a vehicle to transmit test findings. In many current reports, information gained from testing is minimal, or absent. Originally the psychological report took the form of a narrative. Now reports may consist of a terse listing of problems and proposed solutions. Computer derived reports may consist of sequential statements or a profile of characteristics.

Checklists of statements or adjectives are a form of report. Clinical notes, in effect, are reports. The oral relating of impressions also constitutes a report. A physician may ask a psychologist who has just completed two hours of testing, "Do you think he can make it?", to which the psychologist may respond with a nod, a horizontal shake of the head, or a gesture of uncertainty. Such is also a report.[1]

Custom written narrative reports continue as the single most used form. Most typically they are written by a psychologist for another person or persons.

THE TEAM

Team is a loosely structured concept that refers to the multiple input and interaction of two or more persons who share responsibility in dealing with clinical-type problems. There is no immutable definition of what personnel constitute a team, their roles, specific functions and interrelationships, or the power structure of the group. Teams may appear to have a central core composed of key, highly active and influential workers, plus a more peripheral membership, some of whom become involved in specific cases and absent themselves from others.

A psychologist serving as a team member commonly is expected to play a key role through contributing his report, observations, and other inputs. He may be "teamed up"—"permanently" or on an ad hoc basis with teachers or with a counselor, lawyer, probation officer, psychiatrist, or pediatrician. In a mental health clinic the core team may consist of a psychiatrist, a clinical psychologist, a social worker, and perhaps one or more nurses. In a psychiatric hospital the team is likely to be rather extended, consisting of a psychiatrist, a clinical psychologist, a psychiatric social worker, one or more nurses, one or more nursing assistants, and various counselors and therapists. This by no means exhausts the list. A parent or spouse may be asked to participate, and indeed, the patient himself may be regarded as a team member where he actively participates with staff in deliberating on treatment and plans for the future. In special instances an internist or a dietitian may be brought in by a team that normally is not directly concerned with the contributions of these professionals.

One of the most unusual teams coming to the author's attention is known as the Forensic Psychiatry Clinic. Based at the University of Virginia, at the time of this writing its staff includes three psychiatrists, a psychologist, two members of the law faculty, a psychiatric social worker, researchers, and students. With a total input of about 20 to 30 hours per case, citizens involved in both civil and criminal law actions are evaluated. The team is available to courts and lawyers in Virginia and neighboring states.

---

[1] The expression psychological report *writing* is retained in a generic sense. Most still appear in that form.

Another team format, a psychodiagnostic-therapeutic team, has been developed by the author in collaboration with nursing colleagues (Tallent, Kennedy, Szafir, & Grolimund, 1974). Situated in a psychiatric setting, the essence is to involve in the diagnostic process the nurses and the nursing assistants who are in daily therapeutic interaction with patients. Conceived as an expanded role for nurses, in accordance with evolving nursing concepts, all testing and initial interviewing is accomplished by nurses and assistants trained in these functions. This accomplished, the psychologist meets with his nursing colleagues, the test protocols and other inputs are collaboratively evaluated, and tentative conclusions are reached. The patient is next interviewed by the team. Then, in further discussion, conclusions are reached on the nature of the patient's problems, indicated treatment, and plans for the future. These are immediately incorporated in the nursing care plan and are orally transmitted to the psychiatrist and discussed. The psychologist then prepares his report with the dual objective of answering questions raised by the psychiatrist or other personnel, and providing material for the data base of the Problem Oriented Medical Record (discussed in context in Chapter 8).

The roles that the various team members play, the power structure of the team, the interpersonal dynamics of the team members, and personality features of the psychologist and his colleagues, all help to determine the quality of the psychological report and how effectively it and other of the psychologist's inputs will be used. Teams that function in psychiatric settings are particularly instructive in these several regards.

Such teams traditionally have been headed by a psychiatrist member—the captain of the team, as he has been sometimes called. Traditionally medicine has had an authoritative role, particularly with nonmedical associates—so-called ancillary persons, literally female servants or handmaidens. (And here we apologize to Women's Liberation for any unseemly connotations the literal meaning might have, and to any males who might resent being cast in a female role.) The practice of a well-known and respected setting is illustrative. Here a rigid seating arrangement was enforced at staff meetings. The senior physician occupied the chair at the head of the conference table, with physicians of lesser rank arranged in order, toward the far end. Next were seated the various "ancillary" personnel, by profession (from the highest on "down") and by rank within profession; the individuals at the far end of the table could thus entertain few illusions about their status.

Such hierarchical team structure is now largely in disrepute. A more democratic arrangement is widely endorsed and operates to a greater or lesser degree in many settings. It is sometimes referred to as a *wagon wheel*, because all members occupy a comparable position, and none is more distant from the hub of power than any other. In reality, the dominance, other personality features, and/or qualifications of the persons involved come into play, and, regardless of discipline, some are closer to the power center than others. Only in the sense of the lip service to the democractic ideal do all have equality. If the truth be known, a psychologist, a social worker, or a nurse may wield more power than the physician in reaching some sort of group consensus on the nature of the problem and the treatment indicated. A determined physician sometimes falls back upon the legal aspects of responsibility for making a "medical" diagnosis and prescribing treatment.

ROLE OF THE PSYCHOLOGIST

The role of the psychologist has evolved considerably since the emergence of the "testing movement," the high-water mark of the 1920s. At this time the psychologist, identified with an oversold IQ, was commonly known as a "mental tester." Even when projective techniques had well overshadowed psychometrics in many settings, Schafer (1954), writing from a psychodynamic perspective, persisted in referring to the psychologist as "the tester," a term also retained by Rosenwald (1963) and Appelbaum (1970), both psychodynamically oriented psychologists.

The proper role for today's psychologist, as a professional who provides information to others, is that of consultant, as explicated by Towbin (1960), formulated by Matarazzo (1965), and endorsed by Holt (1967). This is in sharp contrast to the role of tester, who is on a par with a laboratory technician. There are a number of distinguishing features.

The laboratory technician functions in a limited, circumscribed role for which the formal and practical preparation is much less lengthy and rigorous than that required for full professional functioning at the M.D. or the Ph.D. level, for example. The training of the technician is always in accordance with the principles and needs of a professional group and the parent group, through various direct and indirect means, influences the training program: the students are trained explicitly to serve the group. In carrying out his duties, the technician is asked to make a particular determination; his procedure will be the same regardless of the purpose. He does not interpret his findings, make a judgment as to which of his findings are relevant and which are not, or make recommendations. He is not sought out by the person who made the referral to discuss possible implications of his findings or the need for additional tests or subsequent retests. It is sufficient for him to give his results along with some indication of their reliability. The report of a psychological technician may contain such material as an IQ, various other requested scores, ratios, profiles, psychographs, or whatever raw responses might be requested. The instruments generating such data would be "ordered," for example, by a physician, an attorney, a school principal or counselor (counselors increasingly are doing their own testing), or a teacher.

The consultant, by contrast, is a product of advanced scientific and professional education designed to fit him for high-level, responsible functioning. He must have a grasp of both broad and specific knowledge and the ability to reach decisions that may be of major importance. His training is under the sponsorship and direction of his own discipline, and he claims a unique competence that is vital to his role. Thus the psychologist is thoroughly familiar with concepts of human personality, carries out psychological techniques with expertise, and works from a background of relevant research orientation. He must be familiar with the nature and the background of the problem at hand and the alternative decisions that might be influenced by his report. He must then decide on what kind(s) of data to seek, which of his findings have relevance, and how these can be most effectively presented.

The distinction between professional, or consultant, and technician is sometimes unclear to the psychologist's associates. One reason is that some continue to perceive the psychologist as a "tester." Another is the notion of test objectivity, which even psychometric instruments only approximate; the scores obtained on these tests need at least some interpretation. Tests can't think, as Schafer (1954) points out. In problems involving disorders of personality we do not have instruments which can be routinely administered and interpreted by subprofessionally trained personnel.

In the clinical-type situation, both the objectivity and validity of our tools have meaning as they relate to specific problems and to the confidence the psychologist is able to place in the relevant conclusions that can be drawn from them. Published indexes of validity for particular research stratagems are but rough guides, for the psychologist must reach his own judgments of clinical validity and meaningfulness in each particular case. Many tests, particularly tests of personality, are subjected to interpretive procedures that yield information not available from standard usage of the instrument, if indeed, in *practice* there is such a thing. Both knowledge and clinical acumen enter all phases of the evaluation process and, inevitably, some psychologists tend to be more effective than others in their clinical judgments (see Thorne, 1960, 1961). How does one assess validity of a test when even superficial familiarity with the process suggests that the individual is evaluated not by tests alone, nor by tests and interview data alone, but by psychologist-test data-interview data (test data typically referring to the information deriving from administration of a battery)? The input of other team members must also be taken into account. It is a meaningless abstraction in the individual case to speak of the validity of (for example) the Rorschach, the TAT, or the WAIS. Evaluation more reasonably involves the basic assessment units of "Rorschach-Psychologist A," "TAT-Psychologist B," "WAIS-Psychologist C," "Interview-Psychologist D," and, more typically, such units as "Rorschach, TAT, WAIS, Interview, Staff Input-Psychologist E."

PERSONAL AND INTERPERSONAL DYNAMICS OF THE STAFF

The mention of a "personal factor" in assessment is but an allusion to the personal and social realities that enter psychological evaluation. Schafer (1954) discusses at length the dynamics of the psychologist and how these bear on his relationships both with the person he is evaluating and with his colleagues. He lists no fewer than eight "types" of psychologists, types in the sense of salient personality failings. He discusses, for example, the psychologist with a defective self-concept, the rigidly intellectualistic psychologist, the psychologist with unresolved dependency needs, the masochist, and the sadist. All of these failings have influence on the sort of report that is produced. The sadist for example sets himself up as a "chief inquisitor." He concentrates on the shortcomings and weaknesses of his subject, and his report reads like an "exposé" or a "denunciation," what is called in this book "the prosecuting. attorney brief." This is discussed more fully on p. 56.

While the personality of the psychologist has frequently been emphasized as a factor in his ability to function as a therapist, in our preoccupation with tests and our zeal to establish their validity, too little has been written on the psychologist's personality as a significant factor in his evaluative work. One of the greater concerns with the psychologist's personality has been with the tendency of some examiners to confuse their own problems with their clients'. Such tendencies are readily seen in "trade-marked reports" (see pp. 55-56).

Perhaps an even greater source of difficulty is the confusion of the self-needs of a psychologist, particularly his role needs, with the needs of the task. It is readily acceptable that one's occupation be a factor in bringing about a sense of personal fulfillment. But in dealing with people who have major problems, who perhaps find themselves in a life-crisis situation, the psychologist must avoid intruding his own personal adjustment problems. Typical are difficulties with the self-concept; this may become evident in role aspirations that are hardly compatible with the specialized, technical functions of psychology. The psychologist may step outside his own specialized area and thereby neglect his duties. Sometimes this sort of problem detracts from effective contribution because the psychologist encroaches on the prerogatives of others rather than gathering the sort of information the team needs.

There are various other problems that seem to detract from the psychologist's function. These include attempts to seek insight through his clients and thus effect self-therapy; the opportunity to try, at some level of consciousness, to work through personal conflicts; the opportunity to see oneself as superior to another (the client); and the opportunity for catharsis, voyeurism, exhibitionism, or hostile expression. Sometimes the problem may be an ineptitude for psychological diagnostic work; sometimes the difficulty is one of lack of personal integrity. These latter deficiencies could go hand in hand, since the psychologist who cannot produce what is required may try to conceal his inabilities. One often effective maneuver is to slant the report in a manner designed to please the individual who has referred the case. Klopfer (1960) refers to such a document as the "Madison Avenue Report."

Any of these personality difficulties may find its way into, and readily be identified in, the psychological report. Often the report reflects self-conflict. Sometimes there is an expression of interpersonal or interprofessional conflict, with the report itself serving as a battleground. Both offensive and defensive maneuvers will be evident, but the aggressiveness is called up by defensive needs. Thus the report that is exhibitionistic and authoritative in tone, displaying apparent knowledge of words and theory, may be a way of saying, "I am as good as you, even better." (It has also been suggested that words and theory may be used to hide ignorance.) But defensiveness in other respects may be even more obvious. The excessively detailed omnibus personality description ("shotgun report") is an example, as is the heavily hedged report.

Needless to say, the mission is advanced only when team members are comfortable with themselves and with one another. There should be mutual respect and compatibility (obviously only a goal in many settings), and each should have a good understanding of the function of the others. But even under favorable conditions, the psychologist has need to interact with colleagues in a persuasive manner. The psychologist is often able to make highly confident statements that are at variance with the impressions of other team members who operate without the benefit of psychological tools. Because of this he has a selling job to do in the interest of his client (see pp. 197-202). Appelbaum (1970) suggests that a psychologist must also be a sociologist, a politician, a diplomat, a group dynamicist, a salesman, and, if you please, an artist. The word "salesmanship," Appelbaum advises, ". . . may denote high pressure, 'activity,' hucksterism; and, indeed, there may be clinical situations that do require some of this. Usually, however, the test report is more akin to institutional advertising, a low key presentation of evident factualness." In the long run, the psychologist's selling job is to sell himself. He can do this best by doing a good job and earning respect.

CONTINUITY, CHANGE, AND EVOLUTION IN THE PSYCHOLOGICAL REPORT

Today's psychological zeitgeist is a far cry from that of the early years of Binet testing. Our key instruments however have shown no particular evolution. The newer Wechsler scales, for example, are built essentially as was the Wechsler-Bellevue of 1939, and the standard Rorschach cards are identical to those that Hermann Rorschach bequeathed to us in 1922. But our understanding and use of these instruments have undergone a veritable revolution. The Rorschach *experiment*, for example, is now conceived as the *Rorschach systems* (Exner, 1969), systems that have traveled far from Rorschach's own modest estimate of the worth of his blots. The uses of assessment and how the psychologist's mission may be conceptualized have also undergone vast change. It should be instructive to note Wechsler's (1944) view of the first duty of a psychologist in a psychiatric hospital: ". . . to define, as an expert, the patient's intellectual level and to indicate whether the I.Q. obtained represents the true or merely the present level of functioning."

In just one eleven-year period, Dollin and Reznikoff (1966) noted a decline in interest in formal diagnostic labels. In 1956, 64 percent of the referrals received requested that a diagnosis be made, while in 1966 only 29 percent of the referrals asked for a label. In another study of referral questions, Korner (1962) found that over an eight-year period requests to clarify diagnosis dropped by some 60 percent, while questions pertaining to ego-functioning and defenses increased by 50 percent and requests to assess organic deficit quadrupled. Studying the topics discussed in psychological reports, Korner noted many changes. Discussion of ego defects climbed from 30 to 72 percent, evidently in response to the changes in referral questions just noted. Discussion of diagnosis dropped by a factor of five and anxiety by a factor of two. Talk of aggression dropped from 42 percent to 18 percent, and discussion of sexuality fell from 48 percent to 12 percent. Since we may assume that eight years could not possibly make much difference in how aggressive or sexual people are, we might conclude that the interests of the psychologists who wrote the reports had changed. In 1950 clinical psychology was a rather new profession with a preponderance of youthful practitioners. Perhaps with increasing maturity there is more mellowness and less voyeurism. But an alternate explanation might emphasize change in both the general and the psychological culture. Freudian concepts, in many settings, have yielded to other interests. Sex has lost much of its glamor, and aggression is all too prominent in our awareness.

In this context of flux there remain a number of persistent, nagging problems, among them the questions of validity and of the utility of psychological assessment. The latter pops up occasionally in the literature and continually in some settings where such assessment is carried out. This question has partly to do with the utility of psychological reports for traditional psychotherapists, but also with their utility for some of the newer therapies, particularly the behavior therapies and the humanistic therapies. These questions are addressed shortly. And modern economics being what they are, the cost of preparing a psychological report— from the initial handshake to the last period of the report—is an increasingly important, if underdiscussed, problem. As a specific example, we may read with nostalgia Odom's (1950) paper on the time required to do a Rorschach examination and be transported back to that halcyon era when a psychologist's time was not worth very much, and his paycheck confirmed it. Odom concludes: "The consensus is that the average test requires a little more than four hours, but that the total time required will sometimes be less than two hours, and at other times over eight hours." Even a leading practitioner like Beck spent at that time, ". . . on the average, from three and one half hours at the minimum to about nine hours at the maximum in completing a Rorschach test." As an exercise, let's translate that into today's costs. And remember that, typically, the Rorschach is only part of a battery. We could just price ourselves out of the market.

Utility of Psychological Reports

Let us consider the matter of utility, for if psychological reports are not useful, or cannot be made useful, we need not continue our discussion. There is a dearth of studies on this important topic, and the limited evidence available is contradictory and can be interpreted in various ways. It also appears that the methods of study themselves need to be evaluated, for the obtained results differ widely, evidently as a result of differences in research design.

Dailey (1953) reported that psychological reports contributed to clinical decisions in 26 percent of the cases referred for psychological evaluation. Cole and Magnussen (1966) state: "Traditional diagnostic procedures are only loosely related, if at all, to disposition and treatment." Breger (1968), examining psychological testing in clinical settings "in terms of its history and underlying assumptions," concludes: "Serious questions are raised about the clinical usefulness, logic and validity of practice." He refers here to the notion that diagnosis is a valid prerequisite to treatment and to psychology's emphasis on assessment and selection. Hartlage, Freeman, Horine, and Walton (1968) found that a sample of psychological reports ". . . was evidently of little value in contributing toward any treatment decisions for the patient." But these studies also concur that this state of affairs is remediable and accordingly make suggestions.

Studies by Dana et al. (1963) and Affleck and Strider (1971) reach quite different conclusions. Studying routine psychological diagnosis and treatment planning in a juvenile probation department, Dana et al. report as follows: "Predictions of prognosis were made from psychological reports with 80.5% accuracy. When recommendations contained in these reports were followed, 82.5% accuracy of predictions was obtained." The Affleck-Strider study also revealed high utility of psychological reports. The authors observe: "About two-thirds of the requested items of information were seen as either providing new and significant information or as providing information which confirmed information previously suspected, but which was not well-established." Further, ". . . it was found that 52% of the reports altered management in some manner, 24% had a minimal effect or confirmed current thinking, 22% had no effect, and 2% were felt to have an erroneous or detrimental effect."

How might such material be understood? With the exception of the study by Dana et al., all of these studies were either done in or had reference to a psychiatric setting. We might then evaluate the obtained conclusions against what little data are available on the utility of other diagnostic procedures in such settings. These are entirely impressionistic; the practical utility of such inputs as the anamnesis recorded by the psychiatrist, his mental status examination, the social history, and nursing notes have not been systematically studied and established. But even if only 26 percent of psychological reports make a difference in patient management and disposition, we might regard the psychological report as a very effective instrument indeed. Most of the diagnostic procedures done in psychiatric hospitals, though expensive, have in most cases little bearing on treating the mental and/or emotional problem for which the patient was admitted to the hospital.

Utility of Psychological Reports for Psychotherapy

Another way to evaluate the utility of psychological findings is to assess their pertinence for the practice of psychotherapy—essentially an open question. A therapist's opinion on the utility of psychological evaluation is recorded when he indicates whether or not he himself requests psychological evaluation for his client. Meehl (1960), on the basis of a survey of 168 therapists, disclosed that only 17 percent of the sample believed that the information provided by testing was of much value to them. Kelly (1961) reported that only half of his therapist sample always or commonly relied on psychological diagnosis. Hinkle, Nelson, and Miller (1968) found that approximately two-thirds of the respondents used tests, and those reporting frequency of usage indicated that they resorted to testing in 50 percent or more of their cases.

Mintz (1968) found that the upcoming crop of new therapists shares the beliefs of those practicing therapists inclined against evaluation. In rating items having to do with the usefulness of psychological reports, on the average, 65-75 percent of the respondents said "not at all." To the item, "In sum, how valuable to you as a therapist were the reports," the overall view was just below "slightly." Mintz concludes: "Thus, the reports seem to have little significant impact on therapy (other than confirmatory, at least)." He notes further: "Once therapy had begun, ratings of value of specific reports were largely a function of general attitudes to diagnostics. Overall ratings were so low that the general utility of such work may well be questioned."

In a later study, Wiedemann and Mintz (1974), surveying student therapists (psychologists, psychiatrists, and social workers) report that "In general the respondents indicated psychodiagnostics could be of significant utility." Other recent views give support to this contention. De Courcy (1971) and Lambley (1974), in case presentations, demonstrate how psychotherapy without assessment can present a distinct hazard. Klopfer (1964) goes so far as to state: "To deliberately blind himself and handicap himself as the psychotherapist by refusing to use the tools of assessment available to him, would seem a practice so questionable as to border on the unethical."

Allen (1942) regards as a "false belief" ". . . that if enough can be learned about situations and happenings and motives, change will take care of itself. Or they [some child guidance clinics] believe that a person can be changed by the 'complete understanding' a therapist acquires through having all these facts." In this regard it should be noted that many therapists, especially psychoanalysts, who routinely seek psychological evalution have little interest in the bulk of the content that finds its way into psychological reports, but seek rather information on the client's ego strength. It is important to assess the possibility that the client will decompensate in intensive, uncovering therapy.

Rogers' (1942) early position is that:

> . . . the place of tests in counseling treatment is not nearly so clear-cut. The disadvantage of using tests at the outset of a series of therapeutic contacts are the same as the disadvantages of taking a complete case history. If the psychologist begins his work with a complete battery of tests, this fact carries with it the implication that he will provide the solution to the client's problems. The point of view consistently maintained throughout this book is that such 'solutions' are not genuine and do not deeply help the individual, but tend to make him either resentful or overdependent.

On the other hand, he sees value in using tests

> with some individuals . . . handicapped in fundamental ways by their own inadequacies or the destructive quality of their environment. . . . In such cases to initiate psychotherapy without a diagnostic study may only plunge the client further into hopelessness as his own lacks are brought into greater prominence by his increasing insight. Consequently, even though the diagnostic study may interfere somewhat with a counseling process, it is definitely advisable here.

In his later *Client-Centered Therapy,* Rogers (1951) retains and strengthens his negative position. It is the client who must "diagnose" himself, i.e., experience a change in his perception. The therapist's intellectual knowledge of his client is for nought, since only self-knowledge can effect change. Rogers sees it as a net therapeutic loss if the client sees judgment and responsibilities as the prerogative of the therapist (the expert). Further, the client's feeling that he cannot know himself—only the expert can—leads to ". . . a degree of loss of personhood. . . ." Rogers even postulates dire social implications in the use of psychological assessment: it may lead to the control of the many by a few experts.

The advent of the behavior therapies and the humanistic therapies would appear to raise fresh questions about what the psychological report can contribute to therapy, or whether indeed it might detract from the process, or even damage the therapist-client relationship. Rogers' position would appear to anticipate the sort of arguments that some therapists in the current humanistic-existential orientation might advance. So far as the behavior therapists are concerned, an a priori guess that this group would have little use for psychological reports seems to be substantiated in numerous instances. Psychological assessment of personality is heavily steeped in the psychodynamic tradition, and, as we know, many behavior therapists have little concern for psychodynamics. Yates' (1970) double-barrelled blasting of psychodynamics and psychological evaluation is a good case in point. Greenspoon and Gersten (1967) observe that "The behavior therapist is generally as unsympathetic to the use of psychological tests as his nondirective colleagues, though for markedly different reasons."

There are other considerations, however, and many behavior therapists do, in fact, see merit in psychological evaluation. The earliest endorsement is perhaps that of Wolpe (1958) who found it useful to assess the degree of neuroticism in those he treats. Since then other behavior therapists have affirmed the value of assessment, and the need for research to link psychological findings to behavioral therapy has been pointed out by a number of workers. Greenspoon and Gersten (1967) set forth a basic position:

It is our contention that psychological tests should be of value to provide the behavior therapist with information that should be of value in doing behavior therapy. This contention is based on the assumption that the behavior on any psychological test should be lawful. We believe this assumption of the lawfulness of any behavior is necessary in a science of behavior, but it is an explicit assumption made by the behavior therapists. Having accepted the assumption of lawfulness of test behavior, we have proceeded to assume that the behavior on a test should be related to behavior emitted by the test taker outside the testing situation. The important issue is the basis of the relationship. We propose to look for this relationship in a realm that is considered critical in behavior therapy, sources of control of behavior. In other words, we believe that it may be possible to determine sources of control of the patient's behavior outside the test situation from his performance on psychological tests. Control is the essence of behavior therapy. That is, the behavior of the patient must be brought under the control of the therapist and/or others who are working with him. To effect this control the behavior therapist manipulates the consequences of a behavioral act of the patient. These consequences may be called contingencies or contingent stimuli.

Goodkin's (1967) position is:

Before employing any of a variety of efficient techniques, the therapist must determine what behavior he wishes to change. . . . Surely, the question of diagnosis is an important one. In discussing various aspects of the patient's life, there may emerge a considerable number of behaviors, which the therapist sees as maladaptive. Which ones are most relevant in aiding the patient? Which should receive attention first? Which should be left alone?

Dengrove (1972) emphasizes the need to identify target symptoms:

All behavioral therapies must be preceded by proper behavioral diagnosis. The application of behavioral principles is so precise that without a proper delineation of the 'target' symptoms one can go astray. It is worth emphasizing that target behaviors involve the identification of 'emotional habits' and faulty cognitions. 'Symptoms' merely denote the patient's awareness of the reactions that go on within him.

Fensterheim (1972), in speaking of diagnosis, includes the establishment of a formal diagnosis. Thus,

A differential diagnosis between a character disorder and a neurosis is often important. Neurotics tend to have anxiety and guilt connected with crucial problem areas and the treatment of choice usually centers around some form of desensitization and tension reduction. Character disorders, when they do show anxiety, usually experience it as a consequence of the symptom rather than as a cause of the symptom. Desensitization may be difficult because of the inability to experience anxiety when picturing scenes or even in the actual situation. At best, the desensitization procedures lead only to peripheral changes in that the patient becomes more comfortable with an inadequate mode of life. The treatments of choice for character disorder usually center around a combination of operant methods, aversive techniques, assertive training, education and guidance.

Similarly, he points out differences between the hysterical and the obsessive-compulsive neuroses, and the implications these have for treatment. A new discovery of the value of old-fashioned psychodiagnostics.

Cautela (1968) is convinced that "there is a widespread misunderstanding about assessment in Behavior Therapy." This misunderstanding, in turn has contributed to a belief that training in assessment techniques is not needed by the behavior therapist. But, "The first task of the behavior therapist is the identification of the specific maladaptive behavior or behaviors and any relevant antecedent conditions which might be maintaining that behavior." Cautela and Upper (1973) have in this regard introduced a behavioral coding system and also present a comprehensive position on assessment (1974).

Goldfried and Pomeranz (1968) present some very incisive reasoning on the relationship of assessment to behavior modification. They assert that

> ... one topic which has been conspicuously neglected by behavior therapists is that of assessment. ... Indeed, our thesis is that assessment procedures represent *a most crucial and significant* step in the effective application of behavior therapy. ... As we see it, the two most significant potential clinical uses of assessment material for therapy are (1) to delineate those target areas where change should take place and (2) to offer some information about the specific therapeutic technique which would be best suited for bringing about such change with this particular individual. In practice, assessment procedures have served neither of these two purposes in traditional therapy.

This latter assertion rests on the belief that the treatment a client in psychotherapy usually receives is more a function of the orientation of the therapist than of the client's problem.

> In the practice of traditional, insight-oriented psychotherapy, we would tend to agree that the need for detail and comprehensive assessment information prior to the treatment itself may exist minimally—if at all. From the viewpoint of the contemporary, behaviorally oriented attempts to *understand* and change human behavior, on the other hand, the development and utilization of appropriate assessment techniques is crucial. [Italics added.]

They quote with approval from Paul (1967): "*What* treatment, by *whom*, is most effective for *this* individual with *that* specific problem, and under *which* set of circumstances." A lofty goal indeed. The ideal case-focused report would address itself to all of these issues, together with *understanding* of the individual, the *why* of the recommendations.

Goldfried and Pomeranz give little attention to the sort of content the behavior therapist needs to fulfill his mission. They do identify thoughts and feelings as the sort of target behaviors that may be in need of direct modification. In presenting a hypothetical case, they indicate that assessment procedures point up a person who might "become anxious in unfamiliar situations" as "the type of person who would prefer to have other people look after and care for him" (a dependent personality). Thus, although the report writer might have to adjust his focus to meet the needs of the behavior therapist, it appears that the sort of content the behavior therapist seeks is not unfamiliar to the personality assessor. Ritchie (1968), for example, shows how conventional psychological evaluation may be used in the successful treatment of a case by behavior therapy.

Mischel's (1968) approach to assessment as a precondition for effecting behavior change is most precise. First, he defines "with *clear* behavioral referents" ". . . the problem behaviors and the desired objectives." His next concern is with " . . . the *exact* circumstances provoking the problem behaviors and to identify the conditions maintaining them. In light of this information the *particular* behavior change operations most likely to produce the desired objectives must be *selected.*" His view " . . . presupposes that different problems require different treatment and that *specific* treatments can be *designed* to fit them— an assumption that is basic to social behavior theory." (Italics supplied.)

The idea of specificity is also uppermost in the view of Goldfried and Kent (1972) who largely reject traditional personality assessment in favor of behavioral assessment; that is, an approach that favors samples over signs and selects items from such sources as direct observation, from role-playing, and self report. They distinguish between "traditional" and "behavioral" approaches to assessment as follows:

> Although the ultimate goal of both procedures may be essentially the same (e.g., the prediction of human behavior), the general approach which has been employed in the pursuit of this goal has differed. The traditional approach to personality assessment has been directed primarily toward an understanding of the individual's underlying *personality characteristics* or *traits* as a means of predicting behavior. This general approach to assessment is reflected in most of our currently available personality tests—both projective techniques (e.g., Rorschach, TAT, Draw-A-Person, etc.) as well as objective personality inventories (e.g., MMPI, California Psychological Inventory, etc.). The behavioral approach to personality assessment, by contrast, involves more of a direct measurement of the individual's *response to various life situations.* The techniques associated with behavioral assessment include the observation of individuals in naturalistic situations, the creation of an experimental analogue of real-life situations via role-playing, and the utilization of the individual's self-reported responses to given situations.

Behavior therapists need not shy away from psychological assessors because assessment so often gives attention to intrapsychic factors which most behavior therapists exclude from their work. Serious differences between the aims of behavior modifiers and those who focus on intrapsychic factors may be more apparent than real. Many professionals attribute differences in theories in large part to differences in terminology and emphasis. Among those who focus on the similarities between psychoanalytic and behavior theories are Shoben (1949), Alexander (1963), Weitzman (1967), Sloane (1969), Marmor (1971), Rhoads and Feather (1974), Abel and Blanchard (1974), and a task force of the American Psychiatric Association (APA, 1973), the latter calling for "crossfertilization" of viewpoints rather than parallel development and wasteful duplication of effort.

A strong case is thus made for the role of assessment in the various behavior modification techniques. Uppermost is the fact that behavior methods stress a logical, reasoned approach and that the steps and the rationale for taking them be expressed. The very concept of target symptoms carries with it the idea of careful aim. The task, then, is to specify clearly the classes of content that the behavior assessor must be able to develop. Further, the psychological report must sharply case-focus on the individual client, identifying the behavior in need of modification, the therapeutic modalities that might best effect change, and the rationale for believing that this is so.

As among behavioristic therapists, humanistic therapists too hold different positions on the value of psychological assessment to the therapist. There are polarized positions, both for and against assessment, intermediate positions, and positions polarized against assessment that nevertheless allow for exceptions. Part of the disagreements noted seems to center about what underlying assumptions are made about assessment methods and psychological reports, and how such instruments are actually used.

Rogers' (1942, 1951) assumptions about assessment—that, generally, it impairs the therapeutic relationship, sets up unrealistic understandings on the part of the client, and compromises the client's responsibility for his own growth— anticipate later views of May (1958), Bugental (1963, 1964), Brown (1972), and Hacker, Gaitz, and Hacker (1972).

May, however, seeks to make it clear that "Nothing we are saying here in the slightest deprecates the importance of gathering and studying seriously all the specific data we can get about the given person." He then gives specific examples of the sort of content that enters psychological reports. But such material, he indicates, is *about* the person, not *of* the person. Whether material *of* the person can be committed to words and to paper is not clear. First we would need clear definitions of *about* and *of*, and a means of distinguishing the two. By *of*, May seems to mean the configuration of psychological facts grasped about an individual in person-to-person encounter; this is a very valuable datum, but less complete than the configuration which also incorporates material gained from the use of psychological instruments. The basic theme of Chapter 5 is that all data in the psychological report should be presented in a meaningful configuration, and not as a listing of attributes or part processes.

Bugental's 1963 paper seeks to explode as a fallacy that diagnosis is basic to treatment. He regards diagnostic information as deindividualizing[2] the person, as "part-function" information. With May, he characterizes assessment information as *about* rather than *of* the person. In his 1964 paper he writes of testing as

---

[2] An etymological note is in order. Tracing diagnosis back to its Greek root, the *Oxford English Dictionary* lists such meanings as to discern, to distinguish, to learn, to know, to perceive. ("Perception is essentially a diagnosis," Herbert Spencer, *Principles of Psychology*, 1872). We know more about A to the extent we distinguish A from B, C, D, and E. Each increment of knowledge about A enables us to know A *more* as an *individual*, and renders us less likely to confuse A with B, C, D, and E.

depersonalizing the relationship and as taking responsibility from the patient. He regards testing as making the patient an object of study, as fostering dependency on the therapist, and as creating (unrealistically) a sense of certainty outside himself—the "certainty" of the one who applied diagnostic instruments or relayed his conclusions. Further, he believes testing takes time from the therapeutic task, interferes with encountering the patient as a total human being, and "the therapist may unwittingly use the test information to bulwark his own resistance to confronting his unsureness concerning the relationship with the patient." Bugental does, however, on some occasions, find a use for tests. Such occasions may arise when it is necessary either for the therapist or the patient to reach a decision on whether psychotherapy is indicated, or perhaps whether some other service might be more desirable.

Hacker, Gaitz, and Hacker are concerned with the effect of testing on the test *users*. They feel that using instruments " . . . themselves encouraged a dehumanizing orientation toward the people we had tested." Brown and Smith (1968), using Kotchen's (1960) 27-item self-report, questionnaire-type rating scale sought to measure existential mental health in Kotchen's terms that ". . . a mind is healthy when it has achieved a sufficient store of 'meaning' to enable it to master suffering and to direct daily action." Nevertheless, Brown (1972) ultimately concludes that ". . . to proceed psychometrically violates the major tenets of humanistic psychology." Specifically, he is concerned that psychometrics violates "the *image of man*, and the image of human relationship." This view is challenged by Craddick (1972) who argues that the ". . . separation of man into parts is antithetical to *both* the humanistic tradition *and* to personality assessment" (italics supplied). Craddick often shares his test protocol with the testee (his term), or with the testee and therapist simultaneously, as implementation of an ethical, humanistic viewpoint. He concludes: "I feel that each of Brown's demands for humanism could be met in testing." At the same time, publications emerge seeking to establish the value of psychometric instruments for gauging humanistic attributes such as self-actualization (Bonjean & Vance, 1968), [the Personal Orientation Inventory (POI) and the Comrey Personality Scales (CPS)] (Anon. EITS Research and Development, 1973). A mixed bag.

Fischer (1970) advocates psychological assessment, but notes that the testee must be a coevaluator of the protocol for ". . . to understand his past behavior, predict his future behavior, or identify feasible possibilities, the client's perspectives must be understood." Mosak and Gushurst (1972) follow a similar procedure. They regard psychological testing, rather than hampering, as helping to establish a therapeutic relationship. They emphasize the humanistic concept of openness: "Psychologic testing can be used very fruitfully as an introduction to the therapeutic process. This is often conducted most effectively in a 'double interview' where the major therapist presents his findings to a second therapist who serves as a consultant. The cards are placed on the table: the therapist says what he thinks, and the client is encouraged to respond with a similiar openness. . . ." Mosak and Gushurst see this approach as opening a relationship on an honest footing, and as engendering in the client confidence in his therapist. He believes the psychological report ". . . can be used in a number of ways to encourage a patient and arouse hope for the future." The humanistic psychologist must incorporate psychological assessment data in this approach as he appreciates their value.

CHAPTER TWO

Pitfalls
in
Reporting

Psychological evaluation, the results of which are formulated and conveyed in the psychological report, is widely accepted and sought as a contribution to the case study. In the opinion of many, however, psychological evaluation frequently could be of more value were the psychological report made a more effective practical document. There are many ways in which the report can fall short of its potentialities. Although these pitfalls are a hardy breed, most can be corrected. A first step in the right direction is to examine the criticisms commonly made of reports. Simultaneously, however, we must recognize that some of the problems in report writing stem from limitations in the field of behavioral science itself, and from shortcomings in our knowledge of how to apply it to practical issues.

The value of the psychological report is variously perceived, both within and without the profession. Dr. William Menninger (1948), during the period of his presidency of the American Psychiatric Association, suggested that "The diagnostic function of the clinical psychologist is now so well established . . . that the competent psychiatrist . . . would no more exclude the special techniques of the psychologist in his diagnostic studies than would a capable internist routinely exclude the findings of the roentgenologist." Since that time there have been gains and losses. Part of the responsibility for advancing the psychologist's contribution rests with the science and profession of psychology, itself. In the everyday conduct of his duties, however, the individual psychologist bears much of the responsibility for the effectiveness of his contributions.

With a positive purpose, this chapter dwells on the negative aspects that are extant in many psychological reports. The concentration of negative comments that follows shortly is an artifact of presentation, and the reader should not reach a pessimistic conclusion about psychological reports, which are widely regarded as doing a needed and valuable job. Rather, the purpose is to highlight those difficulties, often unrecognized, that many psychologists incorporate in their reports and that might be eliminated.

The categorized problems in psychological reporting presented in this chapter are based on returns from a large-scale survey, with an unusually high rate of returns—97.7 percent of psychologists, 81.2 percent of psychiatrists, and 97.2 percent of social workers, a rate achieved with the help of two follow-up mailings (Tallent & Reiss, 1959 c; 1960). Of slightly more than 1,400 clinical workers, psychologists, social workers, and psychiatrists who returned the form, over 700 completed the sentence (or paragraph) root "The trouble with psychological reports is . . . ." The product of this invitation to tell what is wrong is now in the author's files—118 single-spaced pages of pitfalls, which, to be sure, contain numerous instances of overlap. Interestingly, even this slanted sentence completion item, designed to draw negative comments, resulted in a number of favorable, even laudatory observations from nonpsychologists. Mingling with critical, occasionally caustic remarks, are statements like "No trouble at all. They are useful and helpful," "I like 'em," "I find the psychological reports written at this hospital excellent," and "The trouble with psychological reports is . . . there are not enough of them." More neutral are comments that better approximate the author's outlook in that they recognize values, shortcomings, and greater potentialities: "A lot of work to be done, but still valuable," and "I appreciate whatever help they give and would allow their improvement to stem largely from the psychologist's own efforts." Perhaps the most favorable observation to be made is that, of those who contributed their time and thought to completing a lengthy form, almost half did not see fit to complete the sentence root that "pulled" for negative comments.

The primary purpose in trying to find out what workers in the helping professions think is wrong with psychological reports is to develop a rationale for practice. The gathering of such opinions is an example of searching for a rationale by means of the "popularity" approach (Tallent, 1956). This method has certain shortcomings. A compendium of opinions should not lead automatically to conclusions, and certainly not to a systematic approach to practical issues. Reflection on the overall problem of report writing and additional pertinent research are required. The major asset of the popularity approach is that numerous insights may be obtained by "talking" with hundreds of workers through a survey form, yet, just as in talking face-to-face, the person seeking the benefits of the experience and observations of others must weight and measure the information received and act accordingly. In the present instance it is well not to be seduced by the expressions of praise for psychological reports, however well deserved. Several respondents who made favorable comments indicated that they had the good fortune to be associated with excellent psychologists. In other instances, there was a suggestion that the respondents were not sufficiently versed in the methods of psychology; they assumed that the psychologist knew his business and was beyond criticism by members of other disciplines.

The hundreds of negative comments received are particularly interesting. They are a sample of impressions gained by practicing professionals who have had experience in variously constituted psychodiagnostic-treatment settings, and need to be seriously considered. Although much of the criticism may appear valid to many psychologists, some of it obviously stems from disparity in training and orientation among members of the team, and solutions to the difficulties noted would appear to lie in the direction of greater interdisciplinary contact and understanding. It is also interesting that some of the comments are mutually contradictory; what are regarded as superior report-writing practices by some workers are seen as wretched by others. The solicited comments give much food for thought, and the reader of them must be his own judge. The writer disagrees with some of the criticisms as suggesting practices contrary to the effectiveness of the mission. Indeed, whereas in our sample an appreciable number of workers, mostly psychiatrists, criticized the offering of diagnoses, prognoses, and recommendations, Siskind's (1967a) group of psychiatrists questioned whether such practice should be criticized. The justification for accepting, rejecting, or modifying any sincerely made criticism is to be sought in the implication it has for fulfilling the psychologist's mission, which itself is an evolving function.

A second purpose in studying what others have identified as shortcomings of psychological reports is to gain a better understanding of the image the psychologist presents to his associates. Indeed, as we would expect, some of the comments made about psychological reports reflect the psychologist's image of himself. Such remarks bear on the entire group of psychologists working in clinical-type settings and upon the psychologist's role, attitudes, theories, and procedures, as well as on his individual skills. They thus afford awareness of certain value judgments made about psychology and psychologists by their associates.

A number of respondents suggest or imply as a base issue the individual psychologist's personality or a conflict of personalities among staff persons: "The trouble with psychological reports is . . . psychologists," "The trouble with psychological reports is . . . they try hard to be an M.D.," and "The trouble with psychological reports is . . . many are influenced by psychiatrists' diagnoses and comments." In practice, relations between psychologists and team associates range from those characterized by cordiality, mutual respect and interdependence, to hostility. A paper by Moore, Boblitt, and Wildman (1968) cites examples of the latter, more offensive (and amusing) than any received in the present survey. The authors report the following two examples: "[Psychologists] lack training in the basic sciences of medicine and Freudian psychology," and "Psychology is to psychiatry as astrology is to astronomy." (!) Many other illustrations suggesting personality shortcomings of a more serious nature will be found under various headings of criticism.

A comment on psychological services offered by a number of workers made no reference to the quality of reports as such, but pointed out that they often arrive too late to be of maximum use (Smyth & Reznikoff, 1971). This complaint should be borne in mind as the rationale of psychological reporting is studied. Might better consultation practices allow the psychologist to deliver more punctual, and thus more practical, reports?

The categories of criticism of psychological reports presented in the ensuing discussion are summarized in Table 1 at the end of this chapter. Issues of profession and role, and hence of rationale and purpose, find recognition primarily among psychologists and psychiatrists, although these groups tend to emphasize different aspects of the problem. Most of the criticisms suggest shortcomings that should be remedied in large measure through corrective training. Others point to the need for additional research.

THE PERSISTENCE OF PITFALLS

The bulk of this chapter, then, may be regarded as a compilation of pitfalls the report writer should be wary of. (We believe the listing is rather complete but hope that our readers will inform us of any we have overlooked.) While training may tend to reduce the incidence of errors in report writing, in general, available research suggests that they are a hardy breed. Each generation of psychologists must be taught anew. Both human traits and the nature of language itself tend to perpetuate errors. Only by conscientious effort at avoiding them can they be reduced. Other pitfalls will tend to continue, minimized only by diligent concern with certain problem areas, until research provides better solutions.

Thus, Lacey and Ross (1964), in a poll of workers in child guidance clinics, turned up a number of the same complaints noted in the Tallent and Reiss (1959c) study, though the percentages varied. Olive (1972) compared psychoanalysts' opinions of psychological reports in two different years, 1952 and 1970. Her general conclusion was that there is a disenchantment with the psychologist both as a tester and as a writer of reports. In both 1952 and 1970, the analysts' criticisms included "lack of clarity," "vagueness," "excessive use of jargon," "theoretical bias," "unreliability," and "overgeneralized." The 1970 survey revealed additional "bias to pathology" and "overlooking the patient's potential for change" (which we have incorporated in the "prosecuting attorney brief" [Tallent, 1958]), "too pat," and "too intellectualized." Rosen (1973), in a delightful contribution entitled "Alice in Rorschachland" also points out psychologists' concern with pathology to the neglect of health factors. He also chides those psychologists who "restructure reality along Rorschach dimensions of personality and terminology."

One gets similar feelings about report shortcomings from reading Holzberg, Allessi, and Wexler (1951), Garfield, Heine, and Leventhal (1954), Cuadra and Albaugh (1956), and Symth and Reznikoff (1971). Though differing in point of focus, the common denominator is the frequent occurrence of shortcomings in reports. All these articles may currently be read with profit. Similarly, Foster's (1951) succinct, half page of counsel to report writers is as pertinent today as when written. Just as teachers of rhetoric through the generations have been making the same corrections on their students' papers, so too has this writer noticed that students today tend to make the same errors as did students 20 years ago.

The persistence of pitfalls is well established in the faulty use of language. In 1950, Grayson and Tolman studied the definitions of clinical psychologists and psychiatrists for words that commonly appear in psychological reports. The first 20 words on the list were

Abstract	Bizarre	Defense	Father Figure
Affective	Bright Normal	Dependent	Hostility
Aggression	Compulsive	Depressive	Identification
Ambivalence	Constriction	Ego	Immaturity
Anxiety	Control	Emotional	Impulsive

The authors conclude that "The most striking finding of this study is the looseness and ambiguity of the definition of many of these terms." In a replication of this study 15 years later, Siskind (1967b) found that there was no decrease in the ambiguity of the same 20 terms. A study by Auger (1974) in which clinical personnel matched behavior descriptors with psychologists' definitions suggested that "either the behavior descriptors lacked specificity, the definitions were ineffective, or both."

Report stereotypy (pp. 52-56) continues to be a potent danger. A particular form of stereotypy, the Barnum Effect (Meehl, 1956) has been well studied by Forer (1949), Sundberg (1955), Ulrich, Stachnik, and Stainton (1963), Carrier (1963), Dmitruk, Collins, and Clinger (1973), Manning (1968), Snyder and Larson (1972), Snyder (1974), and others. So sturdy is the phenomenon that it seems likely that Barnum material may readily enter the report and escape detection by others. The psychologist needs to be vigilant in guarding against stereotyped material entering his report, and his colleagues should be wary of accepting it.

That many psychological reports are written so as not to be very useful, so as not to contribute to decision making, is a complaint that just won't go away. Dailey (1953), Cole and Magnussen (1966), Breger (1968), and Hartlage,

Freeman, Horine and Walton (1968), all conclude that many reports exhibit this deficiency and suggest solutions that are considered in the following three chapters.

But the ultimate problem is the limitations of the science and profession, aptly put by Holtzman (1964) in the title of his paper, "Recurring Dilemmas in Personality Assessment." His major points are (1) that personality assessment is hampered by lack of a clear, adequate, and consensual definition of personality; (2) that there is no agreement on what are the units and combinations of units needed to understand a person; (3) that personality variance and method variance are not readily separable; (4) that personality and personality assessment are overly culture-bound; and (5) that there are built-in moral dilemmas arising out of the individual's right to privacy and the investigative probing needed to (hopefully) understand his personality. The psychologist's awareness of such shortcomings, if nothing else, might keep him from wading out beyond his depth.

PITFALLS BY CATEGORY

The solicited comments on "The trouble with psychological reports . . ." were classified under five major headings and numerous subheadings. The first four pertain specifically to the performance of the individual psychologist. Problems of science and profession (Category V) have to do with issues psychology must identify and cope with. The matter of role conduct, so frequently commented upon by psychiatrists, may depend partly on how the psychological profession, through teaching and readings, structures the psychologist's role and how the individual psychologist idiosyncratically understands his role.

I. Problems of Content

The psychologist's diagnostic purpose requires that he convey to his readers a body of information or content that will contribute to the team's mission. Study of the psychological report calls for the examination of a number of problem areas that are associated with the use of this tool, but all considerations are aimed toward delivering the content most likely to be helpful in individual case situations. It is therefore appropriate first to turn our attention there.

Raw Data

Whether or not the psychologist ought to include raw data in his reports, or whether current reports contain too much or too little raw data, seems to have become an issue of major importance. To a large degree opinions on this matter are distributed along professional lines, the psychologists tending to be critical that there is overinclusion of such content, the psychiatrists being concerned that reports offer too little raw data, and the social workers being divided on this matter but perhaps siding somewhat with the psychiatrists. The way one views this issue is an individual matter, and there is widespread disagreement as to whether the liberal quoting of patient responses is a major asset or a distinct liability. From a plethora of comments, just a few are needed to capture three basic points of view. First consider these two opposing statements, reflecting as they do differing role concepts. They were written by a psychologist and a psychiatrist, respectively.

> They are too often descriptive rather than interpretive, leaving this job to the reader when really the psychologist is in the best position to interpret results.
> They do not contain enough selected raw material to permit the psychiatrist to draw his own conclusions.

A social worker differentiates himself from those psychiatrists who feel this way by pleading a lack of qualification to deal with data that are not meaningfully interpreted.

> Reference to specific psychological material in reports has little meaning to nonpsychologists.

And similarly, from another social worker—

> When reference is made to test cards, formulas, etc., the reader is often not familiar enough with the tests to understand what significance they have.

Improper Emphasis

Many clinical workers, especially psychologists, criticize that reports are written with improper emphasis. The implications of such a shortcoming might be far-reaching. It would seem to suggest, for example, that the report is not geared to the specific purpose(s) for which it is needed, a criticism mentioned many times and examined at greater length under another heading of this chapter ("Not practical or useful"). Improper emphasis may also suggest a faulty or incomplete knowledge of personality and of clinical operations—for example, what sort of finding is likely to prove clinically rewarding and what sort is not. The occurrence of such errors might indicate a deficiency of clinical judgment, presumably based on an unenlightened approach to the psychological consultation. That is, the psychologist evidently does not discriminate among his findings. There are many ways in which a psychologist may place improper emphasis in his report, at least in the opinion of others, but the following few examples show how report readers are likely to evaluate reports with regard to the appropriateness of emphasis.

> They seem to emphasize the personality state of an individual whereas I think more emphasis should be placed on the functioning of an individual in terms of what he is doing to and with other people. If the patient is to be

seen in psychotherapy, the psychological report should include some predictions about how he will probably act toward the therapist, how he will see the therapist, some goals for the therapist, and how the therapist might try to accomplish these goals and why he might do it in the way suggested. If the psychologist knows something about the limitations of the therapist who is to see the patient, then he should take these into consideration before he includes some of the goals of treatment.

The report of dynamics and structure of the personality is very good. There should be more attention to the strength of defenses or pattern of adaptation, i.e., how well will a reaction formation stand up under stress, for example.

Tendency to emphasize the unconscious to the neglect of the conscious goals and values.

Not enough emphasis is given to conscious, practical controls.

And an impassioned protest—

Too much pressure on sex. I know, I know, it is important, but, for heaven's sake, the world does not spin around the axis of . . . genitals.

Diagnoses, Prognoses, Recommendations

Offering a diagnosis, a prognosis, or recommendations in a psychological report seems to raise numerous objections, almost all of them from psychiatrists. In a sense this reaction is surprising, since many of this group actively seek such information from psychologists (Tallent & Reiss, 1959 a, b) but, as already pointed out, preferences in psychological reports are an individual matter. The dissenting group evidently sees the offering of such content as an encroachment upon its role, although quite often this meaning was not spelled out. A few quotes are more than sufficient to clarify this position.

In my opinion, the recommendation as to plan of treatment, chemotherapy, etc., is not appreciated.

They try to diagnose.

Recommendations should be excluded from psychological reports. It would seem more appropriate a function of a staff decision where other data can be considered.

Omission of Essential Information

Some readers and writers of psychological reports, particularly the latter, feel that reports omit essential information. That is, they evidently fall short of what is required for effective psychological consultation. It is not certain whether this criticism is based chiefly on the supposition that a fixed body of content ought to be conveyed in reports, or whether reports tend not to have information necessary to specific consultations. The following representative quotes, however, indicate what is meant so far as the individual respondents are concerned.

They do not present specific and essential data which would be helpful to a team conference or individual attempting to formulate a plan of treatment and working diagnosis.

They usually do not give any practical recommendations.

Seldom do they make recommendations regarding treatment goals, nor do they specify areas of strength.

In view of the content of the previous section the reader is probably wondering if it is possible to write a report to please everybody.

Minor Relevance

The problem of data selection seems to have arisen in any number of contexts. Some of the content of psychological reports is criticized as being not necessarily inappropriate, but of minor relevance. The flavor of such comments is captured by these statements.

Our prejudices often lead us to make statements which are of little import to the recipient.

They include data that I believe are not an essential part of the report, such as clinical description of the patient, social and medical data. This may be necessary to the examiner conducting the tests in evaluating the responses of the patient, but I do not believe this should be included as a routine procedure.

Unnecessary Duplication

The final criticism pertaining specifically to content, one made by a minority of workers, is that in some reports the same content tends to be repeated unnecessarily. There can be no dispute that where duplication occurs without good reason, such as to provide needed emphasis, its appearance is not defensible. Poor rhetoric can hardly be good psychology.

II. Problems of Interpretation

Irresponsible Interpretation

The psychological report, as the formal document of the psychological consultation, frequently reveals weaknesses in various aspects of the consultation situation. One of the more common of these evidently occurs before the psychologist begins to prepare his reports. The phenomenon is that of eisegesis, faulty interpretation based on personal ideas, bias, and whatnot. It has frequently been noted in the misinterpretation of scripture. Dana (1966) urges that eisegesis be trained out of student psychologists and suggests a way of doing so.

Several meaningful patterns of criticism of data interpretation emerged in the analysis of negative comments made about reports. So many different kinds of alleged interpretive errors were pointed out that for tabular presentation they are simply recorded as "assorted irresponsible interpretations." Of the workers who made any sort of negative comments on psychological reports, no less than 41 percent of the psychiatrists, 27 percent of the psychologists, and 22 percent of the social workers made criticisms placed in this category. An examination of some of the criticisms is informative.

Clearly written to please the psychiatrist for whom it is being written, often interpreting data to fit his known pet theories and thus rendered unscientific.

Tending to find more or less schizophrenia in every case.

They sometimes seem to reflect the psychologist's feelings about the patient rather than the data revealed by the patient's responses to the tests.

They draw conclusions from insufficient data, lack objectivity.

They are frequently too arbitrary, expressing theory as fact.

They are not sufficiently related to the tests they presumably are derived from.

The referral question is frequently vague, and psychologists frequently hate to admit it when the tests don't give much information, and so overinterpret what they have.

Too much "Barnum effect" (see pp. 54-55).

Too much . . . (unquotable) . . . invalid statements, overgeneralizations, stereotypy and evidence of lack of reflection and integration of the material into a meaningful picture of the patient as a person.

Just as the TAT reflects one's feelings, attitudes, desires, conflicts, etc., so do our psychological reports. We project ourselves. If we are integrated then so are our reports; if not—then?

Reaching into the test data certain of the examiner's own conflicts, usually discernible after seeing a few reports in which certain phrases and ideas repeatedly occur, without fitting into the entire picture.

Sometimes there is more of the psychologist than the patient in the test reports.

People who write them frequently feel they have to say something about all areas of the client's life, even those about which they have little or no information.

Occasionally they paint a darker picture than is true, possibly because not enough emphasis is given to conscious, practical controls.

Sometimes sweeping pronouncements are made, and I doubt that the best tests can support such big conclusions.

Overspeculation

A specific type of irresponsible interpretation frequently mentioned is overspeculation. From reading the criticisms, it is somewhat difficult to know what all of the speculating is about, or why psychologists feel impelled to do so much speculating. There does seem to be definite opinion that many psychological reports are characterized by too much speculation, that this practice often irritates readers, and that in some instances it reduces respect for the psychologist's contribution. Just a few illustrations suffice.

. . . speculative assertions beyond the realm of the testing results.

Too theoretical and speculative.

Too much speculation, reading between the lines, personal interpretation rather than reporting facts as observed.

Unlabeled Speculation

Many report readers are not particularly disturbed by speculation, provided that such interpretations are properly labeled. There do not seem to be group differences among the members of the team in this regard.

> Facts, inferences, speculations are often mixed and not labeled.
>
> The distinctions between reasonable deductions from the data, speculative extrapolations from the data, and the psychologist's clinical impression are not clear.
>
> If some indications were given for the bases for speculation and if clearly labeled as speculation.
>
> Many speculate and do not so indicate until questioned.
>
> Data is frequently overinterpreted. One can speculate but should label it as such.

Inadequate Differentiation

Another apparently frequent problem of interpretation is that psychological reports sometimes deal in generalities. It is charged that such reports do not differentiate among those evaluated. Psychologists seem to be roughly three times more cognizant of this difficulty than are their psychiatric and social worker associates.

> Too little individuality of descriptions.
>
> All too often they don't present a comprehensive, logical picture of a unique individual.
>
> Very frequently they are made up of too many stock phrases which do not give any real feeling for the individual client.
>
> They frequently involve too many generalizations about human behavior and fail to describe the specific person who is involved.
>
> They tend to present generalizations that might apply to anyone rather than to the particular individual.
>
> Typically, they present a rather stereotyped picture into which any number of patients—or other people—might fit, rather than describing the individual.
>
> They report in broad generalizations that, although they sound quite profound, really would apply to nearly any patient.
>
> Too often the generalizations are so great that one could visualize the same report having been made on the preceding dozen persons seen at staff. Reaching for psychoanalytic concepts too often is the reason (and I am psychoanalytically oriented).
>
> They tend to rely on vague, psychoanalytically-oriented phrases which fail to convey an individualized picture of the client. Their vocabulary is excellent but what is lacking is a feeling for the client's individuality as a troubled human being.

III. Problems of Psychologist's Attitude and Orientation

A number of difficulties in the writing of psychological reports were singled out as more or less direct reflections of the psychologist's attitude and orientation. That is, many of the criticisms seemed more meaningful in terms of ultimate improvement when emphasis is related to certain personal features of the psychologist than to the end product.

Not Practical or Useful

The most frequent criticism made of the psychologist's attitude or orientation is that his report is not written with a practical or useful purpose in mind. Psychologists identify the existence of such a deficiency far more frequently than do social workers and psychiatrists. The examples which follow reflect some of the more cogent observations regarding this difficulty.

> Our prejudices often lead us to make statements which are of little import to the recipient and to ignore or deal lightly with the objective reason for the referral.
> Their lack of function and value to the person.
> Often lack of comprehensibility in terms of a real life treatment program.
> They are often written without a clear idea of the practical "users" or "consumers" on the receiving end.
> In my view we need to write more in the spirit of an operational approach.
> Many writers forget the purpose(s) of their reports and wander all over the psychic range, even when they are asked for a relatively clear-cut opinion.
> They're too sophisticated, too impractical for the people who rely upon the information they dispense.
> They are not pertinent to the purpose desired.
> They seem at times very professional but useless in terms of the personality of the patient.
> They are too often written to satisfy the interest of the psychologist rather than for the clinical application and understanding.

Exhibitionism

That psychological reports are sometimes seen as exhibitionistic calls up a good deal of comment, especially from psychologists. A number of such comments refer to high-flown terminology in psychological reports, but do not mention exhibitionism as such. Those so disposed should find it easy to interpret a prominent dynamic in a number of psychologists via the following remarks. In fact, gratuitous interpretations are already built into some of them.

> They are written in stilted psychological terms to boost the ego of the psychologist.
> They are attempts on the part of the examiner to show what he can do rather than what the patient is.
> Reports delight in including details of findings which are obviously comprehensible only to one who has made a study of psychological testing or is versed in the finer significance of statistical research expressions.
> Such reports occasionally produce the feeling that words of less than four to six syllables and sentences with less than two thoughts will convince the reader that the writer is too simple.

It is not necessary to impress the reader with the psychologist's mentality.
Their reports reflect their needs to shine as a psychoanalytic beacon in
revealing the dark, deep secrets they have observed.
Reports should be concise and clear without an attempt to impress the
reader with the erudition of the person who performed the test.

Too Authoritative

Reports which convey an authoritative stamp may have a motivation similar to
those regarded as exhibitionistic. Their effect on the reader, however, seems to be
different. Reports which pontificate tend to irritate the reader even more than
those which are merely regarded as show-offy, perhaps because an authoritative
report is likely to be perceived as an affront, while the defensive motive of the
exhibitionistic report is more transparent. Psychiatrists evidently take more
offense at, or at least are more aware of, overly authoritative reports than are
other workers.

They are too positive, confident, assured, as though they were the last word,
irrefutable, authoritative.
Many reports are much too opinionated and obviously reflect the author's
own biased viewpoints.
Some are too dogmatic.
They often are too definite in their interpretations and assume to have all
the answers.
The psychologist feels too superior and will generally write a short summary
of his interpretation forgetting that a psychiatrist reading the report might
differ in interpretation. This feeling of superiority on the part of the
psychologist has alienated many intelligent psychiatrists.
A lack of humility. I never cease to be amazed by the confidence some men
have in their tests and in their own abilities to interpret them. To accept such
reports the psychiatrist would have to lose what little intelligence he is
supposed to have [a psychiatrist's comment].
They attempt to be all things to all men.
I have seen some reports which affected me adversely because of a tendency
to sound pompous with the implication "This is the final word!" rather than
"This is an opinion which is intended to be helpful in understanding the whole."
(and) to be all-inclusive to the point of excluding the specific contributions
of other disciplines—a sort of "I can do everything approach" which sometimes
results in the clouding of the most important observations. A second, though
no less important result, is the impairment or even destruction of the team
function.

Test Orientation vs. Client Orientation

It is perhaps surprising that psychologists complain more frequently than other
team members that clinical reports are too test-oriented rather than client-oriented.
It may be that, since a number of workers from the other clinic groups wish the
inclusion of raw data, they do not find talk of tests offensive.

They usually talk about tests and test results rather than the client's personality.

Talking about the tests too much and the patient too little.

They often describe responses rather than people.

They are test centered too often rather than containing statements about behavior in the non-test environment.

Often the writers feel it necessary to include scoring and other quantitative detail at the expense of providing a useful and helpful picture of the person evaluated.

Psychological reports should reflect the judgment of the psychologist with all the limitations of maturity and experience. The psychologist should proceed as though he knows something about human behavior and tests are aids in his understanding. He should not act as though he is lost without his tests. I think other disciplines want us to give opinions which are free to open discussion and exchange.

Too Theoretical

Sometimes criticisms indicate or imply that reports are not useful or client-oriented because they are too theoretical.

In general, they are too theoretical.

They concern vague hypothetic properties of people.

They often are too theoretical or academic in language to be comprehensible or meaningful in terms of future treatment goals for the client. They occasionally give us the feeling that no client was present at the time.

At times one has the feeling he is reading a biological dissertation on protoplasm rather than about a flesh and blood person.

Sometimes I come across psychological reports which are loaded with textbook phrases, but giving very little clear picture of the particular individual involved.

We sometimes get bogged down in vague, theoretical terminology which has little direct relation to the actual behavioral dilemmas confronting the individual. Also we employ theoretical concepts reflective of basic psychological processes (e.g., oral sadistic orientation) which are so general and so removed from the level of behavior that we write more like textbook theoreticians than as psychologists confronted with the task of making some sense out of a client's behavior.

Overabstract

Similar to the criticism that some psychological reports are too theoretical is the complaint that they are overabstract. Criticisms that reports are too theoretical and overabstract frequently occur in the same statement.

At times they become too difficult and abstract.

They are sometimes too theoretical and/or abstract; and on the other hand, too concrete—as reports of exact performance on tests as such. Ideally, there should be a happy medium.

They are too often lofty abstractions or concrete banalities. In either case, they fail to offer a meaningful, readily grasped, exposition of the subject's psychological condition.

The more abstract and/or intellectual the report is, the more likely the examiner is either defensive or projecting his own conflicts into the report.

Some are unnecessarily involved, technical and abstruse so as to be virtually useless in planning disposition of the subject.

Miscellaneous Deficiencies of Attitude and Orientation

There are a number of aspects of the psychologist's attitude and orientation we term "miscellaneous." Included are criticisms calling his reports too intellectual, too academic, and too pedantic, comments which no doubt overlap those just quoted. Such features may stem from the transplantation of an earlier generation of psychologists from an academic to a clinical setting. At any rate, the academic influence is noted by a number of observers who seem to feel it detracts from the practical utility of reports.

> They are too studiously intellectual.
> Too pedantic—obscure to other professions.
> Usually too involved, pedantic.
> In many instances psychological reports have the tendency to be too academic.
> They are often esoteric to the practice of psychological testing.
> Esoteric reference to statistical mechanisms.

A reluctance on the part of some psychologists to take on the consultant role, or to prepare psychological reports, is suggested by some clinicians as an explanation for blameworthy reports. In individual instances this could be a lack of confidence in or confusion about psychological methods. Such criticism might be seen as part of the psychologist's role problem as discussed below.

> Psychologists feel it is almost below their dignity to do them.
> (The trouble is) that you've got to write them.
> Psychologists appear to have lost confidence and/or interest in testing.
> I have a strong personal dislike for writing psychological reports, in spite of my recognition of their usefulness. Perhaps part of my feeling is due to the excessive length and detail of reports which are seldom read by anyone else, anyway. To me it is the most distasteful part of my job.

IV. Problems of Communication

Many of those concerned with psychological reports conceptualize the matter overly simply in terms of communication. The negative comments already made about psychological reports demonstrate clearly enough that report writing cannot be divorced from purpose or context or from the basic technical competence of the psychologist. The communication aspect is but one of the vital problems to be singled out for study.

Hundreds of workers had one or more negative comments to make about this pitfall. More respondents were concerned with this kind of difficulty than with any other aspect of psychological writing or consultation. Accordingly, there is a tendency for overlap among the subcategories.

Word Usage

The worst offender, according to our sample, is what is classified here as "word usage"—really a variety of offenses against the King's English. Thirty-seven percent of psychiatrists, 45 percent of psychologists, and 65 percent of social workers making negative comments on psychological reports had something to say on this matter. Deficiencies of terminology and wordiness were mentioned with great frequency. Some may be surprised to learn that psychoanalytic terminology is singled out as an offender with great frequency.

> A good report writer uses the language of the novelist, not the scientist unless he's writing for another psychologist. Analytic language is a language of generalities and thus loses the uniqueness we should be striving for.
> Often padded with meaningless multisyllable words to lengthen report.
> Gobbledygook [this expressive term was used by numerous respondents].
> Too much jargon [also a *very* frequently used term of criticism].
> I don't like reports which contain jargon which I can't understand.
> They do not take advantage of simplicity and ordinary words.
> Semantics have a tendency to creep in, and the phenomenon of "verbal diarrhea" occurs too often.
> The appearance of stereotyped phrases.
> They are too often written in a horrible psychologese—so that clients "manifest overt aggressive hostility in an impulsive manner"—when, in fact—they punch you on the nose.
> Too much emphasis is placed on psychological phraseology and such when we could say the same thing quickly, efficiently, and simply.
> They are not frequently enough written in lay language. I believe it requires clear thinking to write without use of technical terms.
> What about describing the person's behavior in terms that one ordinarily uses in describing a person rather than a client?
> Their value depends on whether the psychologist talks English or a special language of his own.

Vague, Unclear, Ambiguous

Many clinical workers are critical that psychological reports are vague, unclear, or ambiguous. No doubt a good deal of this difficulty stems from expressive deficiencies, although there are apparently other ways of writing reports that cannot be understood. How this occurs is a matter about which many respondents are not clear.

> They sometimes are vague and unsubstantial.
> They tend to rely on vague, psychoanalytically oriented phrases.
> New words or new meanings to familiar words are used, leaving the reader confused as to what is meant.
> Excessive wordiness which clouds the findings.
> Perhaps some are a little "veiled" in meaning, so as to attempt to prove the psychologist is truly a professional.

Oftentimes the psychologist has to be interpreted.

They contain too many ill-phrased, hard-to-understand sentences.

Often lack of comprehensibility in terms of real life treatment programs. They are intellectual vagaries.

They are not clear enough to be wrong.

Statements are made which could have more than one meaning, or are difficult to understand.

They suffer mainly from vagueness, double-talk and universality without enough of an attempt being made to specify more precisely what sets this person off from other people (and what does not).

Scores have little meaning even to the psychologist who understands their rationale, unless he also knows how they fit together in terms of cause and effect regarding behavior. To cover up his ignorance he resorts to the reporting of percentages, ratios, etc., and overwhelms his reader with such technical language that little information is conveyed.

Length of Reports

The length of psychological reports comes in for a good deal of criticism. In general, the consensus is that they are too long, but some feel they are too short. The latter scourge does not yet seem to be pandemic.

They are too lengthy—should be concise and to the point.

Many are too long. This usually teaches the reader to look for a summary and ignore the rest.

Too often the completed report is too long. Often I might go to the summary to get the gist of the examination.

Most of them are too long. Few people, if any, will take the time to read them.

Psychological reports should present specific data and specific interpretation. Too many contain omnibus recommendations and universal statements which apply to most people. I'd rather see brief reports with relatively little said than lengthy stereotyped reports which also say little.

A good report should stop when it has run out of useful data.

And one unhappy psychologist is concerned with length, apparently because he does not enjoy reading psychological reports for what he considers good reasons, and therefore would prefer to lessen his burden.

They are:
Over-imaginative,
Over-academic,
Over-syllabic,
And not over soon enough!

Too Technical, Too Complex

A further plea for simplicity and straightforwardness is registered in comments that psychological reports are too technical and too complex.

The more simply the material is presented, the more useful it is.

I have made "Flesch counts" of quite a large number of reports and the level of difficulty tends to be much too high. Psychological reports should not be as difficult to read as our professional papers, but often they are. Many reports of this type are actually meaningless—a kind of polysyllabic illiteracy.

Too technical or too esoteric.

Technical terminology, particularly Freudian or statistical language, where these do not serve as highly specific communications, which implies writing a report for another psychologist or analyst.

I think that it is important that the person write in such a way as to communicate to those who will read the report. In some cases this will require that he write in a much simpler and more descriptive manner.

Documentation makes reports too technical.

It appears that the psychologist prepares the report for one of his own group rather than for the benefit of other members of the team.

Style

Although style is generally regarded to be a rather individual matter, a number of workers believe there are certain necessary style requirements for effective communication. Psychologists are evidently more concerned with this matter than are members of other groups.

The reports tend to sound very much alike—to represent a personal "style."

Style is a matter of choice, but since we are supposed to be literate people, we should have certain standards of excellence to meet—too often this is not the case.

Too concerned with literary style.

The art of report writing should be akin to caricature.

They become too "flowery."

They all sound too much alike, as though the writers are adhering to a standardized model instead of allowing the form of their reports to be determined by the individual subject and the circumstances.

Too many reports follow a stylized form without due consideration to the real needs of the patient for which psychological testing had been requested.

Their formality, when the psychologist feels he must stick to form, often clouds his expression of what he feels is really important in the case at hand. It seems to me that rigid structuring of the report should ordinarily be minimized, unless structuring is to serve as a training procedure. Perhaps a definite structure is more desirable in the initial attempts at report writing in order to gain practice in the various aspects of the report. What is communicated as well as the manner in which it is presented should vary, depending upon the nature of the referral problem, the theoretical orientation of the particular staff who will use the report, the amount of educating which the psychologist deems advisable—in the direction of his own orientation, case load demands (reflected in the amount of time both psychologist and staff can spend with a report), and whether or not the report is apt to be included in further research efforts. Generally effective standards of form should be freely varied as personal and singular factors in one's working situation require.

Too often they seem to satisfy the writer's literary, "expressive" needs rather than communicate adequate description.

They give one more the impression of poetry than of scientific writing.

Under the guise of "capturing the flavor of the patient," appropriate scientific writing is sacrificed for style.

Organization

Psychologists are evidently more prone to the belief that psychological reports are not well organized than are other members of the team.

Often they are not coherently organized in terms of a personality or psychoanalytic theory and hence become meaningless jumbles of bits of data and information.

Frequently they are not organized—thought out—before they are dictated.

Too often they are so poorly organized that the reader has a difficult time to get a clear psychological picture of the client.

The analysis is in fragmented form rather than being integrated.

Write-ups frequently are not really organized, but formulations are "faked" in a sense by the use of syntax and grammatical construction.

They are often not organized around a central pattern characteristic of a person. Each paragraph seems a separate, discrete, unrelated part which could be clipped out and inserted in any other report.

When several tests have been administered, many psychologists cannot integrate the findings without giving separate results for each test.

Hedging

The final elicited problem of communication is that of hedging. A number of workers feel the psychologist should commit himself at one level or another, and not straddle the fence.

Some writers refuse to take a chance and say anything definite. They beat about the bush, include every possible descriptive or diagnostic phrase.

Psychologists seem too often to "play it safe" and include so much in their reports (or so little) that they can never be wrong, refuse to make specific predictions, and therefore can never really be right either.

They too often are riddled with qualifications—"it appears that," "it may well be," "the test reports indicate." This is fine when speculation is being introduced, but many reports merely convey the inadequacy and timidity of the writer.

We seem to be afraid to commit ourselves in a few words; using too many qualifying statements and thus avoiding ever being wrong, but never actually predicting anything at all.

Can't they be more confident in their findings, i.e., when it might appear from testing that the patient may be homicidal or suicidal and may act this out, to say so clearly? It's better to know before than later—or too late.

Often no definite conclusions are reached and the reader of the report is left as bewildered as he was prior to requesting psychological examination.

V. Problems of Science and Profession

Problems of Science

Our survey shows that primarily psychologists made observations to the effect that the trouble with psychological reports is not entirely the faults of individuals. Rather, a number of respondents see the need for a number of basic advances in areas such as psychological theory and the validity and applicability of tests. This latter problem is of great moment to many of the psychologist's team associates.

There is too little research on effective report writing. This would make an excellent thesis topic.

I suggest that a "sociologist from Mars" would find the test reporting behavior of psychologists quite as "weird" as any of the rituals and customs and beliefs of many so-called primitive societies.

They are not consistent. No one group has agreed what they should contain.

There is lack of agreement, even among members of a small staff, as to how they should be written. Clinical psychology doesn't have an adequate basis, either in theory or tools, for writing simple, straightforward, meaningful reports.

Most people, including psychologists, don't know what they are for or how to use them once they are written.

It has never been convincingly shown that the type of information contained in a psychological report contributes information which can improve the validity of decisions beyond that possible on the basis of interview impressions and a good case history. The trouble does not lie so much with psychological reports as with the material we have to report.

Primarily that their utility is unknown and untested. Few encouraging reports of prediction studies have been noted lately. Assuming validity and reliability (mighty big assumptions) psychologists are still in doubt as to the purpose of their own diagnostic efforts—particularly in a team setting.

Their usefulness is limited by the validity of the inferences based upon test performance. Formulations of test findings in terms of some general conception of personality processes appropriate to the issues raised in the referral are always preferable in my mind to showing description of test responses and behavior in the test situation. Such formulations must, however, be explicitly tentative in the light of doubts one must entertain about the dependability of inferences drawn from test responses—especially in the area of projective techniques.

Interpretation is too often based on theories which are yet poorly validated.

Essentially the same trouble as is found with psychiatric and psychological theory and terminology in general. That is, theories and concepts are vague and of low reliability and validity.

We have too many concepts, none of which can be regarded as demonstrably fundamental. Thus we write confused reports which depend on literary excellence more often than scientific knowledge.

The greatest defect is inadequate and unsympathetic personality theory on which to hang our observations.

Problems of Role Conduct

An insight into psychological consultation, far broader in scope than the psychological report, is gleaned from an observation of comments classified as "Problems of Role Conduct." These relate to what is regarded as encroachment of psychology upon the functions or prerogatives of other professionals.
It is the psychiatrists who feel most abused in this respect. An appreciable number of social workers also feel that the realm of the psychiatrist has been invaded by the psychologist, but some social workers see their own functions as assumed by the psychologist. Even more, a number of respondents are of the opinion that the psychological report encompasses the function of the entire team. None of the psychologist contingent indicated that they felt there was psychological encroachment upon the duties of any of their associates.
The author personally disagrees with some of the following statements, but it is important to know how one's team associates might feel. A number of psychologists are concerned that their role is not adequately defined, and they do see their effectiveness as being compromised by their equivocal position.

Too enterprising, perhaps too flavored with clinical feeling.
Many psychologists tend to digress in other fields.
They frequently do not mind their own business and go beyond their ken—invading territory properly allocated to the M.D.
Some reports go to the extreme of becoming a clinical summary of the client, including social and personal history and mental status.
They often contain medical and/or psychiatric diagnoses, prognosis, and, at times, treatment.
Some even suggest medical and other treatment.
They often try to give purely medical advice to physicians.
They make specific recommendations that an M.D. or a psychiatrist should do, and psychoanalytical insights or formulations that a psychoanalyst should do.
There is a tendency to avoid the very purpose for which psychological testing exists. Namely, to present laboratory data codified in its original terminology so that the physician who has requested such testing for his own purpose of treating the patient may add to his clinical estimate of the patient. In my opinion, the recommendation as to plan of treatment, chemotherapy, etc. is not appreciated. Psychological testing and reporting is certainly a highly specialized and technical field which adds a great deal to the doctor's knowledge of the patient and should confine itself to this area.
They tend to make diagnoses rather than furnish specific data supporting a certain diagnosis. They are requested by the M.D. to help him make the diagnosis, prognosis, etc. The M.D. is not interested in what the psychologist things, but why he thinks so. History and behavior are already available on the patient. The skilled psychiatrist knows how to interpret the data.
If the psychologist feels his M.D. does not know what all this means, he should first give the data and follow it with a polite interpretation beginning such as "This data suggests . . . etc. . . . ."

Some psychologists seem to take offense and think it too menial to perform I.Q. tests. Their reports reflect their needs to take over the functions of a psychiatrist.

The psychologist tries to do everything else but an evaluation of intelligence, which is what he is best equipped to do. I personally feel that psychiatric diagnosis does not fall within the realm of the psychologist.

They try to make psychiatric formulations instead of assist.

The frequency with which the psychologist attempts to be a psychiatrist and does not use his legitimate observations from his testing materials to provide a picture of one or more samples of behavior. Most psychiatrists feel psychologists and their tests have value as such. Why don't psychologists feel this way?

They are too much concerned with matters unfamiliar to the psychologist and familiar to the psychiatrist. Thus the reports are too often replete with amateur psychiatric data, and deficient in psychological data, which had been requested and presumably are needed by the physician. On several occasions, I have been surprised, if not shocked, to see included in psychological reports "Patient should be helped by E.C.T."

On the other hand, one psychiatrist sees the "trouble" as quite the opposite from that expressed by his colleagues quoted above. This is definitely a minority opinion.

Too many psychologists are afraid they'll tread on M.D.'s toes. The properly trained psychologist will prepare better psychological reports as soon as he is liberated from the fear of overstepping certain unwisely defined professional bounds. Once liberated, he will have no need to fill space with social data. His reports will then reveal his full understanding of the patient based on observation, experience, plus the skillful interpretation of special tests.

Where social workers make comments on the psychologist's role conduct, they are likely to be concerned with the same matters which trouble many psychiatrists, or to have very similar feelings. They feel, for example, that an invasion of social work territory, the taking of social histories, has occurred. One social worker, however, sees a problem of role dissatisfaction which affects a number of groups:

Our hospital has six psychologists and many student trainees. They have a wide range of duties and responsibilities but can't keep inside their own yard! Our staff has six social workers, one researcher, and an anthropologist.

The social workers all want to be psychologists.

The psychologists anthropologists.

The anthropologists social workers.

And only God knows what direction we are all going in.

TABLE 1   Criticisms of Psychological Reports*

		Psychiatrists	Psychologists	Social Workers
I.	Problems of Content			
	A. Unnecessary duplication	<1	<1	<1
	B. Minor relevancy	5	5	2
	C. Offer diagnosis	8	<1	<1
	D. Offer prognosis	4	0	0
	E. Offer recommendations	8	<1	<1
	F. Improper emphasis	10	13	10
	G. Too much raw data	5	12	5
	H. Too little raw data	20	4	8
	I. Omit essential material	5	13	7
II.	Problems of Interpretation			
	A. Too general (reports do not differentiate among patients)	9	30	9
	B. Too speculative	13	6	3
	C. Speculation not labeled as such	3	7	1
	D. Assorted irresponsible interpretations	41	27	22
III.	Problems of Psychologist's Attitude or Orientation			
	A. Overabstract	3	2	0
	B. Too Authoritative	4	2	2
	C. Exhibitionistic	4	6	2
	D. Not patient oriented	0	3	<1
	E. Test oriented	0	5	<1
	F. Too theoretical	2	3	2
	G. Not written with practical or useful purpose in mind	8	41	16
	H. Miscellaneous (Especially: too intellectual, lack of interest in communication)	1	5	2
IV.	Problems of Communication			
	A. Defective communication (reasons not given)	2	3	2
	B. Word usage (Especially: deficiencies of terminology and wordiness)	37	45	65
	C. Style deficiency	3	9	2
	D. Vague, unclear or ambiguous	14	15	21
	E. Too technical	5	4	5
	F. Too complex	2	4	5
	G. Hedge	2	3	2
	H. Too long	13	15	7
	I. Too brief	1	1	1
	J. Poorly organized	<1	8	<1
V.	Problems of Science and Profession			
	A. Problems of Science (Especially: psychological theory, validity of tests)	2	10	0
	B. Problems of Role Conduct	12	0	4

Source: Based on table in Tallent, N. & Reiss, W.J., Multidisciplinary views on the preparation of written clinical psychological reports; III. The trouble with psychological reports. *Journal of Clinical Psychology*, 1959, *15*, 444-446. Reproduced with permission.

*Figures represent per cent of respondents of each category who made a negative comment or comments about psychological reports.

CHAPTER THREE

Responsibility
and
Effectiveness

The effectiveness of the psychological report may be enhanced by attention to a number of factors. Everything is subsidiary to the matter of the psychologist's understanding and fulfilling the mission of meeting responsibilities in the case. In order to do this, the psychologist must provide an individualized report rather than one heavily saturated with some form of report stereotypy. Always important is the need to guard against personal factors compromising the value of the report. Responsibility also demands that the psychologist focus on practical requirements, carefully consider the use (or nonuse) of raw data, and decide on the proper terminology and report length. If the report is to be an effective instrument, the psychologist must even take into account its cost and its timeliness.

Primum, non nocere — First, do no harm. The sage admonition of Hippocrates to his medical students is very much applicable to psychologists today. Typically, psychological evaluation of a single individual occurs when intervention in another's life is taking place or is contemplated, an awesome responsibility. The psychological report thus may be a powerful instrument for good or ill. The points the psychologist makes and how effectively he gets them across may influence such decisions as the sort of schooling or vocation an individual is to enter, the treatment he is to receive, or the nature of his living conditions. In the formative years, the school psychologist's understanding of a child, and his ability to effectively convey that understanding, may contribute importantly to shaping the child's future. At stake may be an individual's very life. It is a matter of some moment, for example, when a psychologist is able to identify a client who has suicidal propensities and is able to relate his conclusions unambiguously and convincingly to his colleagues.

To meet his responsibilities to produce an effective report, the psychologist must be aware of the many pitfalls we have discussed that might compromise his efforts. But the thrust of the report should be positive, not just to avoid errors, but to produce the most faithful results in order to fulfill the psychologist's mission to serve the needs of his client. To this end, we must devote much attention to the development of the sort of content that will best advance the mission. This is the topic of Chapter 4. How best to conceptualize the report, a crucial factor in maximizing report effectiveness, can be very difficult indeed for many students and professional psychologists. This is the topic of Chapter 5. In the present chapter, we deal with two rather basic issues: (1) the responsible interpretation of data (one aspect of learning to present conclusions effectively) and (2) some considerations on the rhetoric of presenting those conclusions. There is quite a logical relation between the two. Rudolf Flesch (1972) entitles his book on the art of writing *Say What You Mean*. Before one can say what he means, he must know what he means.

Responsible interpretation has many facets, the most basic being a well-trained, knowledgeable interpreter. The psychologist must know his mission, his colleagues, his client, his client's total situation, and available resources for dealing with the client's needs. He must know personality theory but not be ruled by it. He must be able to differentiate what he *can* interpret from what he *should* interpret. He must be able to present his client as an individual, with individual needs and goals, and not travel the easy road of stereotypy. Undoubtedly, he has seen hundreds of "psychopaths" or schizophrenics or students who do poorly in school or have faulty social relationships. But, though many in each category have prominent features in common, each has his (often important) differences.

The psychologist, if he needs to improve his rhetoric—as many do—had better learn from a teacher of rhetoric or from any good book on rhetoric. We are somewhat partial to Flesch's *Say What You Mean* and to his earlier work *The Art of Readable Writing* (1949). What appeals most is the emphasis on simplicity, directness, and what must be good common sense. Of particular interest in *The Art of Readable Writing* are scales for measuring the ease of reading and the level of interest of content.

Style or rhetoric, admittedly, contributes to (or detracts from) the psychological report. As a basic point, it is well to point out to the psychologist the words of Sydney Smith: *Everything which is written is meant either to please or to instruct. The second object is difficult to effect, without attending to the first.*

THE CLIENT IS AN INDIVIDUAL

In the diagnostic/treatment situation the psychologist's reason for being is to represent the client in the relevant terms of his unique behavior, overt and covert. Perhaps the meaning of uniqueness as used here should be defined in terms of an orientation to human behavior. This is based largely on the idiographic approach to personality, which stresses that each human being has a personality different from all other personalities; this individuality distinguishes one person from another as do fingerprints. Widespread traits, factors, clusters, constellations, complexes, types, pathological dispositions, and temperaments can be identified and ascribed to persons, but such descriptions must remain general and tend to omit much of what is personally important. Concern with these descriptions, in the applied area, most probably will yield results in a group setting but is only the first step in understanding an individual in his own right. The clinical approach, with its interest in the generally recognized human qualities, stresses that these are different in strength, in idiosyncrasies (which may be subtle but of the greatest importance) in terms of level, and configuration, and in forms and occasions of expression. In working with the living personality, our attention is drawn to the specific features of traits. These are often clinically significant.

In a previous publication the writer summarized some of the more common practices involved in general rather than individual clinical descriptions (Tallent, 1958). What is probably the most common of these was termed the *Aunt Fanny Description*. This designation seemed appropriate because the report reader, on noting the characteristics ascribed to the client—what the client *has*—might well think "So has my Aunt Fanny!" Thus, "The client has traits of immaturity," or ". . . he has dependency needs," or "has latent homosexual strivings." Such statements can hardly differentiate among people or point up what is unique— a person's specific needs, deficiencies, strengths, stresses, or implications for the treatment of a troubled person. A study by Davenport (1952) lends support to this impression held by many psychologists. This is not to say that all statements in a report need be of differentiating value in and of themselves, for even the most objective statements take on additional meaning as they are appropriately modified and integrated with other findings. For example, you don't really know much about a person when told "His I.Q. is 115." This statement is true of millions of people (or at least would be if we tested many millions of persons). The information is not sufficient to judge whether the person might make a superior teacher or regularly get lost between the bus stop and his house. But when a statement about an individual's I.Q. is appropriately linked with other information—perhaps his interests, attitudes, goals, defense mechanisms, formal thought processes, memory function—the contribution can become highly meaningful.

The following "psychological report" is a hoax. It was prepared by Dr. Norman Sundberg along with an accompanying explanation and is reproduced with his kind permission. It was selected as a good example of the Aunt

Fanny technique. Overlooking the fact that Fanny is a female appellation, this particular case report is, at least to a degree, applicable to many schizophrenic persons. Dr. Sundberg comments, "We had a lot of fun presenting it and discussing it at the Oregon Psychological Association meeting. It was quite impressive how it seemed to fit the case when it was actually presented."[1]

Completely Blind Analysis of the Case of a Schizophrenic Veteran
—Norman D. Sundberg

(Written before knowing *anything* about the patient except that he was a new admission to the Roseburg VAH and was to be worked up for an OPA meeting.)

This veteran approached the testing situation with some reluctance. He was cooperative with the clinician, but was mildly evasive on some of the material. Both the tests and the past history suggest considerable inadequacy in interpersonal relations, particularly with members of his family. Although it is doubtful whether he has ever had very close relationships with anyone, the few apparently close relationships which he has had were tinged with a great deal of ambivalence. He has never been able to sink his roots very deeply. He is immature, egocentric and irritable, and often he mis-perceives the good intentions of the people around him. Projection is one of his prominent defense mechanisms. He tends to be basically passive and dependent, though there are occasional periods of resistance and rebellion against others. Although he shows some seclusiveness and autistic trends, he is in fair to good contact with reality. Vocationally, his adjustment has been very poor. Mostly he has drifted from one job to another. His interests are shallow and he tends to have poor motivation for his work. Also he has had a hard time keeping his jobs because of difficulty in getting along with fellow employees. Though he has had some affairs, his sex life has been unsatisfactory to him. At present, he is mildly depressed, although a great deal of affect is not shown. What physical complaints he has appear mainly to have a functional origin. His intelligence is close to average, but he is functioning below his full capacity. In summary, this is a long-time inadequate or borderline adjustment pattern. Test results and case history, though they do not give a strong clear-cut diagnostic picture, suggest the diagnosis of schizophrenia, chronic undifferentiated type. Prognosis for response to treatment appears to be poor.

This completely blind analysis is based on the following assumptions:

1. The veteran being referred for psychological testing is not likely to be an obvious or clear-cut diagnostic case. There is no need for testing unless there is some indecision. Consequently, hedging is to be expected on a report anyway.

2. This is a schizophrenic case. Given the general class of schizophrenia, one can work back to some of the characteristics which belong in that class and have a fair chance of being right.

3. There are some modal characteristics of patients coming to VA hospitals. In placing bets on what the patient is likely to be like, the best

---

[1] Personal communication.

guess would be a description of the modal personality. For instance most of the veterans coming to Roseburg are chronic cases who have not succeeded in jobs or in family life. Also, the best guess on intelligence would obviously be average intelligence, but since the person is a psychiatric patient it is likely that he is not functioning at his best.

4. There are also certain modal behaviors of the clinical staff. They use certain words, certain jargon; they have a preference for certain diagnoses. Oftentimes, a large percentage of the cases wind up with the diagnosis of schizophrenia, chronic undifferentiated type.

5. There are some "universally valid" adjectives which are appropriate for almost any psychiatric patients, such as "dependent," "immature," "irritable," and "egocentric."

6. In the less clear areas where modal characteristics are not known, it is more safe to write a vague statement or one which can be interpreted in various ways. Readers can be counted on to overlook a few vague misses and to select the descriptions which jibe with their own preconception.

7. All of this is intended to say that we have much in common with the old fortune teller, and that what we need is better ways of dealing with individuality. Knowing modal personalties is very useful; it certainly adds to ease of social communication; however, we are sometimes fooled into thinking that we know persons when actually all we know is our own stereotypes.

A good definition for the Aunt Fanny description might note that ". . . descriptions from tests are made to fit the patient largely or wholly by virtue of their triviality; and in which any nontrivial, but perhaps erroneous, inferences are hidden in a context of assertions or denials which carry high confidence simply because of the population base rate, regardless of the test's validity." It is, however, Meehl's (1956) definition of the "Barnum report." We prefer the definition of the Barnum report quoted below, because its essence is to give the customer what he wants. The use of high base rate statements is but part of the technique. Paterson's report—the original Barnum report quoted below—also sought acceptance by the use of flattery, which is not a feature of Aunt Fanny statements. If there is a real distinction between Aunt Fanny and Barnum, it is important that such distinction be recognized for the implications it might have both for research and for teaching psychological report writing. We can also sometimes note a negative Barnum effect, as for example, when a psychiatrist or an administrator is "sold a bill of goods" to confirm for him the negative views he holds on an individual. This might be an instance of Klopfer's (1960) "Madison Avenue Report" (p. 15).

The Barnum report has been viewed by the present writer (*1958*) as a method "to describe a personality by using a few mildly negative generalities which are quickly neutralized in a matrix of acceptable, even flattering remarks, both types of comments being apparently applicable to almost everybody." In short, a Barnum report is readily "validated" by the subject about whom it supposedly is written. This was demonstrated, to the writer's satisfaction, when he passed out to members of a college class Professor Paterson's original Barnum report, with the explanation that it was an individual personality analysis which the instructor had arrived at through inspections of samples of the students' handwriting. The report was unanimously accepted as accurate by all 39 class members, with the exception of two students who indicated very slight error. The potency of the evaluation was punctuated by several of the more startled (or least inhibited) students making exclamations like "Uncanny!" and "This is me all right!" This sort of "validation" has been studied under more exacting conditions by Forer (1949), Sundberg (1955), Carrier (1963), Ulrich, Stachnik, and Stainton (1963), Snyder (1974), and by Snyder and Larson (1972). Paterson originally used the report as a lesson to businessmen on irresponsible personnel evaluation practices. Passing out copies to groups of businessmen, he obtained excellent results by asking how many were fitted by "their" personality descriptions. (Professor Paterson's report has been reprinted here by permission.)

Abilities: Above average in intelligence or mental alertness. Also above average in accuracy—rather painstaking at times. Deserves a reputation for neatness—dislikes turning out sloppy work. Has initiative; that is, ability to make suggestions and to get new ideas, open-mindedness.

Emotions: You have a tendency to worry at times but not to excess. You do get depressed at times but you couldn't be called moody because you are generally cheerful and rather optimistic. You have a good disposition although earlier in life you have had a struggle with yourself to control your impulses and temper.

Interests: You are strongly socially inclined, you like to meet people, especially to mix with those you know well. You appreciate art, painting and music, but you will never be a success as an artist or as a creator or composer of music. You like sports and athletic events but devote more of your attention to reading about them in the sporting page than in actual participation.

Ambitions: You are ambitious, and deserve credit for wanting to be well thought of by your family, business associates and friends. These ambitions come out most strongly in your tendency to indulge in daydreams, in building aircastles, but this does not mean that you fail to get into the game of life actively.

Vocational: You ought to continue to be successful so long as you stay in a social vocation. I mean if you keep at work bringing you in contact with people. Just what work you pick out isn't as important as the fact that it must be work bringing you in touch with people. On the negative side you would never have made a success at strictly theoretical work or in pure research work such as in physics or neurology.

What may be called the "trade-marked" report (Tallent, 1958) has long been commented upon. This is a report that may overemphasize the psychologist's personal concerns, conflicts, interests, dynamics, or shortcomings at the expense of accurately describing the client. It is an example of eisegesis gone wild. Some psychologists are known in their organizations for always including and loud-pedaling a specific theme—hostility, heterosexual immaturity, homoerotic impulses, compensation for inferiority, presentation of a false façade, or conflict with father, mother or authority. That this phenomenon exists seems well established (Filer, 1952; Hammer & Piotrowski, 1953; Robinson, 1951; Robinson & Cohen, 1954). It is perhaps some comfort then that such tendencies appear to be shared by clinicians of other disciplines. Observed at a staff conference: a nonpsychologist who appeared to interpret sex as the crucial dynamic in every case but could not seem to "see" the role of "hostility," impatiently asking a psychologist who had just read his report where he "got" all the hostility. The instant reply: "The same place where you 'get' all the sex."

Nonindividualized reporting may also be seen in what has been called the "prosecuting attorney brief." "Such reports are saturated with . . . negative dynamics . . . but give little or no attention to positive features, to commendable conscious strivings, socially valuable compensations, and other well-used defenses. These reports consistently reflect the motto 'always interpret at the lowest possible level of psychosexual fixation or regression.' They are prepared by psychological simians who hear no good, see no good, and report no good" (Tallent, 1958). Apparently this sort of reporting is equivalent to what Klopfer (1960) calls the "maladjustment bias." These observations, of course, refer to the extent to which reports are saturated with pathology. It goes without saying that a patient in a clinical setting does in fact have severe difficulties, impulses, and strivings that we may regard as unfortunate, and maladaptive defenses. These should be reported as they are meaningful. The point is that *appropriate* emphasis ought to be given to *relevant* positive features. But certainly all of the favorable qualities are not relevant. One probably need not write of a neurotic patient as being "in contact," as showing no thinking disorders, as having a satisfying heterosexual adjustment, or as having an I.Q. of 135 (if the problem is in no way related to intelligence).

POINTS OF VIEW ON INTERPRETATION OF PSYCHOLOGICAL DATA

One of the major issues in the writing of psychological reports centers about the presentation of raw data (or of incompletely interpreted data). If raw data are to be offered to the person who referred the case or to other team members, the next questions are: "How much raw data?" "How shall such raw data be selected?" "For what purpose(s) shall raw data be utilized in the report?" Or, from a different viewpoint, to what extent shall the psychologist interpret his data for the consumers of his report? On what basis may the psychologist decide what is to be interpreted and what not interpreted? Shall he present only interpreted data? Shall he, at the other extreme, present no interpreted data? Does the presentation of raw data obviate the need for its interpretation, or should (or may) an interpretation be accompanied by raw data either in a supportive or illustrative role?

Before attempting to cope with these questions, a definition of raw data and the range of possible "rawness" should be considered. English and English (1958) define "data/raw" as "data not yet submitted to logical or statistical analysis." In working with an individual client, it is the logical analysis of data that concerns us. Thus, the data with which the psychologist deals differ vastly in terms of how much logical analysis is required before they can be viewed as meaningful or can contribute to useful action.

At one extreme are data that require highly skilled interpretation and have to be considered only in the context of a battery protocol. What competent psychologist would offer an interpretation of 4 Rorschach M responses without considering also their form level, popularity or originality, whether "easy" or "hard" M, the cards where seen, possible associated determinants, preceding and succeeding responses, the content, the particular verbalization of the content, color usage, pathognomonic signs, intelligence level, fantasy content, and so on? At the other extreme are responses that require minimal interpretation. Such responses often occur in interview, or on sentence completion tests, which are, in effect, controlled interview situations. Thus the completions "Most people I know . . . can't be trusted," and "Those I work with . . . are out to get me" are apparently quite simple matters for interpretation. Yet even here the psychologist must utilize some logical analysis, such as judging whether the person is sincere, malingering, or otherwise trying to create an impression, how consistent the particular responses are with the full test protocol and other information had on the patient, and what significance the material might have. Data perhaps intermediate in the level of interpretive skill required are represented by statements such as "On four TAT cards the hero was depicted as in conflict with a father figure." Commonly appearing in psychological reports, statements of this sort are really descriptions of raw data, not the basic raw data themselves. To offer statements of this sort, the psychologist must use professional judgment, hence some degree of interpretation takes place. Intermediate between raw data and interpreted data, we may speak of "incompletely interpreted data." Other statements in this class are "loose use of color," "concrete thinking," or "syncretistic thinking."

Psychologists do not generally present raw data without what they consider an adequate interpretation of such material. Thus, taken from a report: "Rorschach responses such as '. . . Two wolves . . . they both have their teeth dug into some person as though they're trying to tear him apart . . . a person who has taken on the wings of a butterfly . . . deformed embryos inside the womb . . . an infected vagina . . . a faint suggestion of evil spirits inside the womb . . . octopuses with horse's heads . . . two snakes seem to be trying to gain access to this vagina-like symbol'—are evidences of a severe formal thought disorder when personal material is involved. This is marked by primitive, symbolic and dream-like associations and percepts, and by an accompanying loss of appropriate distance from stimuli which results in his making poor judgments in terms of the total situation."

Even though there are copious amounts of such raw data in some psychological reports, psychologists tend to feel that the appropriateness of including them depends on their purpose. There is widespread feeling among this group that it is all right to present material such as in the above example, but for illustrative reasons only. Had the conclusion preceded the data here, it would have been more evident that they were meant to illustrate, not to carry the freight. On the other hand, themes like:

> On the Object Assembly subtest, the patient seemed at a loss as to where to begin. He picked up pieces at random and attempted to fit the parts together in an unplanned fashion. Finally, he stated his inability to solve the problem and gave up the task.
> This patient's verbal I.Q. is 91 and his performance score is 105. The Comprehension score (11) is five points greater than Information (6). The high subtest score is on Object Assembly, the weighted score being 14, while his lowest is a 3 scored on Arithmetical Reasoning.

are currently taboo among most psychologists, although other team members, particularly psychiatrists, might find them more acceptable.

In general, many psychologists feel threatened by the idea that they must present such data to others presumably more qualified to make the proper interpretations. Similarly, there is widespread objection to being required to support one's conclusions with data, since this procedure might also imply that other professional groups have qualifications to judge the adequacy of the psychologist's interpretations of his own data.

There is a case frequently presented for the use of raw data in psychological reports. The psychiatrist points out correctly that it is traditional for the physician to coordinate findings from diverse sources—his own examination, consultants' reports, laboratory findings, social history—and to reach his own conclusions. He accepts responsibility for these and for the actions which stem from them. The medical consultant therefore helps a clinician by presenting a narrative report which makes liberal reference to the data on which his impressions are based. Notice by way of illustration the ratio of incompletely interpreted data to final interpretation in the following report written by a pathologist for a surgeon.

> Specimen consists of a 2 cm. cyst lined with soft cheesy material.
> Microscopic: Section reveals the cyst to be lined with flattened epidermis and the contents to consist of hyalinized, lamellated, desquamated, keratinized, epithelial cells.
> Impression: Skin, sebaceous cyst.

It therefore particularly behooves the psychologist who is working in a medical setting to examine whether a departure from what physicians do is justified.

The experienced psychologist is in a position to cite a number of pertinent differences between medical and psychological consultations. Most obvious, personality is made of stuff which is patently different from physiological-anatomical variables. Meaningful personality findings are deduced only after hundreds of bits of discrete data are sifted and pondered, studied for consistency and the meaning of apparent inconsistencies, and all of the data units studied as they are given significance or are modified by the data of the entire protocol and other pertinent information.

The logical extreme of presenting raw data to support conclusions or to help the person who referred the case reach his own conclusions is of course to present *all* of the data available on any given client. This practice would yield an unwieldy document of many pages, with little practical utility. Most psychologists would oppose such use of data, even when offered to associates highly trained in personality, contending that test data should be interpreted only by those expert in personality *and* psychological assessment methods.

A potent objection to presenting raw data so that the person who made the referral can make his own interpretations, "follow" the interpretations of the psychologist, or judge their correctness, is simply that the practice is not valid. There is not a one-to-one relationship between datum and interpretation; neither is there universal symbolism which would permit direct translation from test material to personality referent. The raw data on which interpretations are really made are far more extensive than test data. They include an experienced knowledge of the stimuli which elicited the data, an awareness of the relationship and effects of test stimulus and examiner stimulus, all sorts of behavioral variables, such as the person's tone of voice and facial expression, the entire context in which responses occurred, and all other relevant data.

A major factor pertinent to the question of presenting raw data—a factor which should be disconcerting to the person who would use the data to draw his own conclusions or to check on the psychologist's conclusions—is that the psychologist in the presence of volumes of data must, of necessity, be selective. And herein lies a telling criticism of the procedure. It is the psychologist's judgment which determines what raw data should be selected for presentation—certainly an uncontrolled procedure of questionable validity. The psychologist cannot decide on what raw data to include in his report until *after* he has weighed the merits of some particular data. Unfortunate selection could come about through insufficient competency, or be used nefariously by one having need to present certain conclusions and to justify them.

There is considerable feeling that raw data may legitimately be used for illustrating conclusions, perhaps linking the two in such fashion that the source of the conclusion is explicit (Mayman, 1959). This procedure may often have much to recommend it, and in some instances may be as close to imperative as can any rule for report writing (see the case of Mr. W, p. 197). Particularly vivid or transparent material, judged by the psychologist to be a valid illustration of the conclusions it is intended to bolster, can be most effective. For example, "All the cards remind me of death, just sorrow and death." However, a response like "two bears with their tails cut off" may be transparent to the psychologist, particularly in the light of other data he has, but all readers may not reach similar conclusions. There is a danger that the use of such material may "backfire," a reader gaining quite a different conclusion from the psychologist, or feeling that the illustration is not sufficient to support the psychologist's conclusion. Since the material is selective, the reader should be made aware that the illustrations are not fully supportive of the conclusions they advance.

A frequently safe and helpful procedure is for the psychologist to share his raw data with an interested associate on a personal basis where the material may adequately be discussed. The central principles involved in the offering of raw data are (1) careful attention to the appropriateness of the circumstances of the procedure, with the wisdom of the illustrations used considered carefully from the standpoint of both validity and effectiveness, and (2) the inability of the psychologist ethically to relinquish any responsibility for his own conclusions. Just as the physician, for good reason, is charged with coordinating all available clinical data and reaching conclusions based on them, the psychologist must coordinate all psychologically relevant material available to him and reach his own conclusions.

THE FLAVOR OF THE REPORT

What may be called the flavor of the report comes in for a good deal of attention, from the readers if not also from the writers of psychological reports. The greatest importance of the flavor is that it may readily influence the attitude of the reader. Such additudes, positive or negative, may then contribute to what the reader derives. In addition, the flavor is inextricably enmeshed with such other matters as technical level and orientation, terminology, psychologist's attitude, and role concept. All of these have implications for the acceptance and effectiveness of the report.

Background, training, self-needs, and personality idiosyncrasies all may influence the flavor of the report. These contribute to reports which may be described by such adjectival expressions as "abstract," "theoretical," "academic," "intellectual," "erudite," or "learning theory oriented." Typical are reports with a concrete psychometric emphasis, or reports which are more or less psychoanalytic. There are also reports which exude an authoritative tone or are exhibitionistic. Although any of these flavors may arouse disapproval, disinterest, or antagonism in the reader, the latter two are regarded as particularly defeating professionally, not only because others are not likely to respond kindly to them, but also because such writing is incompatible with scientific tentativeness and modesty.

Styles of Reports

Psychological reports are sometimes categorized into one of three basic styles, (although it would be easy to nominate others). These may be called the clinical style, the scientific style, and the literary style—which at the extreme may perhaps better be labelled "dramatic" or "flowery." No general agreement exists concerning the relative merits of each, but one does overhear comments, and the opinions of clinical workers may be formally surveyed (Tallent and Reiss, 1959b). For example, the following statement, intended as a specimen of literary writing of a somewhat dramatic sort, achieved significant popular support from clinical workers, yet many others did not feel that it suited their taste: "Crushed and defeated by telling setbacks, the patient feels unable to continue to fight what he sees as an oppressive environment."

The clinical style focuses upon pathology, deficiency, and equilibrative processes, and some would say that the report more nearly describes a case than a person. The orientation, of course, is basically medical and normative. An emphasis in this vein might make it hard to account for such behavorial variables as attitudes, sentiments, or relationships, unless these are diseased or associated with disease.

The scientific style, by partial contrast, is more closely related to the academic psychologist's discipline. This approach stresses the normative, and sometimes also the pathological. It differs from the clinical most in its relation to a conceptual scheme of personality or to a theory of assessment. This style would apparently be particularly compatible with approaching a personality through its segments or part processes and dealing with these in some detail. Here the psychologist becomes involved with what, for convenience of study, might be regarded as discrete functions—intellection, perception, emotion—or finer divisions of these—much as the physician may be concerned with units of clinical study like the cardiovascular system, the genitourinary system, or the neuropsychiatric system.

This approach is subject to attack from a number of directions. It would seem to do violence to the concept of personality unity (this most important matter is considered in Chapter 5) and may also appear to many to be overly "cold" and impersonal. This approach may cause the reader to feel there was no person present at all. We must be aware that many clinical workers, particularly those in disciplines other than psychology, do not have empathy with scientific-sounding reports. Another hazard is that a scientific presentation with an unusually strong laboratory flavor may reinforce the commonly held impression that psychology renders laboratory rather than consultant services.

The scientific emphasis of modern experimental and quantitative psychology is the basis on which many clinicians and others, in and out of psychology, argue that the psychological report is a scientific document. As such, it is thought proper that the report be exclusively concerned with the "findings," that which is factual; any mention of application, or of an emphasis on application, is regarded by some as latter-day sophistry. But a great distinction needs to be made between science and its application to workaday purposes. The psychological report is a practical document, and when it is not designed to be effective its very purpose may be defeated. It is understandable that the more palatable and comprehensible the report, the more usable it is. To merely present ideas or conclusions is not enough; they must be "brought home" or "gotten across" to the reader or they are lost, and the psychologist's mission is aborted. The psychologist must write in whatever style he judges to be appropriate and effective, using literary, clinical, and scientific styles in whatever combination he judges to be effective, using material that is objective, phenomenological, or whatever, again, as he judges it to be effective and appropriate.

Archibald MacLeish suggests that the purpose of education is to weld the fact with the feel. The function of the psychologist is perhaps similar, it being his task to present an integration of the facts about the individual with a feeling for him. Many psychologists presumably operate on this premise. Recoiling from the scientific, they tend in the direction of, and sometimes get lost in, the literary. Unfortunately, they sometimes fall into the obvious methods of the previously given example of literary writing. Sometimes a literary twist may help in capturing the flavor of the person, but to do this effectively, using facts about him to instill a feel about him, involves presenting him in his uniqueness. This objective is accomplished partly by the fortunate use of language, but mostly by developing the proper content, by understanding what are the clinically relevant personality processes and how these relate to one another, and finally by organizing these so that what is most vital stands out, and what is less vital supports the essence of the presentation. The psychologist has to understand the person (a much bigger job than test interpretation) and then to help someone else to understand him.

The Use of "Human Interest"

We may profitably borrow from the newspaper people some methods of conceptualizing and presenting a theme. The traditional news item is a cut-and-dried affair concerned only with the "facts" (somehow the meaning or understanding of events usually do not come under this heading). Generations of cub reporters have learned their five W's—Who, What, When, Where, and Why—and the accounts of two reporters assigned to cover a fire on Main Street probably would read very much alike. Psychologists might even commend such similarity as evidence of a high degree of interobserver reliability.

But all newspaper stores are not the same, and some strive for effect, for deeper understanding, or even for the development of understanding in the reader through "human interest." The latter can be valid enough (not detracting from the accuracy of the story and sometimes contributing to it), even though some psychologists tend to oppose reason and feelings, or to stress the manner in which feelings hamper reason.

Writing can, and often ought, to include both factual and affective elements—a point which Flesch (1949) has developed well in his book on readable writing. Each field must develop its own styles. But since the subject matter of psychology, like that of journalism, commonly involves the emotions of people, these can be utilized to describe people effectively and more realistically than when the emotions are exsanguinated in the objectivity of a specimen analysis. Even feature articles about events, new machines, or industrial processes can be "humanized." We shall see in Chapter 5 how even some engineers knowingly allow the intrusion of subjectivity both to color their reports and aid them in conceptualizing their tasks. Indeed, great scientists like Einstein may rely heavily on the subjective and even the intuitive. He writes: "I very rarely think in words at all. A thought comes, and I may try to express it in words afterward. . . . During all these years there was a *feeling* of direction, of going straight toward something concrete. It is, of course, very hard to express that *feeling* in words; but it was decidedly the case and clearly to be distinguished from later considerations about the rational form of the solution" (Wertheimer, 1945, italics added).

In view of the objections raised here to literary, clinical, and scientific approaches, the reader might wonder what style would be suitable. Why not a simple, matter-of-fact approach based on everyday expository writing? Such an approach can readily incorporate scientific information as necessary, give pathological manifestations appropriate representation, and retain the flexibility or even sedate license allowed for in any creative writing. A psychological report is, or at least should be, a piece of creative writing. There is no logical reason why the tone may not approximate the conversational.

An overly specialized tone seems to be both a barrier to communication and to understanding, and not infrequently antagonizes the reader. The demand is for simplicity. This, of course, is distressing to some psychologists. It disturbs them to consider, even if not to admit, that the complexities of personality revealed by the psychologist's probing can be expressed in something less than an involved presentation, that might even be comprehensible to the psychologically unsophisticated. It is likely that large numbers of psychologists, because of training, or for reasons of conviction or personal dynamics, cling to these views.

ORIENTATION OF THE REPORT

An issue related to the problem of flavor is that of orientation, particularly person-orientation versus test-orientation. The person-oriented report deals with the functioning of the person and with such real, pertinent matters as the outlook and recommendations that might prove helpful. The test-oriented report, by contrast, places its emphasis on test responses, test scores, and perhaps on relations among test scores. The first kind of report talks about the person, the other about the person's performance on tests.

Although the test-oriented report is still quite common, there is considerable feeling that reports ought to be person-oriented. Test-orientation probably harks back to the early days of psychometrics and school psychology, when the IQ was regarded at a premium and the various successes and failures on test items supposedly had some obvious and practical meaning.

The early days of clinical psychology in psychiatric settings again saw "mental testers" very much concerned with scores and proficiency levels. The orientation was essentially that of a technician, where the data were delivered to a clinician for interpretation. Such an orientation frequently leads to incomplete interpretation of data—an entirely unacceptable procedure in personality evaluation, at least according to our point of view. However, many psychologists have carried over from early psychometric procedures to projective techniques a propensity to talk about tests rather than about people. This can also be viewed as a negative practice because talking about tests may confer on the person making the referral or other team associates part of the psychologist's responsibility for interpreting his preliminary data. This was discussed more fully under the heading, "Points of View on Interpretation of Psychological Data." At worst, test talk may be made to serve as a veil to conceal the examiner's lack of understanding of his client or lack of ability to present his conclusions effectively.

THE MANNER OF PRESENTING CONCLUSIONS

The reporting of conclusions must be from the standpoint of a psychologist who has achieved certain impressions, or has *not* achieved impressions, about some areas of the client's life he feels he should throw light upon. In any event, the psychologist's report ought to concentrate on what he knows, not on what he does not know. It is hardly necessary that he recapitulate his agonies in weighing data, accepting conclusions, rejecting conclusions, and holding other tentative impressions in abeyance. There is no need to hedge or to be indecisive, or even to "let the reader in on" the decision-making process. The process is complicated, but the major contradiction to a democratic approach is that it would take too many pages to convey the gross and subtle data that could permit the qualified reader to retrace the psychologist's steps. (As already indicated, however, it is desirable, when the personal relationship permits, to discuss such matters with team associates). It falls upon the psychologist to state his conclusions, together with appropriate modifying terms to indicate verbally the degree of confidence with which he offers them.

Speculation

Speculation refers to tentatively held conclusions for which adequate dependable evidence does not exist. Sometimes the psychologist's basis for such conclusions is little more than "impression," which might even stem from features of his own personality, or from one or two test responses that are interpretively equivocal. Hence speculation refers to conclusions offered at a low level of confidence. One of the greater sins a psychologist can commit is to fail to point out when he is speculating.

In perusing the thousands of negative comments made about psychological reports (some of which form the basis for Chapter 2), one might readily conclude that a major job activity of psychologists is speculating. If there is truth in such a conclusion, so much the worse for psychology. Then what is the occasion for speculating? Legitimately, speculation may be in order when few definitive data are available and an important issue requiring attention is raised by the person making the referral, or when the psychologist becomes aware of such an issue during his examination procedure. An uncertain answer may be better than none in *some* cases, particularly if it is not misleading. It may be important in certain cases to speculate about such matters as suicide, homicide, antisocial sexual acting out, cerebral pathology, or rehabilitation potential. Inadequate information about such matters may suggest the need for further investigations by a social worker, a medical specialist, or another who might be able to throw light on the topic. But speculation about matters which are not especially relevant may not be defensible. An example of this might be speculation about developmental events in a patient who is being seen in a setting where treatment is almost entirely by drugs.

Transfer of Responsibility

A final comment on the manner of presenting conclusions pertains to the transfer of responsibility for conclusions from the psychologist to his tests. For example, "Psychological testing reveals . . . ," "The Rorschach shows . . . ," "Stories given to the TAT point up a person who. . . ." It is hardly quibbling to insist that psychological tests reveal or indicate nothing. The psychologist uses tests, but reaches his own conclusions for which he, not the tests, is responsible. (Typically, in fact, his conclusions are based more on a battery than on individual tests.) Sometimes the above quotes are little more than a manner of speech, but in other cases they reflect a psychologist's lack of confidence in himself or in some conclusion(s) he plans to offer. He is hiding behind his tests. The effect on the reader might not always be what the psychologist desired. In fact, this way of presenting conclusions might prompt referrals asking for administration of certain tests because of the sort of information they are thought to reveal. In the case of nonpsychologically trained readers, lawyers or judges for example, the notion that decisions affecting a person's life turn on a test (whose validity might be challenged in the literature) rather than on a psychologist, a responsible human, may lead to some unsought outcomes. Ulrich, Stachnik, and Stainton (1963), in a study of gullibility to generalized personality interpretations, point to results that indicate " . . . the awe with which personality tests per se are viewed by the naive student or others of comparable test sophistication"—i.e., many readers of psychological reports. Snyder and Larson (1972) report similar findings.

PRIMARY PRESENTATION OF THE REPORT

The mode of primary presentation of the report may have a bearing on how it is written, though this need not be so. Many persons find it easier to absorb technical material by eye than by ear. When a report is requested for oral staff presentation, or is likely to serve this purpose, special attention is necessary in the preparation. Reports heard in staff meetings may often be characterized as "involved," "complex," or "saturated," and many are difficult to understand when presented orally. However, it is often possible to derive meaning, sometimes important meaning, on reading these same reports. It would be a worthwhile objective, then, to write reports suitable both for written and oral presentation.

TERMINOLOGY IN THE REPORT

Everyone probably agrees that a piece of writing ought to be comprehensible to its intended readers. Psychological reports are read by persons with various kinds of training and backgrounds, hence it is not possible to project, or to write for, a specific audience. Terminology obviously is one of the matters related to comprehensibility, and the question of appropriate terminology has not yet been settled. Psychological terminology is viewed by many as highly technical and specialized, complex, and esoteric (Tallent & Reiss, 1959c). Is it possible to substitute something simpler?

Sargent (1951) thinks not. At least in writing for consumers familiar with psychological constructs, she observes that, in the context of relating, "the degree and kind of abnormal psychological functioning . . . technical terms and concepts are . . . considered to be more economical and cogent carriers of meaning . . . than if they were to be translated into everyday language." Hammond and Allen (1953) go further. They contend that "Technical vocabulary is indispensable for three reasons: first, it is precise; second, it can communicate concepts that are virtually impossible to convey in ordinary language; and third, it is economical." These writers do point out that the amount of technical verbiage used should be gauged by the ability of the intended reader(s) to understand, and should be appropriate to the context, but for communicating "complex technical concepts with precision to a qualified reader," such a vocabulary is "indispensable."

A case can also be made against the use of technical terminology. Hammond and Allen themselves discuss frankly the shortcomings of such language as used in psychological reports, and suggest some remedies. These writers effectively point out the difficulties the psychologist may face in the use of such words and the lack of understanding or the misunderstanding they may cause in the reader(s) of the report. Cited is variability in sophistication and orientation among the readers, the specialized meaning of certain terms, and the multiple meanings as well as technical meanings which differ from lay meanings. There is also a demonstrated tendency for professional persons to assign individualized meanings to words commonly used in psychological reports. Here the work of Wendell Johnson (1945) and of Grayson and Tolman (1950) is pertinent. As an example of word ambiguity, Grayson and Tolman classified definitions of "anxiety" contributed by psychologists and psychiatrists—a word which appears in a very high percentage of psychological reports—into no fewer than seven categories of meaning. It would seem that the psychologist must indeed step lightly!

Another meaningful study that gives some understanding of at least the current effects of using technical verbiage is one by Davenport (1952). She found that interpretive statements taken from case reports frequently did not differentiate adequately among persons and were ambiguous, with psychoanalytic-type expressions the worst offender. This observation calls attention to a special problem about technical words—the issue of analytic terminology. Many psychologists are sharply against its use. Writing that incorporates analytic terminology is more fashionable in some quarters than in others; in some settings it seems to be the expected mode of expression. But the inexact, nondifferentiating use to which such a vocabulary may be put has caused considerable discussion. There has been for some years now a trend away from psychoanalytic terminology, and many psychologists may find it fashionable *not* to use it.

It may be true that technical words are precise, but such precision is to be found only in a carefully defined context associated with *discrete* orientations. It would be a prodigious task to train all writers and readers of psychological reports, even those at the professional level, to accept and learn some common meanings for several hundred words. At present, report readers—teachers, administrators, legal and correctional persons, medical people, and even psychiatrists and psychiatric social workers—typically do not have a large technical *psychological* vocabulary. Further, the multitude of schools, orientations, and loyalties which abound in the psychological domain would be a telling barrier. Nor would the eclectic, whose understanding reflects a number of viewpoints and glossaries, some of them contradictory, fare any better. Indeed, the same writer may use the same word with different meanings. Freud, for example, uses "ego" in various senses. Erikson uses "identity" somewhat differently in different contexts.

But what about the argument that technical words "communicate concepts which are virtually impossible to convey in ordinary language" and that they are "economical?" Hammond and Allen point up specific examples: the words "empathy," "rapport," and "subliminal." These words are said to be "virtually impossible to express in plain English: They may, by means of a lengthy paraphrase, be approximated, but the communication thus achieved is far less complete and *satisfactory* than that produced by use of the terms themselves *when they are fully understood by the reader* (italics supplied)." It does seem that paraphrased technical terms would be longer; how much longer would be determined from the context. The question is, who finds the technical terms more "satisfactory," since the study on "The Trouble with Psychological Reports" compels the belief that very large numbers of readers, and writers, do not. The crucial phrase is, "when they are fully understood by the reader." The findings of the Grayson-Tolman study are too overpowering to suggest that such conditions are readily attainable. The answer to the question of economy is, can fewer words be regarded as economical when they fail to do the job?

Technical psychological words used in a theoretical or a general context are wholly different than what is called for in clinically oriented usage; even in a theoretical context such words are meaningful only because they are in a consistent, theoretical framework. Theories, by definition, deal with general phenomena. Clinically oriented psychology deals with the application of specific knowledge of general phenomena to persons. Technical names are certainly appropriate for abstract ideas or occurrences or for scientific notions, or occurrences which are subjected to special study. Technical names are appropriate for many ideas or concepts, or for phenomena the understanding of which can suitably be modified with words to meet the individual instance. Individual personality study may be importantly different only because of the numerous ways and occasions in which generally identified behaviors or other psychological phenomena are expressed.

Considering the example of "empathy," to the extent our knowledge of an individual permits we may describe specific situations in which particular usages of this word are identifiable and contributory to the understanding of a unique person. We may glibly talk of an empathic person, but does he exhibit empathy in all situations—does he experience empathy for Hitler or for modern-day terrorists? It would be better to talk of the surface correlates of empathy, of the depth of the experience, of the kinds of situations which call forth empathic experiences, and of the kinds of situations in which the "empathic" person experiences feelings quite different from empathy. This approach to personality description is appropriate to clinically oriented psychology. Clinical description has to be specific because it is supposed to be useful, a basis for decision and action. In clinical prediction, where there may be a question of assaultive behavior or suicide, it does not help much to talk of generalized and somewhat ubiquitous psychological phenomena like sadomasochism, hostility, narcissistic wounds, or inadequate empathic development, because Aunt Fanny and perhaps her psychotherapist too may "have" these.

In the clinically oriented mission it is necessary to spell out each conclusion in terms of the occurrences, levels, nuances, and interrelationship of events with the rest of personality. Such an approach is less economical of syllables than is one that relies on technical words to transmit insights. A more careful approach, in fact, may utilize technical verbiage to help establish a set or emphasize a personality component, but not really as organic to the description. For example, "This patient is narcissistic *in the sense that . . ."* or, "He has little confidence in himself and is dominantly oriented to seeking all sorts of support, guidance and reassurance, essentially an oral person." Notice that the ways in which the person is "oral" are spelled out. In how many ways, grossly, subtly, disguisedly, can one be "oral"? In our view words like "oral," "narcissistic," "masochistic," "immature," "compulsive," and "schizophrenia" are often more concealing than revealing.

Technical words do not cause, but readily lend themselves to, imprecise or incomplete thinking. There is the 'error of nominalism," wherein we simply name a thing or an occurrence and think we understand something of the real world. Of course, this patient is anal, or immature, or insecure, or sadistic. But really, what is this living person, John Jones, *like* when he is anal, or immature, or insecure, or sadistic, and what does he *do*, overtly or intrapsychically? Do the terms differentiate, make for understanding? Can not two persons have dominant traits of sadism, one of them awaiting capital punishment stemming from this characteristic, the other the respectable warden charged with carrying out the sentence? It may be countered that if the psychologist is careful to define the term *as he uses it in a particular case*, them the term *would* differentiate among persons. But then the term itself would become superfluous except, as suggested above, that it might be used to help establish a set or emphasize a personality component. In this sense, "sadistic" may be employed as a strong word of dramatic quality to help focus on a central personality theme of personal or social significance. Too many such words obviously cannot be used in one report.

This point of view perhaps requires more evidence, although hopefully the arguments developed at least pose a real challenge to what we regard as the continued irresponsible use of technical language. Two specific questions follow from this challenge. The first is whether it would be desirable to write reports in lay language. It is criticized that such writing permits the least common denominator to set the level of the report. In a sense this is true, but since even professionals trip over technical terms, plain English would seem to meet the need for a clear understanding shared by all readers of the psychological report.

Since technical language is often presumed more scientific, it is well to note Block's (1961) rejection of this point of view and his use of lay language in a quantitative research method (Q-sort technique). He notes "The orientation of the presently proposed descriptive language is, as Lewin would say (1943), a 'contemporaneous' one. *The subject is described as he appears and is understood by the observer at the time of observation."*

Technical language is sometimes defended as necessary or at least useful as a "professional shorthand." If so, does it have a place in psychological reports, many of whose readers have not been trained in this shorthand? Worse still, in view of the Grayson-Tolman study, showing as it does intraprofessional variation as well as interprofessional variation in the understanding of professional terms, it becomes necessary to redefine the various symbols.

In its current stage of development, the mental health profession, considered collectively, has an appreciable tolerance for terminological looseness, and unambiguous usage of technical words is not yet the rule. It seems to cause little concern to label as "paranoid" one who is defensive in interpersonal relations and cautious, and as "compulsive" a person who is careful, conscientious, ethical, and reliable. You may even hear that all psychologists or all graduate students are "compulsive"—that one has to be in order to negotiate the curriculum.

Such loose usage raises yet an additional question. What is technical language? Is "compulsive" still a technical word? Or "paranoid?" Or "identity?" These terms have drifted into the language and are freely used by the layman, sometimes no more carelessly than by the psychologist. They may be used in psychological reports, if used responsibly and meaningfully as suggested in the foregoing discussion. On the other hand, "cut-off whole," "sex shock," "position response," certainly are technical terms, test talk. They can only confuse or befuddle most readers. They have no place in most psychological reports.

There is a common-sense approach to the use of words. Words can be our servants or our master. They are supposed to stand for real phenomena, things, or ideas, and as such they can help us to conceptualize our ideas in terms of real events, or we can allow them to confuse us with generalities, vagaries, ambiguities, and imprecision. There is not necessarily a one-to-one relationship between word and referent, as *a* stands for the side of a given triangle. These facts are further complicated because many words, big words, little-known words, impressive sounding words, have long been used by psychologists as currency and have an appeal not based on their communication value.

Having noted all this, we might as well conclude, that at least in the present state of the science and the art of psychology, and of language, our word usage is going to be something less than perfect—even as is word usage in many everyday documents. It is difficult in our field to get away without at least occasionally using such stock-in-trade words as "anxiety," "defense," or "affective," even though there is inadequate consensus as to their meaning. But knowing this, we can be careful how we use them. In-context usage well might result in less ambiguity than the out-of-context studies that defined these terms as ambiguous. And we may rationalize that we are still far from perfection in many other areas of human endeavor. Our interpretations are often not perfect either, and we are too aware of the many pitfalls that await the unwary psychologist. But the responsible psychologist can produce an effective psychological report.

This discussion of terminology, then, is not intended to be totally proscriptive of technical terminology. But the heavily technical reports that were all but universal yesteryear, and which, alas, linger on here and there, clearly are not appropriate to most practical missions. We use some technical terms *in communicating among professionals who can be expected to know these terms* simply because there are no substitutes. In the report on Henry Dennis (p. 210) terms like "form constancy" and "position in space," and the scores obtained on these are highly meaningful to the intended reader, but the psychologist attenuates the technical psychological material in reporting to the child's physician (p. 210-211). It is difficult to document an organic brain syndrome (or to do without the term "organic brain syndrome") without using some technical material. Diagnostic terminology is frequently appropriate in a psychiatric setting, school terminology in a school setting, counseling terminology in a counseling setting. Even though there is insufficient understanding of schizophrenia with accompanying semantic confusion about the term "schizophrenia," we have no substitute ("split personality" will hardly do!).

UNFAMILIAR CONCEPTS IN THE REPORT

The use of unfamiliar concepts or materials from the psychologist's tool box can be as great a barrier to effective communication, and evoke much the same personal reaction, as the use of unfamiliar words. Unfamiliar concepts that psychologists are prone to use, to the detriment of the clinical mission, stem from (1) theory, (2) tests, (3) statistics.

Theoretical concepts that give trouble are often carried into the report by equally troublesome words. Many readers remain unenlightened after reading about "projection in the classical Freudian sense," "an inverted Oedipal complex," "unconscious fantasy," "an external super-ego," or "identification with the aggressor."

Simply recording test results may suggest to the reader that perhaps he should but doesn't know what is being talked about. After hearing about perseveration, constriction, shading shock, coarctation, experience balance, scatter, the reader remains no more enlightened. The latter concept is familiar to many report readers, but do they understand its significance?

Other unfamiliar matter presented to the reader presupposes familiarity with the physical nature of tests and score sheets. This includes talk of the client's performance on the Object Assembly test, a particular response to Card

VI (Is that the one with the butterfly?), or a clear spike on the psychopathic deviate scale which is accentuated by unusually low scores on the neurotic triad. Some thoughtful psychologists try to take the reader into consideration by a description intended to be meaningful: "on a test involving the assembly of pieces such as in a jig-saw puzzle . . ." or "on a card showing two male figures commonly seen as father and son. . . ." It is uncertain to what extent these humanitarian essays bring the reader closer to understanding.

Statistical expressions cause a certain amount of dismay too, although this is not as widespread. Unfortunately, but understandably, reporting in terms of T-scores or percentiles would not be appreciated (Tallent & Reiss, 1959b), although from a technical standpoint these have much to commend them. Talking about people in terms of norms, standardization data, or standard deviations will probably not be confusing to the untrained inasmuch as such persons will not become sufficiently involved to become confused.

THE LENGTH OF REPORTS

A certain business executive likes to relate the anecdote about the occasion when he assigned a new employee to prepare a report for him. In due time a voluminous piece of writing was returned. Dismayed, the executive pointed out that the required information could be presented on one, or certainly not more than two, pages. "But sir," pleaded the young man, "I don't know that much about the matter you assigned me to."

On purely impressionistic grounds, there does not seem to be a necessary positive correlation between the length of documents and the quality of their content. Some observers insist that in the case of psychological reports the relationship is a negative one. At any rate, report readers tend to dislike overly long reports, even when they are otherwise good.

The often noted "length compulsion" probably has a dual etiology. Teachers often demand long pieces of writing, probably with the idea that this will lead to coping thoroughly with the assigned task. Is it possible to assign a term paper to a college class without a hand going up and a student asking how long it must be? The present-day psychological consultation also seems to encourage long reports. The nonspecific referral is one factor; another would seem to be a defensive attitude in many psychologists which gives rise to unnecessary inclusiveness of topic coverage, heavy detailing, hedging, and superfluous qualifications that are wasteful of space. The long document may then be identified as the "exhaustive report," or, more commonly, the "shotgun report."

Some common-sense considerations might help to reduce the length of reports. But when is a report *too long? It is often too long when it is not conceptualized in terms of the mission.* It probably is too long when the psychologist is unhappy over the length of time required to write it and he experiences difficulty in organizing a multitude of details for presentation. It is too long when it contains content that is not relevant or useful, when the detailing is greater than can be put to good use, when low confidence statements (speculations) are presented without an excellent rationale for their inclusion, when the writing is unnecessarily repetitious, when the organization does not evidence "tightness," and when the reader is irritated by the length or limits his reading of the report to one or more smaller sections like a summary, a diagnostic impression, or a statement of recommendations.

The Ten Commandments are expressed in 297 words. It took 300 words to write the Declaration of Independence and 266 words to compose the Gettysburg Address. Surely the modern psychologist can try to approach this standard.

CHAPTER FOUR

Content of
the
Psychological Report

There is presently no consensus on the appropriate topics for a
psychological report. Even so, if the psychologist will consider the
various purposes to which his contribution may be put, and the roles of
several definable classes of content in the report, he may better know
what kinds of material to include. Is his choice of topics legitimate and
defensible? Can he define, for the particular case, his principles of
selection? The report writer can gain insight into these matters by
studying reports that have been traditional in psychology. He can also
try to decide, on a rational basis, what content should enter his report.
In so doing, it becomes apparent that while certain issues are never
appropriate, other topic categories may frequently be discussed.
The choice and the appropriate emphasis of report content depend on
the case and the mission.

The psychologist, in his evaluative role, is a source of information about people.
He is consulted when it is thought that he can supply needed information that
would not otherwise be available, or simply when a supplementary opinion
would be helpful to another. This kind of information properly makes up the
basic content of psychological reports.

Some, however, think the task of the psychologist should be to merely pass along his "findings." Such a view suggests that the process of clinical communication is a more basic matter than the issue of what to communicate. Quite to the contrary, adequate guidelines for determining what content the psychologist should communicate can be discussed only in general terms, and must be developed in terms of the various missions or the settings in which psychologists work. Yet an emphasis on the techniques of communication may imply that the proper content of psychological reports is merely what some battery of tests yields; that the psychologist administers and scores tests, interprets them, then gathers up the "results" and transmits them to others. To think this way neglects the fact that when the psychologist accepts a consultation he is charged with a mission. The products of assessment probes—the conclusions of the consultation—therefore ought to be *selected* interpretations arrived at through consideration of both the raw data *and* the evaluative goal. This chapter scrutinizes the development of report content—the appropriate conclusions of the consultation—in relation to the mission of the psychologist.

THE MULTIPLE PURPOSE OF REPORT CONTENT

The usage of psychological reports dictates that content be developed in accordance with (1) the needs of the immediate mission, (2) the anticipation of questions and future needs, and (3) the creation of a record.

Needs of the Mission

The immediate mission must be regarded as having the highest priority, for this is understood in relation to a felt need and is therefore the only purpose (other than research, or sometimes training) that justifies the seeking of psychological information. Unfortunately, the full scope of the mission is not always easy to define, particularly when information is not requested in specific terms. But the request for information, even when quite specific, does not necessarily circumscribe the mission. The specific request or statement of problem may profitably be modified as a result of discussion between the psychologist and the person who has referred the case. Beyond this, the psychologist must exercise judgment and decide how he understands the case in terms of his own experience, background, and theoretical and value systems.

Anticipation of Needs

Often the psychologist might wish to add to his understanding of his mission in anticipation of further immediate or short-term uses that might be made of his report, or of further questions that he feels might arise in current work with the case. If he is writing about a patient he feels is likely to present problems in nursing care, these might be explained in anticipation of difficulties. Similarly, problems might be foreseen in the areas of psychotherapy, rehabilitation, social behavior, or diagnosis. Suggestions might be included on the best approaches in psychotherapy, in occupational therapy, or in diagnostic interview techniques.

Creation of a Record

The final, but essential purpose of the report is the creation of a record for long-term use. A record is valuable as a means of comparing a person's condition from one evaluation period to another. The psychologist must anticipate further questions and uses, but such anticipations are more easily found in short-term considerations of the case than in projections of its usage over the long run. A person who had earlier been regarded as showing a functional reaction may, some years later, be examined for organicity, and the psychological record searched for earlier evidences or suspicions of such a disorder. Or a person who commits a crime of violence might have his earlier record consulted for an understanding of personality tendencies which might help explain such behavior. The psychologist's record may eventually be used for research, in a court case, or for its further direct contribution to a case, as in a patient's readmission to a hospital. The difficulties of anticipation may therefore appear to be great, but the discussions of relevance and appropriateness later in this chapter will hopefully make the task easier.

DEFINITION AND CLASSIFICATION OF CONTENT

Before delving further into the topics of content, we should differentiate among the various meanings of the term. Content can be thought of in a rather broad sense, or in a more limited way. In a broad sense, content is anything the psychologist writes into his report—perhaps statements on such topics as the reason for referral, why a person is under treatment, how well a child cooperated, an IQ, an F percent, a diagnostic impression, a discussion of scatter, what the client saw on Card II, or the fact that the client had to be excused twice to go to the bathroom. In the limited sense, content refers to the conclusions that are transmitted to the person who has referred the case.

It is perhaps most useful to think of content in the limited sense as the *primary* (organic) content of the report, and everything else as *secondary* content. This makes it easier to concentrate on the mission and to relegate other material that the psychologist feels ought to be transmitted to its rightful auxiliary position. Making the distinction will help to highlight the conclusions and to de-emphasize whatever else is required to make the report complete or effective.

The primary content may also be thought of as the psychological core content, since it is the basic (and original) contribution the psychologist makes to the case study. In many instances all or a substantial part of this may be congruent with the findings of others. When this occurs, so much the better! The psychologist's contribution is original, not necessarily for the information it supplies—since personality information may be gained in a number of ways against a number of orientations—but because his conclusions derive from his expertness in utilizing psychological methods for understanding the personality of individuals. It is as much a contribution when the psychologist, in agreement with a child's teacher, suggests that the child's poor classroom deportment is a desperate attempt to achieve recognition (which the teacher might make a direct effort to provide), as it is to report that a child's reading difficulty is based on brain dysfunction.

Various items of secondary content round out the report. Such material is not vital in the sense that the conclusions are so regarded. Nevertheless, the information may be important in developing and supporting the conclusions, and just as a fortunate choice of words and pleasant readability add effectiveness, so can information of secondary importance help to "put across" a report. Such nonorganic items as the date evaluation was made and the reason for referral can have great bearing at some future time.

Orienting Data

First to be considered is orienting data. These refer to judiciously selected items of information (probably available elsewhere) which may help put the conclusions in appropriate context. For example, it may make a difference on how the conclusions are understood if the reason for referral or something of the client's social or educational background is given. A prosaic matter like the client's age might be highly relevant, since behavior or goals which are fully appropriate and expected at one age may be regarded as inappropriate, ludicrous, pathologic, or socially incongruous at another. To illustrate further, a request for vocational appraisal is often a straightforward matter, but sometimes it is not. How shall we understand the findings that might be obtained on a 35-year-old woman who appeared at the writer's office and asked for "vocational guidance testing"? Asked the nature of her vocational and educational background, she disclosed that she had just been awarded a Ph.D. in anthropology.

Illustrative and Persuasive Content

Illustrative material, the use of which has already been discussed in a more general context (pp. 56-60), may also be regarded as secondary content. At some unknown point such matter shades into persuasive writing, which, at the extreme, is neither objective nor scientific. Some would argue that the reader should be allowed to reach his own conclusions. A good thought, until we consider the process of reaching conclusions, and the ingredients which go into these. The psychologist is responsible for forming his conclusions, and to the extent he has confidence in them he has the responsibility to try to be an effective contributor to the case study. Let us look at the case of W, p. 197, for support of this principle. The psychologist had obviously reached some conclusions (not reached by other team members in whom the patient did not confide) to the effect that the patient might be dangerous and that it was imperative that he be observed carefully. He therefore felt it as his *responsibility* to the community and to the patient (in this order) to convince the team of the necessity for special measures. The dramatic material presented is persuasive as well as illustrative. To utilize all of this material for just illustrative purposes would probably not be defensible.

Subconclusions

Judiciously used illustrative material may be considered secondary content on a par with the necessary subconclusions which contribute to one or several of the major conclusions of the report. Major conclusions require support, not in the sense that raw data may validly support conclusions or that the psychologist's impressions are otherwise suspect, but because these conclusions are more comprehensible and useful when presented in the context of their components. It would be unthinkable, for example, to suggest, for no apparent reason, a diagnosis of schizophrenia. Mention should be made of such observed deviancies as a formal thought disorder, bizarre content, pervasive and exaggerated suspiciousness, and grossly inadequate insight. Nor would it be well to suggest that a patient is capable of destructive acting out without first pointing to such (possible) factors as severe undercontrol of thought and conduct, a tendency to projection and strong accompanying hostile ideation, and belligerence in the examination situation.

SOURCES OF CONTENT

A number of sources of content are available to the psychologist, although there is by no means agreement as to what constitutes the proper sources of content. Three of these sources are directly available to the psychologist through his examination: test data, interview material, and observed behavior. In addition, the psychologist may observe the client in nontest situations; he may even know him as a member of the community. Finally, there are a number of nonpsychological sources of information ordinarily available to the psychologist. These may include a social history, psychiatric and medical reports, nursing notes, staff conference proceedings, reports from various therapists, or discussion with a physician, psychiatrist, teacher, principal, lawyer, nurse, attendant, therapist, or social worker.

Some workers, generally not psychologists, do not look at all kindly upon the practice of the psychologist seeking out and using data other than that elicited through testing. Those few who hold this attitude in its most extreme form would have the psychologist do fully blind diagnoses, and not see the client or know anything about him. This position is held because psychological tests are regarded by these persons as objective tools, and the psychologist's function is seen as "testing"—a laboratory procedure where extraneous information might bias the "readings." Besides, expressing interest in the data or conclusions of others, or even in the psychologist's own interpersonal observations, to some co-workers smacks of dishonesty or calls into question the competency of the individual psychologist or the validity of testing. Presumably, if it is not practicable for one psychologist to test the client and turn over the protocol to a colleague for interpretation, then at least he should attempt to shield his objectivity from what he sees while testing the client.

Most psychologists flatly reject this point of view, pointing out that blind diagnosis is (1) a training device, (2) a stunt, and (3) a research method. Blind evaluation can, however, supply pertinent information. Some psychologists might wish to examine the protocol in the presence of minimal data available from other sources before completing the evaluation by utilizing all pertinent material. A comparison of conclusions arrived at blindly with data available from other sources may permit him to estimate the proper confidence which may be placed in various aspects of the integrated conclusions he offers. In general, where practical decisions are to be made which may have temporary or lasting effect on a person, he should have the benefit of being evaluated by the psychologist under conditions where conclusions and recommendations are most likely to be realistic, accurate, or helpful—a matter of basic human ethics. The psychologist who functions in this manner is clearly a high level professional, not a technician.

Recognized, but perhaps not adequately appreciated by many psychologists, is the fact that tests are merely devices to help understanding. They represent contrived samples of behavior, some of which can responsibly be regarded, with a good degree of confidence, as having meaning for more typical life situations. Others, however, are of more tenuous value. In general, and within practical limitations, the more behavioral samples observed in the psychologist's office and elsewhere, the better, and the more meaningful and responsible the conclusions. Tests help us to understand the meaning and purpose of behavior in the person's everyday life situation; knowing something of a person's life in advance adds meaning and significance to test performance, thus increasing its practical implications. Tests are predictors of significant behavior only in the sense that they show potentialities; otherwise there would be a one-to-one relationship between test response and behavior, or between test interpretation and behavior. A Rorschach protocol may suggest a potentiality for behavioral undercontrol, but seen against a background of the person's history with regard to this variable, a more precise and practical estimate of future conduct, or an understanding of present or past conduct, may be offered. The value of testing is based only partly on tests, and partly on the circumstances of testing and the collateral material available to the psychologist.

Certain cautions are necessary in using data which are or may be available elsewhere. The danger is repetition or unnecessary duplication, which is wasteful of time, increases report length, and may be offensive to those who feel that certain kinds of information (for example, clinical appearance and behavior) or social history are more properly identified with professions other than psychology. The psychologist may therefore reflect on what such material adds to his report.

What, for example, does the psychologist tell Frank's teacher that she has not observed over and over since he has been in her class, the psychologist's last observation, incidentially, being the reason the child was referred?

> Frank is a neatly dressed, eight-year-old boy whose left eye constantly squints. He is courteous, perhaps overly courteous, and is most cooperative. When he doesn't know an answer he becomes noticeably upset, sometimes appearing to be on the verge of tears.

What is added to the psychologist's contribution to the case study when he reports as follows on Patient A?

> The patient says he came to the hospital because for the last three months he has become extremely "nervous"—couldn't eat, couldn't sleep, "started hitting the jug again," has been quarreling with his wife, his boss and fellow employees, and last Tuesday night struck his wife during an argument although he "didn't mean to do it."

This information is no doubt available from the intake or initial examination interview. What is added to the case study when a psychologist in a psychiatric hospital writes about Patient B?

> The patient enters the office with apparent apprehension, glances furtively about the room and asks if it is wired. He several times inquires about the examiner's purpose with questions like "What's this for?" He is guarded and evasive in responding to questions.

Isn't such material routinely noted in the psychiatrist's report? And, of course, it is usually the physician or the social worker who reports:

> The patient is the youngest in a family of five children, the four older sibs being girls. All during school he was teased by his classmates because of certain effeminate ways and he was taunted with the name "sissy." He admits that he doesn't have much interest in girls and thinks that this is why he was rejected by the army. He volunteers that the medical examiner asked him, "Do you go out with girls?"

There is great distinction to be made, however, between repeating or duplicating what is usually the property of others, and utilizing such material *in the context of a new integration*. This sort of content can be employed for strengthening conclusions and insights suggested by tests, for understanding the practical significance of behavioral trends as indicated by test data, for showing how underlying psychological factors may relate to overt behavior which is of concern, or as illustrations for presented conclusions.

Thus, for Frank:

This child's perfectionistic strivings, if not modified, can become a way of life, crippling spontaneity and ability to relate with warmth and satisfaction. He could develop a very serious breakdown as early as adolescence. He has the feeling that catastrophe awaits him if he does not achieve at an exaggeratedly high level, that somehow such performance is expected of him. Seeking to minimize fear, he sacrifices the positive feelings and true interest in his scholarship, for being correct is what is important to him and not the meaning of the work. This child has need for warmth, kindness, and acceptance— especially when he does not know the answer. He needs to learn that he can be accepted for himself rather than for his performance. He should be involved in play therapy, particularly in contact and rough-and-tumble games where getting dirty is assured. Finger painting might also be helpful.

For Patient A:

. . . anxiety centering largely about his sex role, conflict over his adequacy as a male, and dependency needs for which he cannot secure adequate gratification is most usually not too troublesome to him because a pattern of life emphasizing order, meticulous attention to details, and achievement tends to prevent the experiencing of acute distress. However, this defensive pattern is currently not sufficiently effective to control either strong subjective responses—anxiety and tension—which are apparently evidenced in his being "nervous," in his inability to eat or sleep well, and in drinking. Similarly, rather pervasive negative feelings toward others, about which he usually has no particular awareness, are now associated with an acting out potential. He currently ascribes his own antagonistic feelings to others and perceives people as a threat to him. Though according to the information now available he has expressed hostility only verbally with the exception of one temporary lapse of control when he struck his wife, he is seen as potentially capable of serious assaultive behavior and he should be closely observed for these tendencies particularly during his period of acute upset.

It should also be pointed out that the medical data of a physician influenced the writing of this passage, though there is no direct reference to it. The "nervousness," insomnia, and eating difficulties which the patient reports could have a physiological basis, but since the medical examination was essentially negative, these symptoms may tentatively be ascribed to the psychological state with which they are consistent.

Consider the following passage written about Patient B.

. . . he ascribes these unbridled hostile impulses to others, which causes him to experience his relationships in a context of severe threat. With the loosening of ties to reality he seems to see threat everywhere and is beyond rationality in his suspiciousness, a factor which no doubt aggravates his ability to function socially. This was observed during the examination where he was guarded and evasive, queried the examiner several times with "What's this for?" and especially when he entered the office, furtively looked about the room and asked if it was wired.

This integration of test conclusions with clinical observations makes real and alive the psychological defense maneuver and its social consequences. The purpose here is hardly to tell that Patient B is paranoid, which everyone knows, but to present the condition in a context where it is more understandable and its severity illustrated. This presentation differs from the more common practice of noting clinical behavior prior to offering test conclusions, and then reporting the latter without reference to the patient's clinical behavior, which is kept separate from these (exclusively test) conclusions. The psychologist may feel the need to put forth much effort to illustrate or support his "independent" (test-derived) conclusion that Patient B is paranoid. This may be accomplished by offering test data, the meanings of which are less obvious (and also less valid) than the overt paranoid behavior of the patient. This overt behavior would probably lend in this instance excellent support and illustrate his test-gained diagnostic material were it not regarded as out of bounds to psychologists. Thus, "on the Rorschach he sees a number of faces and the rear end of a bee; on the figure drawing there is eye emphasis, spearlike fingers, and concern is expressed over the size of the buttocks on the male figure; and one of his TAT stories depicts a character as an F.B.I. agent." This practice may be likened to determining a person's job qualifications by giving him an aptitude test, when actual job performance records on the subject—the sort of criteria against which the test is validated—are available.

This discussion of the source and the appropriateness of the content that the psychologist presents is to be understood in the context of an adequate, functioning team and in relation to a setting. In a traditional psychiatric setting, it is not the psychologist who is usually charged with integrating the total data of the various disciplines. In other kinds of settings, the psychologist, by choice or not, may do many things usually regarded as beyond his role in traditional psychiatric teams. The psychologist in current team practice often may be more selective, and utilize the contributions of others or material ordinarily available to others only as these help to round out and make more useful the basic psychological conclusions.

SELECTION OF CONTENT IN TERMS OF RELEVANCE

The problem of what is relevant for a given psychological report often is not broached. This is because of the tendency of psychologists to see their role as reporting the "findings"—whatever their tests happen to yield, such as IQs and other raw and partially interpreted data, rather than developing and interpreting content in terms of a specific mission. What content goes into a given report may depend on any or all of the following: (1) the orientation of the psychologist, (2) the orientation of the person who makes the referral, (3) the particular immediate problem which is under consideration, (4) the anticipated use(s) to which the findings will be put, (5) habit.

When the psychologist wishes to select his content on the basis of a firm rationale, he may often, if he wishes, establish himself within liberal limits as the sole judge of relevancy. On the other hand, he may be subject to pressures from other team members and the person who makes the referral may take quite an active role in the determination of relevancy. If the latter is a Freudian he may let it be known that he is interested in such matters as psychosexual development, drives and dynamics, the unconscious in general, and the client's defensive structure and ego strength. If his orientation is primarily descriptive he may lay heavy emphasis on diagnosis or classification, and expect the psychological report to work toward these ends.

Despite the strong orientations of many readers of psychological reports, the interests of the client and the goals of the setting should receive priority. In a setting where rehabilitation is emphasized, depth evaluations often detract from the main purpose. Instead, what is probably needed is information to help the staff understand the client's personal and social skills, his attitudes toward rehabilitation and assuming a position of greater independence, and perhaps his interests or the ability to learn new skills. In settings where psychotherapy is practiced, it is often desirable to learn through psychological evaluation of the individual's ability to profit from this form of treatment, the nature of the defensive structure, the basic personality integrity (ego strength), and hints to the psychotherapist. Where mental deficiency seems to be the problem, a detailed qualitative and quantitative evaluation of intellectual and social skills might be in order.

Because of the possibly differing orientations among psychologists and other staff members, and also the wide range of problems clients may present, there may exist a difference of opinion on what would be relevant information in a given case. A conference between psychologist and the person who makes the referral, or indeed a preliminary staff conference, might be the best way of determining what kind of data are needed. Of course, after the psychologist starts his examination pertinent material not previously seen as important might emerge.

The determination of relevancy is a very practical problem when we consider the scope and complexity of personality, to say nothing of the various ways in which we try to understand it. The full personality can hardly be approximated in a psychological report, even when the psychologist resorts to the presentation of an exhaustive list of conclusions he has derived. Nor would it be easy in practice to visualize where full or global coverage might be desirable, apart from the economic difficulties such an attempt would entail. Reports that include more content than is required consume too much writing time and are too long to read. They impose on the reader the task of separating for his use that which is essential from that which is not—a duty that really belongs primarily to the psychologist, to the extent he can anticipate what is needed.

What sort of conclusions should the psychologist report? There is no general answer to this question. The sort of information that might be indispensable in one case is probably superfluous or quite out of place in another. It is often appropriate to report on such matters as the self-concept, how others see the person, intellectual prowess or shortcomings, interests, life goals, frustrations, anxieties, defenses, and interpersonal and sexual adjustment factors. Frequently it is not. Sometimes it is well to discuss acting out potentialities, self-destructive tendencies, impairments, relative skills, range and qualitative features of affective response, diagnostic category, intellectual level, or intellectual functioning, but often it is wasteful and an imposition on the reader to do so.

Fortunately, it is possible to be more specific than this. Much of the remainder of this chapter is given over to a discussion of the sort of content often found in reports. We can assert quite definitely that certain kinds of content sometimes found in reports *never* belong there, and it is not at all likely that any particular primary content category ought to be represented in *all* reports. It is constructive to talk about the kinds of content which are frequently appropriate. Further, we often should not think about content on an all-or-none basis, but in terms of how much emphasis ought to be given to various kinds of content in specific case situations.

AN EVALUATION OF COMMON CONTENT CATEGORIES
IN "TRADITIONAL" PSYCHOLOGICAL REPORTS

A systematic evaluation, specifically of psychological report content, might begin with an examination of what constitutes the "traditional" psychological report. The "traditional" report apparently came into its present form by accretion rather than by formulation and development of a rationale. This was of concern to Taylor and Teicher, who in 1946 noted that "Clinical psychology . . . appears to have given little systematic study to the manner in which test findings are organized and formulated to provide necessary records and to render the data easily and fully understood by professional associates." Their solution to the problem was to offer a report-writing outline quite similiar to the many now in existence. Apparently there was then no concern with what content is appropriate for *specific* reports, since the authors made reference only to the "test findings" and to "the data."

Many current psychological reports contain abundant "archeological" indicators of the origins of psychological practice. The early school background and the influence of the testing movement are evident in the prominent concern with matters of the intellect, and especially with the exalted position of the IQ. A more recent layer of development (1939) building on the Binet-Terman foundation is seen in the assignment of three IQs per person rather than one, and in the eager interest as to which of his skill groupings—verbal or performance—is better. With the appearance in this country of the inkblots, and the publication of the TAT, prominent new foci were what the person sees and the stories he tells. After the association of psychology with psychiatry, Freud was welcomed into most clinics, and the emphasis shifted to personality, albeit one aspect of personality—such impalpables as the drives which trouble the individual and society, defenses, and retrospective developmental reconstructions. All of these accretions commonly make up modern reports. Just as taxes, once enacted, are hardly ever repealed, content categories, once they find their way into a report, seldom find their way out.

Test-by-Test Reporting

Content categories do sometimes change, however. In many settings emphasis has shifted from discussion of clients' performance on tests to contributions derived with the help of tests. Test-by-test reporting has lost favor. Now the battery report is utilized by most psychologists. Nevertheless, content categories based on tests still seem to exist, although not formally divided into such units. It is sometimes easy to read reports and silently observe that "now he (the psychologist) is talking about his WAIS data (the client has a good fund of information, superior vocabulary and conceptual ability . . . her knowledge of cultural precepts is somewhat better than her ability to manipulate concrete materials, and visual-motor coordination is poorer than her verbal skills . . .)." Similarly, the reader might be aware that "now he (the psychologist) is talking about the Rorschach," even though intellectual factors are again under discussion —and though the material appears in a section of the report so labelled as to suggest that some other content, i.e., "personality" or "emotional factors" is the focus (respect for reality is basically good, but there is a poverty of fantasy and creativity, the patient tending to restrict her range of interest and to understand and deal with events in simple, stereotyped terms . . .). But the almost complete demise of the test-by-test report is at least a step in the right direction. Reports, as a result, now tend to be less test-oriented and more person-oriented.

Reporting in Terms of Part Processes

Another type of broad content categorization still finds acceptance in many settings. This is the report which focuses upon part processes—for example, intellection, drives, dynamics, affective responses, defenses, or sex adjustment. Objection is raised to this kind of report usually because some readers have difficulty in reconstructing the "whole person" from the segments. This kind of reporting predetermines what categories of content are important in *all* cases, largely relieving the psychologist of the necessity of questioning which of his conclusions are relevant and which are not.

Content Categories in Traditional Reports

The more typical traditional reports tend to contain a number of narrow content categories and two major categories, the first (typically appearing first in the report) labelled something like "Intellectual Aspects," and the second "Emotional Aspects," or simply "Personality." These common content categories may serve as a stable reference point against which revised categories may be compared.

Preliminary Part of Report

The first item of a report is often a statement of the reason for referral. This can be a valuable piece of information, since the psychologist's mission is (or should be) largely defined by the referring person's need for help with some specific problem. A statement of the reason for referral, therefore, may orient the reader on the sort of material likely to follow.

Following this may be a section on clinical behavior, various kinds of identifying information, or social data. Sometimes these heterogeneous classes of information are combined, appearing under the same heading or the same section of the report.

What the client does or says during his stay in the psychologist's office is commonly reported under a label like "Clinical Behavior," "Behavioral Note," "Behavioral Observations," or "Clinical Observations." The length of the section ranges from a few lines up to perhaps two single-spaced pages. But the sort of material found here may vary widely from report to report and from psychologist to psychologist. In addition to behavioral information, this section often contains identifying information (e.g., age, city of residence), descriptive information (e.g., dress, attractiveness, how make-up is used), impressions (e.g., the client has an underlying hostile attitude), matters of social history (e.g., the peson ran away and got married at 16), or the reason the person is being seen in the clinic, in the counselor's office or wherever, in the individual's own words. In many instances such information is unjustifiably repetitious (e.g., the date of admission to the hospital, height, body build) or what is elsewhere conveniently available, and such data are usually raw, uninterpreted, and often of doubtful value. Thus, "The patient readily entered the examining room and took the chair assigned" (few patients are dragged in, even when they are negativistic about being examined; in a school setting, however, a child's approach to an examiner is sometimes such as to challenge the validity of intelligence test results). Another example: "He wore a loose-fitting, faded blue bathrobe" (the one issued to him); and was unshaven" (the patient is not permitted to shave himself and is shaved by an attendant three times weekly).

The behavior commented upon may be normal behavior (the patient responded appropriately to questions, or showed appropriate affect, or gave no evidence of delusions or hallucinations); pathological behavior (the patient sat staring off into space, but with some difficulty could be induced to respond); common behavior (the patient smoked four filter-tip cigarettes during the two-hour testing session); or distinctive behavior (the patient was unusually ingratiating). Verbalizations commonly appear here too. ("He spoke at length about his war experiences: 'I can still see the way the sergeant looked with his guts hanging out.' ")

Presumably, the material selected for reporting has some interpretive meaning which is best translated into clinically significant conclusions by the person who requested the evaluation or by other associates. This abrogation of responsibility is, of course, out of keeping with the consultant role as discussed in earlier contexts. This practice goes so far as to at times strain the interpretive resources of even the most imaginative clinician ("the patient wore a bright red tie," or "the patient was excused during the testing period to go to the bathroom"). It should also be a matter of concern that there is no rationale or consensual basis for what should appear in this section; this becomes obvious when we consider how much irrelevant and unoriginal data are found here.

There is apparently more rationale in reporting on the client's test behavior and test attitudes (the client moved the blocks about in random fashion, sometimes forming a correct beginning for the required design, but then breaking up the pattern and starting over; or, the client usually responded overly quickly, often being in error, and then usually asked for permission to correct his answer; or, he was vehement in his objection to testing, referring to the procedure as "brain picking," and "in violation of the spirit, if not the wording of the Fifth Amendment"). Here too, however, the psychologist is asking another to interpret data which are clearly part of his realm of training and competency. It may be very wasteful of such significant data to present them uninterpreted and apart from the important conclusions to which they may contribute.

Fresh Fish Sold Here

Before proceeding further, a word of caution and logic may help reduce the sort of superfluous content we have just seen work its way into reports. It should be a rule that the psychologist quiz himself about each bit of content he presents: "Does this contribute useful information?" It is here in the preliminary section that superfluous, totally useless material can be nipped in the bud. The psychologist is not really contributing, qua psychologist, when he tells the client's age, the number of his sibs, the accent with which he speaks, or the amount of hair he has on the top of his head.

There is the tale of the young man who went into the fish business. He rented a store, erected a sign, FRESH FISH SOLD HERE, and acquired merchandise.

As he was standing back admiring his market and his sign, a friend happened along. Following congratulations, the friend gazed at the sign and read aloud, FRESH FISH SOLD HERE. Of course it's *here.* You wouldn't sell it elsewhere, would you? Impressed with such astuteness, the young man painted over the obviously superfluous word. The next helpful comment had to do with the word *sold.* You aren't giving it away? Again impressed, he eliminated the useless word. Seemingly that was it, but the critic then focused on the word *fresh.* You wouldn't sell stale fish, would you? Once more our hero bowed to the strength of logic. But finally he was relieved that he had a logic-tight sign for his business; FISH. His ever alert friend, however, audibly sniffing the air for effect, made a final observation: "You don't need a sign."

"Test Results"

Following the preliminary part of the report—such content categories as "Reason for Referral," "Descriptive Data," "Identifying Data," "Social Information," and "Clinical Behavior"—psychologists commonly shift gears and move to another realm of reporting which employs a sharply different flavor and vocabulary and examines the client on a wholly different level. This section of the report may be introduced by a heading such as "Test Results," "Findings," "Test Interpretation," or "Evaluation." Whereas the report up to this point made obvious reference to the client in various concrete ways, it is in this section that the consumer of the report frequently feels he is reading about matters like tests and theories, with the client an incidental, a vehicle to carry information about the psychologist's instruments and beliefs.

This broad content category is then commonly subdivided into two smaller categories. Let us call them, as they often are, "Intellectual Aspects" and "Personality" or "Emotional Factors."

"Intellectual Aspects"

Almost always found in the section on intellectual aspects is an IQ—or more usually IQs—along with considerable discussion about the number(s) offered to the reader. Commonly it is thought important to let the reader know whether the number is truthful or not, but to report a number in any event. Thus the writer recently saw a psychological report prepared on a poorly accessible patient; the obtained IQ quite obviously did not have meaning or utility in its usual sense and was no indicator of the person's potential under more fortunate circumstances. Nevertheless, the psychologist felt he could not omit the expected IQ. He wrote, "the patient obtained an IQ of 58, which is regarded as invalid.

Then why present it? Is it not like the old technique of Jack Benny who
always reported that he was 39, the humor residing in the fact that
everyone understood this to be a broad falsification. (This is not to deny
the pathognomic significance of the impaired intellectual functioning.)

Also prominent in this section of the report, if one of the Wechsler scales is
used, is a statement about the variability or "evenness" of intellectual functioning
(scatter), and about the patient's relative proficiency in the verbal and performance
areas, and in certain heterogeneous skill groupings which may be subsumed under
various descriptive headings, such as visual-motor function. Frequently there
is no apparent rationale for the inclusion of such material, and what are
presented as conclusions are more akin to raw data. Heavy scatter, for example,
as determined either by inspection or by a quantitative index, is without
any necessary meaning, even though there is a tendency for a high scatter
index to be associated with schizophrenia (Trehub and Scherer, 1958).
Nevertheless, the prudent psychologist will not conclude that his patient is
schizophrenic solely on the basis of scatter; he will consider other data.
On including a report about scatter, the psychologist must therefore consider
what conclusions he expects his readers to reach from this raw datum.
If he is using a report of scatter to support a conclusion, then he also needs
to report the other main components which brought about that conclusion.

Some psychologists report in this section personality implications of intelligence
test findings, matters like personality organization and factors related to
adjustment. Such material is, in nonschool settings, more in keeping with the
psychologist's mission than what is usually reported in the discussion of
intelligence. This more meaningful approach may, however, pose problems of
content organization, since many such conclusions are less matters of the
intellect than what is generally considered, report-wise, to fall under
"personality." But some psychologists are not very much concerned about
such matters, and report *all* conclusions gained from intelligence tests
under "Intellectual Aspects," and *all* conclusions derived from general tests
of personality under "Personality"—even basic information on intellectual
function gained through, for example, the Rorschach.

"Personality" or "Emotional Factors"

The section often entitled "Personality" or "Emotional Factors" may cause
discomfort to the purist solely because of terminology. The objection is that
personality is generally regarded as encompassing a larger field of study, perhaps
something like ". . . the dynamic organization within the individual of those
psychophysical systems that determine his unique adjustments to his
environment" (Allport, 1937), and therefore to exclude what may be vital
information on the role of cognition in adjustment (excluded because
it is already neatly tied up in the previous section in a discussion of levels of test

achievements, assets, shortcomings, and impressions about abstract heterogeneous skills) is hardly to give an adequate picture of personality. As for the term "emotional factors," it should be obvious that much of the vital personality material described here—goals, interests, psychological properties of the parents, or cultural factors in the home—are not necessarily more related to emotions than is the intellect or the IQ.

The sort of content which appears in this section may vary somewhat among psychologists, but stereotypy is frequent. Commonly written about are such topics as psychopathology, unconscious drives, attitudes, conflicts, frustrations, guilt, anxiety, defenses, psychosexual factors, and significant relationships. These topics may frequently be related to the mission, but often they are not. In many instances this section does not integrate significant environmental factors, the content of consciousness, and surface behavior with the deeper elements of personality.

"Diagnosis"

In diagnostic/treatment settings, the psychological report commonly gives some attention to a formal psychiatric diagnosis, usually after the discussion of "Intellectual Aspects" and "Personality," and somewhere toward the end of the report. As we have already seen (Chapter 2), this contribution sometimes is not appreciated. This objection apparently does not relate to the psychologist's ability to diagnose, for it seems he is as well qualified as other experts in this respect (Wiener & Raths, 1959). The issue seems rather to be one of role and of responsibility. The psychiatric diagnosis is a medical prerogative, and is sometimes based on information not ordinarily available to the psychologist or on information which the psychologist cannot competently or ethically utilize (e.g., neurological findings, blood chemistry, or blood pressure). The official psychiatric diagnosis *is* legally entrusted only to physicians. In practice, however, the formal diagnosis frequently reflects the contributions of various team members.

The psychiatrist is much less likely to be offended by a diagnostic impression or by a suggested diagnosis. It is possible to be overly obsequious in suggesting a diagnosis: "Such a pattern is commonly found in patients diagnosed as schizophrenic." This apologetic suggestion of a diagnosis may imply either (1) that the psychologist is convinced this is a case of schizophrenia but hesitates to say so, or (2) that diagnoses stem from tests and not from psychologists. The verbal maneuver is not necessary. Some psychiatrists might be offended only when the psychologist authoritatively indicates that schizophrenia is the diagnosis, thus usurping the psychiatric function. It is hard to know why there is so much concern over formal diagnosis, particularly since many psychologists and dynamic psychiatrists minimize, or are even critical of, this contribution to the case study.

There are obvious instances where nosologic material is superfluous, even in settings where diagnosis is an administrative requirement or a matter of firm orientation. One occasion of this sort is when the person presents clear-cut classificatory characteristics or he is already well-known or "well-diagnosed." Another occasion when the psychologist's suggested diagnosis contributes minimally, if at all, is when the emphasis is on understanding some personality characteristic, for example, when it is more important to know the meaning of a symptom than to know that the patient has a hysterical neurosis of the conversion type.

"Diagnosis" and "evaluation" are terms sometimes used interchangeably, in which case "diagnosis" usually includes much more than a formal nosological statement. In such cases the term often refers to a major evaluative conclusion and tends to occur near the end of the report, as do statements of formal diagnosis. Sometimes such contributions may consider what is appropriate as a formal diagnosis in a discussion context rather than offering a clipped nosological entity. In all cases the appropriateness of this diagnostic contribution depends partly on its pertinence and partly on the psychologist's qualifications to render it. In no case is the psychologist qualified to render what is properly a medical diagnosis.

Consider the following quoted material, which is takent from a discussion in Sarbin, Taft, and Bailey (1960). A seventeen-year-old girl had been referred to a psychiatric clinic because of "hysterical manifestations" after the examining physician could find no organic basis for her complaints of abdominal pains. As part of the total evaluation process the patient was seen by a psychologist who reported, in part, "the patient's unresolved oedipal conflict is apparent in her responses to the Thematic Apperception Test. The 'abdominal pains' *are* at one and the same time an identification with her departed father and a way of getting love from her mother (italics supplied)." Unfortunately for the patient, and for the validity of the psychologist's diagnostic statement, she was soon found to have a far advanced cancer in the region of complaint and succumbed to this condition the day following its discovery.

Now it may be that the psychologist's psychodynamic explanation was based on a sound understanding of the person. In fact, we are told that the girl's mother reported that her daughter had always been given over to dramatizing her problems and that she had been close to her father, who died as the result of a perforated ulcer. Such collateral information is similar to what the psychologist concluded with the aid of his tests, but should have been regarded in the light of the original medical findings only as *suggestive* of the nature of the girl's ailment, what it *might* be. How much better it would have been if the psychologist had not rendered an unqualified opinion on the nature of a bodily complaint, but had offered the opinion that his findings were consistent with a functional complaint, or even, in the light of the medical conclusion suggested, that hysteria was a *possible* explanation of the complaint.

"Prognosis"

Prognosis often follows diagnosis, as is frequently the case in medicine.
Again, the objection from psychiatric associates rests on how the content is
presented. Certainly the psychologist's understanding of the individual's
personality permits him to make certain predictions about his future behavior.
The psychiatrist may welcome these. What the psychiatrist may object to is
wording to the effect that the psychologist is charting the presumed course of a
diseased state. When behavioral deviancy is regarded in this manner, clearly a
declining point of view, the psychologist is evidently out of his element.
Hence the manner in which predictions are made—even the heading under which
predictions are recorded—may influence the reader's perception as to just what
sort of content is being reported. What can seem to be subtle differences are
sometimes of great practical moment.

"Recommendations"

Recommendations often appear as one of the final content categories of the report.
In some settings, in schools, for example, psychological consultation is sought for
the help the psychologist can give in dealing with a problem. In other settings,
notably psychiatric settings, however, there is dispute about the psychologist's
presenting such content. Some psychiatrists actively solicit this kind of material
while others denounce it as inappropriate and an encroachment upon medical
function. There is no doubt that the psychologist does have information he is
able to translate into practical terms that have meaning for treatment, disposition,
or other special considerations. And the psychologist's purpose is specifically
to present that content which meets the needs of the person making the referral.
The manner of presentation, particularly the tactfulness of presentation,
must be reemphasized. Thus "psychotherapy along with treatment directed
at symptomatic anxiety reduction may be beneficial" probably is a more palatable
statement to most psychiatrists than "this patient ought to have psychotherapy
along with Librium 25 mg. t.i.d.

The working relationship will determine in part "just how far the psychologist
should go." In the context of many relationships it is probably appropriate to
write something to the effect that "the prominent and incapacitating depressive
features in this patient suggest that he might respond to E.C.T." But it is
doubtful that a recommendation such as ". . . the patient should be started on a
course of insulin therapy with participation in group psychotherapy and
occupational therapy. . . ." appearing in Garfield's (1957) textbook of clinical
psychology would be well received. Insulin treatment can have serious
physiological consequences (the recommendation, incidentally, does not
specify whether subcoma—"subinsulin"—is being called for or whether the
psychologist wants the patient to have comas—"deep insulin"). Treatment with
insulin requires intimate medical and nursing control.

"Summary"

Generally, the report is concluded with a content category labelled "Summary," or sometimes "Summary and Conclusions," which may imply that new major material not dealt with in the body of the report, perhaps some diagnostic considerations or some recommendations, is being introduced. It is hard to argue against the use of summary content since this is so well entrenched in writing practice, and since many clinical workers seem to feel the need for such a statement (Tallent and Reiss, 1959, a, b). However, the use of a summary may often be injudicious, and it should be considered for use with discretion.

The major objection raised against the use of a summary is that it may serve with some degree of effectiveness as an antidote to an otherwise inadequate report. This seems particularly true of reports which are inadequate because they are too long, too difficult, and too involved, the summary by comparison being readable. The reader is soon trained to ignore the report proper and to be content with the summary, even though by definition this section can hardly be expected to carry the legitimate freight of the report. The fact that a number of readers are apparently content with first perusing the summary suggests that perhaps this briefer version of a report often more closely approximates the felt requirements of report readers than does the main body.

An opposite objection to the use of a summary may be made when the summary concludes an otherwise succinct report. There is now a tendency among some psychologists to present a concise, content-loaded report, though without omitting the traditional summary. The result may appear ludicrous, at least visually if not also logically, when the length of the summary approaches the length of the report. In terms of actual measurement, one may find reports of six, seven, or eight inches in length to which is appended a summary statement of three, four, or five inches!

When a summary statement is used, Hammond and Allen's (1953) suggestion for an "opening summary"—what is sometimes called an overview—is well taken. This technique seems to be used effectively in journalism, particularly in feature articles, in scientific journals, and with book chapters. It is thought that presenting the essence of the material at the beginning will create in the reader the proper set needed for understanding, and will entice him to delve into the main body of writing. By contrast, many are of the opinion that a summary at the end, when read first, tends against turning back to the text itself.

FREQUENTLY APPROPRIATE CONTENT

From consideration of the traditional report, we may profitably turn to a discussion of the kinds of psychological content commonly thought to be helpful by social workers, psychiatrists, and psychologists. The data which form the basis for the ensuing discussion are from a survey of these three groups of clinical workers (Tallent and Reiss, 1959 a). No doubt some of the expressed needs reflect familiarity with traditional reports, but many who offered advice on appropriate content had ideas of their own. All of the categories suggested with a degree of frequency are examined closely in terms of their positive and negative potentialities, and with a view to their proper usage. The kinds of content mentioned are not appropriate for all reports, since each report is a highly individual matter. Nor is it implied that reports be limited to these categories, which are meant only as general guidelines. It is better to think in terms of what sort of content is *frequently* appropriate.

Clinical Behavior and Descriptive Material

Report readers are evidently interested in a broad range of behavior, both current and potential, and the reporting of the client's clinical behavior, and other descriptive material, continues to find favor among a number of them. This area of data, dealing as it does with overt material, presents the hazard of duplicating the contributions of other team members. Such observations are best presented—if relevant to the evaluation goal—in a unique context elicited in some special way, or one that offers some special insights (for example, in response to test stimuli or in association with unique psychological findings).

Three subcategories of such material are specifically mentioned as appropriate: appearance, general behavioral observations, and a description of the examiner-patient interaction. Of these, a discussion of a client's appearance (probably noted elsewhere, particularly if highly unusual) is least likely to be fruitful. This is especially true of those aspects of appearance without apparent psychological correlates or not reliably interpretable.

General behavioral observations are frequently unique material because of the inherent differences between a psychological examination and the contacts of other workers. A psychological examination involving a full battery of tests is, in general, more time-consuming than other examinations, or the interviews carried out by the psychologist's associates. This longer period of observation offers the possibility of noting behavior which might not occur in procedures which are cursory by comparison. The length of examination also presents opportunities for noting variations in behavior, particularly when the patient is seen over a period of two or more days. Unique behavior is frequently elicited because the psychological examination is ambiguous to the client, in spite of the psychologist's efforts to structure it. Many clients find it hard to understand the role of the psychologist, his purpose, or the rationale of his tools and procedures. Their perception of the overall activity, the frustrations occasioned by length, the difficulty, and the ambiguous totality in itself present a projective situation to which people make diagnostically useful responses.

The examiner-client interaction is a vital datum, especially to those psychologists who stress the role of interpersonal relationships in the understanding of personality. This interaction is regarded as valuable, as a partial sample of both the role the person tends to take in social encounters, and of the response repertoire available to him. Thus the unique personality of the psychologist is as much an examination stimulus as his various test stimuli. The client's test productions are quite reasonably regarded as based in part on the interaction between examiner and client. This situation, skillfully understood, can contribute valuable conclusions to the case study.

From the point of view of the current presentation, all such behavior description is generally best offered as interpreted material, except where it is used for its illustrative value. Some readers of the psychological report ask for the psychologist's impressions, which are, in effect, interpreted observations. Such interpretation no doubt involves a greater subjective element than is often regarded as proper in the interpretation of test data.

Intellectual Factors of Personality

Various intellectual factors of personality continue to occupy many clinical workers, in nonschool or nonrehabilitation settings, although the specific things they want to know sometimes differ from the information found in the traditional report. Their concern with intellect usually has less important consequences than does the concern of the teacher or the rehabilitation worker, for example. Yet some workers are particularly interested in learning about the intellectual assets of their patients. This would seem to be most valuable when rehabilitation measures involving training and/or placement are at issue. They may be helpful when any change in the life situation is contemplated, since cognitive resources are definitely a factor in adjustment.

Intellectual liabilities seem to call up more interest among clinical workers, perhaps because of the "maladjustment focus" of the diagnostic/treatment setting. Data on low native intelligence, for example, may help to explain the person's frustrations, which may be significant to the case study. Planning for the future is thus facilitated. Similar interest centers about acquired intellectual deficit—various kinds and degrees of previous resources not now available. This type of difficulty may or may not present adjustment problems (particularly vocational adjustment problems) similar to those often occasioned by low native intelligence. Of importance here is the extent of deficit and the nature of the requirements placed upon the person. An isolated statement of deficit may not be very valuable practically, since persons can often carry on adequately in well-practiced areas of function, sometimes even in occupations involving a fair degree of responsibility, in the presence of appreciable loss.

Information about another aspect of deficit, that of the premorbid intelligence, seems to be spontaneously requested by clinical workers far less frequently than such discussions occur in samples of psychological reports. An estimate of premorbid functioning, or of the relationship of current to premorbid functioning, is mainly of value as a crude, nonspecific index of the extent of psychopathology, and is perhaps best expressed in qualitative terms. Certainly figures presented on deficit are not directly translatable into terms with practical clinical meaning, particularly when they are presented out of context of the functioning personality.

   The interest of many clinical workers is in some specific aspect or aspects of intellectual functioning which they feel is of importance. A psychiatrist or a social worker may wish further information on such matters as abstract ability, memory function, or the ability to learn. Such more or less specific requirements point up the desirability of specific referrals. Many workers nevertheless express a general interest, such as one in the "current intellectual status." Presumably such a request gives the psychologist latitude in deciding which of his findings about the intellect ought to be reported.

   Surprisingly, when asked about the sort of content that ought to appear in psychological reports, 58 percent of the replies from psychiatrists indicated that an IQ or the intelligence level be specified, whereas only 1 percent of the psychologists so replied. This is surprising because a much higher percentage of psychologists *do* apparently give this kind of datum high priority by presenting it before there is any discussion of other findings. Is it possible that psychologists do not really believe in this generous offering of the IQ, but are under the impression that it is supposed to be done? The psychiatrists' apparent eager interest in numbers purporting to tell how intelligent their patients are is also surprising, since it is uncertain what practical use they make of this information. It may be that this interest is a residual of the great emphasis psychologists and educators had put on the IQ in an earlier era, or it may reflect the interest in intelligence emphasized in the middle class cultural background of many psychiatrists.

   Whatever the sources of differing opinions on the need for various kinds of intellectual data, it is appropriate that we reexamine the role knowledge of the intellect plays in the appraisal of personality in practical (clinical type) situations. There should be almost universal agreement that knowledge of the functioning of the intellect offers information on (1) skill-interest-motivational complexes of efficiencies, (2) the functioning of various personality processes, and, as a special case of these, (3) the kinds and degrees of both functional and organic disruption of the personality.

   The relatively infrequent need for detailed knowledge of efficiencies and inefficiencies, in diagnostic/treatment settings has already been mentioned. The common use of individual intelligence tests, which require over an hour to administer, score, and interpret, would hardly be justified in many cases were the main purpose to determine intellectual level. There are more economical ways of obtaining such information.

   On the other hand, individual intelligence tests of the Wechsler group are being used effectively to gain personality information of the sort presumably related to intellectual function, but usually thought of in a noncognitive context.

Information on personality, such as dependency traits, attitudes toward society, suspiciousness, impulsivity, and defense mechanisms, may be gained through intelligence tests. The manner in which such traits are intimately tied up with the client's intellectual resources often constitutes valuable datum for the person who makes the referral. The emphasis of these trait complexes, however, is generally most profitably placed on the functioning of the general personality, as opposed to isolated efficiencies.

An analysis of intellectual functioning is sometimes the key contribution the psychologist can make to the case study. This contribution is arrived at essentially through a study of deficit, both quantitative and qualitative. Certain quantitative deficit patterns, often considered together with observations of functioning on an intelligence test, may be identified as the effect of cerebral pathology. This item of information is of particular interest to many psychiatrists and teachers and is regarded as one of the more valuable contributions of the psychologist.

In the functional disorders, psychiatrists are often interested in learning from the psychologist about the formal thought processes. The official criteria for the diagnoses of the schizophrenic psychoses include alterations in the thought processes (*Diagnostic and Statistical Manual, Mental Disorders,* Second Edition, 1968, American Psychiatric Association), and these are often best evaluated through psychological procedures. Sometimes, in fact, this kind of malfunction is not evident in samples of well-practiced interpersonal relationships and is seen only in performance on psychological tests—intelligence tests and other psychological tests. Similarly, the full effect of a neurotic process, or of a personality disorder, is more thoroughly understood through the effects on the cognitive processes.

Nonintellectual Factors of Personality

Those personality factors generally considered nonintellectual are mentioned as proper content by large numbers of report readers, although sometimes one professional group places more emphasis on certain classes of data than do others. The separation of these data from intellectual operations is merely a habitual way of thinking, a result of the dichotomization of the personality in psychological reports (or perhaps more basically of the "isolation" of intelligence from the rest of personality years ago). Many clinical workers mention as proper content a "general personality picture."

Interest in psychopathology is widespread in psychiatric settings; and there are a number of discrete areas that are often specified. These include general description of the psychopathological process, discussion of the areas of disturbed functioning, behavioral symptomatology, reality contacts, and etiological information, although, perhaps significantly, the psychological group was the only one to suggest the latter category.

The underlying psychological processes are regarded as an appropriate topic by all professions of the classical clinical team. Many think in terms of a partial dichotomization of evaluative function between psychologists and other team members, the former being charged with illuminating deep activities of the psyche while psychiatrists and social workers focus on more palpable behaviors—historical information, affect, or stream of consciousness, with some inferential penetrations into the unconscious. Preferably, these descents below the surface are made with the support of the more direct and reliable depth tools of the psychologist, such as the Rorschach. This view is inaccurate and unfair to all concerned. All levels of behavior are the province of psychology, and psychological examination is often invaluable in describing important but essentially overt manifestations of behavior, functions such as memory, behavioral control, the intensity of surface hostility, and the channels through which it is expressed. The psychologist, if he seeks an integrated view of his client, explores the unconscious too, often contributing valued information. Instruments such as the Rorschach frequently give him a significant advantage in his subsurface explorations, but he holds no deed on this section of the personality.

One of the more vital content areas, in the opinion of our respondents, is the conflicts of the patient, although for some reason psychologists and social workers mentioned this topic far more often than did the psychiatrists. Presumably both unconscious and conscious conflicts are alluded to here, though the unconscious conflicts are generally the more important ones in shaping psychopathology.

Various categories of direct adjustment variables were deemed to be appropriate by all of the groups of our sample. The adjustment variable most frequently suggested as proper content is the defenses, and, on the importance of this topic in the psychological report, psychologists, psychiatrists, and social workers are in apparent agreement. The defensive structure is truly one of the major highways leading to an understanding of personality. A knowledge of the defenses permits one to gauge the stability of a person, and may also have a direct relationship to psychotherapeutic activity. The sort of controls exercised by a person, and their effectiveness, can be of key significance. Some think it may be advisable to discuss the appearance or the role of anxiety in adjustment.

The motivational factors in personality also come in for a good deal of attention. Again these would seem to be of central importance in understanding the personality and its key problems. In general, there is much stress on the importance of drives or dynamics, but some point out the importance of motivational elements which are largely conscious, such as the person's interest areas and goals. It certainly would be remiss of the psychologist not to emerge occasionally from the depths of the unconscious to assess the molding power of forces about which the person has awareness and which are probably significant to his life. His diagnostic probings might then return to the unconscious, where basic dependency and independency pushes are to be found, where the malevolent forces press for expression, and the underlying sexual identities reveal themselves.

The personality assets and liabilities of the client, aside from purely intellectual assets and liabilities, are commonly proposed as important psychological contributions to the case study. Interestingly, the psychologists in the sample far more frequently suggested the appropriateness of assets than they did of liabilities. This contrasts with the notion that many psychologists show a "maladjustment bias" in their reports. Psychiatrists and social workers in particular comment on the importance of learning from the psychologist about the person's "ego strength," an item of information that would be especially important when psychotherapeutic intervention is contemplated.

Many of the social workers and psychologists, and some psychiatrists, in our sample spontaneously indicated that the presentation of social variables is of importance in the psychologist's report. These data would bear special scrutiny, particularly from the point of view of the social worker. It has already been pointed out that at least some social workers are sensitive to what they perceive as the psychologist's encroachment on their area, and so could hardly be sympathetic to his reporting parallel or duplicated material. There is no doubt, however, that social workers advocate the importance of social data to the understanding of behavior. May it be presumed then that they would favor the thesis presented here, that social variables ought to be presented in the psychologist's study, but only when they are integrated with other personality data?

Perhaps this does represent the view of some, but the sort of social variables mentioned also might suggest that the respondents intended these items of information to be elicited independently by the psychologist. About half of the social worker respondents suggested the appropriateness of data on interpersonal relationships, and about one quarter of this group indicated they would like to read in the psychological report about the client's relationship to significant life figures. Possibly the social worker is thinking of integrating the psychologist's findings on this topic with his own. This would not and should not preclude the psychologist from integrating social work data with his findings any more than it ought to keep the psychiatrist from his long-established practice of utilizing the findings of his associates to add to his understanding of the patient.

Arbitrarily separated (for discussion) from the topic of the person's interpersonal relationships is the matter of his interpersonal perceptions. Psychologists understand that a person's perception of the environment is vastly more important than the physical facts of environment. This area of personality function appears central to adequate case study in many instances. Often of similar basic importance is the self-concept and self-image.

Diagnostic Material

The reaction of many psychiatrists to the offering of a diagnosis by the psychologist has already been presented in several contexts. It is well to note the other side of the coin, the expressed interest in obtaining diagnostic information from the psychologist. None of this negates the earlier notations on this topic, particularly on the need for tact. Rather it would seem to emphasize the individual focus of psychological work. Much of the diagnostic information sought is not formal or in terms of an official classification.

Approximately one fourth of the psychiatrists responding did request that formal diagnoses be offered. The percentage of psychologists in agreement with this view was somewhat greater, while the proportion of social workers who expressed a desire for a psychological diagnosis was somewhat less. About one in eight of the psychiatric group would like a psychologist to suggest a differential diagnosis, where required, while the social workers recorded no interest at all in this matter. In many situations, the psychologist will justifiably feel that he ought to suggest a diagnosis, if indeed such content is not routinely expected or required in his report.

Some psychiatrists would also have the psychologist render an opinion about the existence of an underlying psychosis. Some wish to be informed on what the psychologist thinks about the presence of an overt psychosis. The medical orientation of many psychiatrists is particularly evident in their interest in securing from the psychologist diagnostic information on organicity. Forty-two percent of the psychiatric group indicated that the psychologist ought to give information on the presence of such conditions. It is good both that psychologists are able to deliver an informed opinion on this important topic and that psychiatrists are so much aware of this fact.

Predictive Material

The cautions mentioned with reference to the offering of diagnoses apply also to predictions, although the giving of a prognosis may be a delicate matter. Social workers, however, seem to be more accepting of such contributions than are psychiatrists, hardly a surprising finding. Social workers also emphasize the practical and the environmental in the way of predictions, and ask for such information as the vocational and educational outlook. Thus the reception of various areas of prediction is an individual matter among report readers. Many are interested in several of the different forms of acting-out potential, such as homicide, suicide, or sexual deviancy, and others want to know about treatment prospects.

Recommendations

The objections raised to the psychologist's offering of recommendations have already been suggested. Some potential strain is seen in clinical relations, because psychologists in general seem to want to make recommendations more often than their team associates, particularly psychiatrists, might wish to have them. Thus, 74 percent of the psychologist sample suggested that it is appropriate to offer recommendations regarding treatment, while only 14 percent of the psychiatric respondents spontaneously mentioned the need for such help. Teachers and others who so eagerly seek the help of psychologists must find all of this strange.

The appropriate content for the psychological report depends on the workers involved in the case, on the reasons for which the person is referred, and on the available conclusions from which the psychologist has to select.

INAPPROPRIATE CONTENT

It is far easier to make pronouncements on what is never appropriate in a psychological report than to offer opinions on what may be appropriate. The most helpful generalization is that the psychologist never renders conclusions which are outside his actual or defined limits of function or competence. Admittedly, the borderlines are sometimes vague and subject to personal interpretations that may be at variance with group consensus. The overall psycho-evaluative competence of the psychologist has not been generally challenged, however, and at this late date is not likely to be. Yet the establishment of certain conclusions based on personality data—for example, the declaration of the legal competency of patients and the making of medical treatment decisions—are functions legally proscribed to the psychologist. Thus there exist some clear external guidelines to show the psychologist what is beyond his qualifications or functions. This observation is consistent with the fact that psychologists may be, and are, asked to contribute information or opinions to decisions which are ultimately outside their scope.

Then there are matters that are within the broad purview of psychology but which may be beyond the competence of a given psychologist. Generally the decision here is based on the psychologist's awareness of his limitations and on his adherence to ethical principles. A psychologist not skilled in the Rorschach ought not to present conclusions based on the use of this instrument. A psychologist not enlightened or practiced in psychoanalytic usage ought not present his conclusions in such a framework. Many psychologists cannot give sound direct treatment suggestions in cases of speech disability or reading disability, but psychologists who have had adequate training and experience in these areas might be specially employed for their ability to render conclusions on such problems.

THE APPROPRIATE EMPHASIS OF CONTENT

In report writing it is helpful to think not only in terms of what to include or exclude, but also of what contents to emphasize or de-emphasize. The topics which comprise the psychological report should, according to our present frame of reference, try to meet the perceived present and future evaluation needs of the client. This requirement ought to be true of the various emphases in a report too. If we take into consideration the different orientations held by psychologists, however, it is understandable for the psychologist to present his findings in terms of *his* approach to understanding personality. This is probably not wrong *so long as he is still able to fulfill his mission.* This argument is not meant to defend the habitual emphases of a psychologist who has no clear-cut orientation, or of one who emphasizes certain kinds of material solely because this was his early impression of how psychological reports are supposed to be written.

We could consider any number of classes of content in terms of what influences their appropriate emphases in psychological reports. But a discussion of a few of the more commonly emphasized topic areas should illustrate the nature of the problem.

We may consider, for example, emphasis on developmental content versus emphasis on contemporary content. A psychoanalytic orientation might focus on developmental stages and apparently suit the requirements that prevail in an analytically oriented setting; even here, though, the therapist will probably be more interested in the strength of the individual's defensive structure. Where behavior and certain humanistic therapies, as well as medical therapies, are used, we should be aware that these treatments may be blind to the individual's developmental history. Even where traditional psychotherapy is the chosen approach, many therapists, including analytically oriented workers, now tend to believe that treatment centering about contemporary problems offers the greatest therapeutic leverage.

An emphasis on unconscious content often appears in reports to the exclusion of concern with consciously directed behavior, the content of consciousness, and surface behavior. Unconscious content is typically related to the origins and to the deepest reaches of psychopathology—perhaps the major of the predisposing factors. Yet to dwell on this topic may be unjustifiable. Other significant clues to psychological problems, such as the precipitating factors and other significant aspects of the condition, its future course, and therapeutic possibilities, can often be effectively approached through the content of consciousness and the surface behavior. The practical relevance of content may then properly dictate the emphasis. Consider, for example, the matter of drives or dynamics, or, as a specific instance of this, the term "hostility," which appears so frequently in psychological reports. The form this trait takes may be central to the understanding of a particular problem, for example, hysterical behavior; otherwise this ubiquitous trait is often unworthy of emphasis or even of mention in a report. Much the same may be said of the common content categories of defenses and structure. A discussion of these topics can be crucial to the psychotherapist who wishes to strengthen a functioning personality and needs to know how well his client can cope with stress developed in the therapeutic situation. But of what value is the presentation of unconscious content to the symptomatically oriented chemotherapist or behaviorist?

CHAPTER FIVE

Conceptualizing
the
Psychological Report

A flexible approach makes for better psychological reports. This view, along with some ways to implement it, is offered as a contribution to the old problem of how to organize reports. Apparently the difficulties involved in this task have not been alleviated by various general report outline schemes presently available. What is proposed here is that the report be case-focused, conceptualized in terms of the mission. In such a report the roles of issues like content selection, theoretical orientation, and organizational form will readily take on meaning.

The responsibility of the psychologist—to the person who makes the referral or to the team and to his client—is the central theme of this discourse. The foregoing discussions have dealt with many of the elements that comprise such responsibility. This chapter ventures to round out the points already made and to suggest for them a framework to provide some additional rationale and further guidance for the effective preparation of a psychological report.

THE RATIONALE FOR FLEXIBILITY

"There is, of course, no one way to write a report, just as there is no one form or organization that will always suffice. *Each writer's personal characteristics*

will determine, in part, how he will attack his problem (italics supplied)."
The source of this quote is perhaps as important as the idea which it expresses.
It is taken from *Technical Report Writing* by James W. Souther (1957), a
guidebook prepared for engineers. Engineering, as the layman understands it,
utilizes precise methods based on the physical sciences and mathematics.
The sort of things engineers write about in their reports are machines, a
factory or mine installation, or an industrial manufacturing process.
Where should one be more systematized and objective? Yet engineers are
trained to be flexible and to allow their personalities to color their reports,
while psychologists are frequently exhorted to deny their participant-observer
role, to standardize their report procedures, to be objective. We are frequently
reminded from within and without our profession that the psychological
report is a laboratory report or a scientific document.

General outlines for dealing with large areas of personality at various levels, as
is typical with traditional reports, are to be regarded as Procrustean schemes,
and none will be found on these pages. How can a rigid outline accomodate
the protean complexities of personality, take cognizance of the variability
among people, circumstances, and practical needs. Such outlines, especially
if well detailed, may be welcomed because they partly or totally relieve
the psychologist of the necessity of thinking about how to organize his
presentation. But they also force him to fit findings where they may
not belong if optimal meaning and effectiveness is to be had.

When we deal with problem-oriented, prescriptive reports, the situation is
different. Here we deal with well-defined, circumscribed areas of behavior
such that the psychologist is in a position to juxtapose problem areas or
symptoms and plans for remediation. Such reports are of particular value in
the behavior therapies (examples on pages 214-219), but are also appropriate
to other problem-oriented, prescriptive approaches, for example the bioenergetic
approach (example on pages 219-220). But Souther's observation still applies.

Have you ever noticed how many of the psychological reports that
you have seen start the body of the report with a statement of IQ(s) and a
stereotyped discussion of intellectual functioning? Why? Is it because these are the
most important findings about the client? Is it because such matters appearing
later in the report after a discussion of more meaningful personality content
would be anticlimatic and are thus best gotten out of the way as soon as
possible? Or is it that this is the way we have been doing it for over a
generation and don't really know what else to do? In any event, second (or
third) generation generalized report outlines continue to place, after
"Test Behavior" or "Behavioral Observations," a report of the IQ and data
on intellectual functioning (e.g., Carr, 1968; Lacks, Horton, and Owen,
1969; Sturm, 1974).

Let's look at it this way. The psychologist has a creative, custom-job to
do, and following an outline approaches the mechanical filling out of a form.
Perhaps the engineers can help us again. Dr. L. B. Headrick (1956) of RCA

advises, "Consider the writing of a technical paper as an engineering problem. Analysis of a problem is essential to understanding and to an organized plan of attack." Souther amplifies this point while at the same time presenting a rationale and general guide to the kind of report he proposes. ". . . The point of attack is always identification of the problem and analyzing the writing situation. Material must be gathered and evaluated, and the report must be designed and written. Failure and confusion often result because the writer starts in the middle of the process or overlooks major considerations. Thus the application of the engineering approach to the solution of writing problems is certain to produce more effective reports, for a report, like any other engineering product, must be designed to satisfy a particular industrial function with its own specific set of requirements. If the analysis is accurate and extensive, the investigation complete and thorough, the design detailed and purposeful, and the application careful and ordered, the report will effectively communicate to its audience, play its industrial role, and fulfill its purpose."[1] To which a psychologist can but meekly add— "writing, communication itself, is also a psychological problem."

HOW TO ORGANIZE REPORTS: AN OLD PROBLEM

The discussion to this point has extolled the merits of flexibility, albeit in general terms, and discouraged rigid outline schemes. "But how then are we to get help in organizing our reports?" the reader might be justified in asking. An unpublished survey of ours among student psychologists, and psychologists at various levels of experience, indicated that a prominent concern of report writers is difficulty in organizing their reports, and a prominent criticism of training programs is that they do not offer enough help on how to accomplish this task. (These observations in themselves would seem to imply that report-writing outlines are not felt to be satisfactory, for there certainly are enough of them to be had!) One cannot give a simple answer on how to organize the report. This depends on how the individual consultation is conceptualized, which, in turn, depends on one's philosophy of the consultation function itself.

THE BASIC SCHEME OF PSYCHOLOGICAL CONSULTATION

The psychologist is a contributing and interacting member of a professional group. Persons with psychological problems of various sorts, are, in effect, assigned to the group with the expectation that it can help, in some degree, to overcome or cope with their problems, or even that it can manage or care for them better than they can do for themselves.

---

[1] From James W. Souther, *Technical Report Writing* (New York: John Wiley & Sons, Inc., 1957). Copyright © 1957 by John Wiley and Sons, Inc. and reprinted by permission.

To accomplish one or more of these goals, different kinds of information about the person may be required. Sometimes information about various aspects of his psychological function is thought to be especially pertinent. At this point the psychologist may become consultant to the group, and his task is to help determine the nature of the problem(s) about which practical, useful information needs to be obtained. In gathering the requisite information, the psychologist utilizes a number of tools as aids, but he himself is the principal evaluative tool employed. On obtaining his conclusions he presents them to the person who made the referral (or to the team as a whole) in as effective a manner as possible.

When the psychologist accepts a case, he must set his own evaluation goal; it cannot be set for him. The various members of the team may have different understandings of the person's problem, and therefore of what additional information might be helpful. It is for this reason that the psychologist may contribute his understanding of the nature of the problem; perhaps even before he sees the client, he may modify this view at any time during his evaluation procedure. His evaluation goal is a compromise among the views of the several team members and his own view of the problem at various times, which in turn is influenced by his orientation and his diagnostic modalities. As he elicits data his goal may shift, sometimes radically. He may start out to evaluate the capacities of what is thought to be a neurotic patient, but soon discover that there are schizophrenic inroads in thinking, and that this is really the area which requires understanding.

Typically, the psychologist uses a test battery as a major aid to arriving at conclusions. He pre-selects the battery in terms of economy and in accordance with the information he desires, since certain tests yield more or less circumscribed classes of information, while others contribute quite different content. But most tests and test items can be, at least to a degree, unstructured and permit some freedom of response. Thus some tests may not yield the data they are expected to yield, while others divulge information that is not anticipated. This fortuitous nature of data sources may cause the psychologist to add to or subtract from his battery as his testing progresses. Obviously, the psychologist cannot in most circumstances reasonably be asked to administer a particular test or battery.

The next step is interpretation of the derived data in light of the client, his problem(s), and the overall circumstances of the consultation, including the anticipated uses to which the psychologist's conclusions will be put. The focus is on interpretations rather than data, since it is best for the psychologist to relate his data to the problem as he understands it. The team may later utilize his conclusions as one aspect of a larger picture.

The interpretations themselves are not directly conveyed. The psychologist selects from his reservoir of interpretations only those he believes will contribute to the mission, and omits those that are apparently not relevant, or add unnecessary length and confuse the issue. The presence of deep castration anxiety—with which the person will no doubt die—would not ordinarily be pertinent when a patient's emotional stability is being evaluated to help determine the advisability of hospital discharge. In fact, the busy psychologist, on spotting raw data that would apparently not contribute to his evaluation goal, might not wish to develop further interpretations in this area. In addition, he may wish to eliminate low confidence conclusions, perhaps retaining them with appropriate qualifications only if he feels they are sufficiently pertinent.

At this point the psychologist will resort to some sort of weighting of his interpretations, placing them in a hierarchy of importance and perhaps reevaluating a few of the conclusions he had earlier judged to be relevant. Again he asks himself how much confidence he has in his conclusions and how pertinent they seem to be. In most cases only a few key conclusions constitute the essence of the report, and the minor conclusions often are best eliminated lest they add bulk and detract from the central theme(s) of the case.

The psychologist is now ready to set pen to paper. It is here that the problem of effective presentation might seem greatest. Chapter 4 discusses the problem of what content may or may not be appropriate, and also broaches the topic of emphasis of content. Only in working with a specific case, however, does the psychologist face the problem of final acceptance of conclusions to report, their organization, and the composition scheme that will enhance the appropriate emphases. It is at this point that he seeks a final conceptualization of his responsibilities to this particular client. He formulates goals for his report that are in addition to his preliminary evaluation goals. Not only does he set about to obtain certain information but to bring about certain effects in accordance with his felt sense of responsibility. Such effects may include the diagnosis assigned to the client, the assignment or nonassignment to therapies, the therapeutic approaches to be taken, assignment to special tutoring, or environmental intervention. It was proposed earlier that it is often well to follow the written report with a conference with the person who has referred the case in order to facilitate understanding of the conclusions. In this context the psychologist might also discuss decisions to be made on the client's behalf.

SOME BASIC CONSIDERATIONS IN ORGANIZING THE REPORT

Prior to organizing his case presentation with an eye to its effectiveness, the psychologist must review his mission. He should focus on what is important in the case, emphasize that which needs to be emphasized, and eliminate that which is not immediately or potentially useful.

Parsimony is basic to organization in addition to whatever other virtues it might have. Parsimony will not only save the time of the report writer and reader, and cut down on bulk, but will also eliminate some of the possible sources of confusion and misunderstanding in the report. Parsimonious writing will tend to emphasize the central problem(s) and personality issues in the minds of the psychologist and his reader, whereas shotgun reporting tends to dilute the main conclusions and place them on a par with matters of minor relevance. Where, for example, a patient who had been economically and socially successful, is now being evaluated for discharge following hospitalization brought about by an acute break, a recitation of the relations among his intellectual skills will probably not add and may detract from, attention to the main problem. Similar value probably attaches to knowledge about psychosexual development, feelings of inadequacy as a male, fear of heterosexual contacts, or oedipal status in a patient who is being evaluated for protective institutional employment.

At this time it is also well for the psychologist to be specifically aware of his theoretical orientation, his biases, and his viewpoint of the overall mission and of the consultation function in psychology. These must be related to what the psychologist can do for a specific person with a specific problem or problems, in the particular setting where he is being evaluated and perhaps treated; There is often temptation to conceptualize the consultation in terms of what the psychologist regards as ideal rather than in terms of the perceived limitations of the situation. A psychologist can think, perhaps rightly so, that psychotherapy (perhaps even a certain "kind" of psychotherapy) is a method of choice, or the method of choice for most of the clients he sees. But it would be unrealistic to conceptualize the typical mission in terms of evaluating the indications for psychotherapy or specific recommendations for psychotherapy in a setting where the availability of this form of treatment is very limited.

The language in which the psychologist *thinks* is also a major issue, influencing as it does both the conceptualization and the presentation of the case. The inexactness and multiple meanings of jargon are well established. When the psychologist thinks in terms of these inexactitudes, can the quality of his writing be any more precise? Is it feasible to think through a case using words which are variously used and variously understood, and then *translate* these into words which have but one meaning and are in the experience of the report reader?

The same sort of consideration applies to the theoretical constructs in terms of which the psychologist *thinks* about his clients, particularly if these are complex and removed from the experience or perceived requirements of his associates. The psychological report is a practical document prepared for use by persons with various amounts of psychological knowledge. Many of them are not expected to be sophisticated in psychological theory. When the psychologist conceptualizes his case in terms of theoretical constructs he would, if interested in communicating to his reader, have to translate, simplify, or dilute his conclusions. Again the question is raised whether the maneuver of translating can be accomplished satisfactorily. Simplifying or diluting the conclusions might tend to call forth a condescending attitude on the part of the psychologist. Theoretical constructs are most useful when dealing with theoretical matters, and they are often helpful, probably indispensable, in making it possible for the psychologist to understand his client. Such use of theory, often implicit, is to be distinguished from conceptualizing the case in terms of theoretical constructs. The psychologist may frequently find himself turning to personality theory or to test theory to find meaning in his data. But he cannot dwell at this level, for the needs of the setting and the client are sometimes far removed from even clinically derived theory.

The counterproposal is that the psychologist think about his client in terms of a simple operational approach. In the interest of relevance the client may be described both in terms of what he *does* and in his potentiality for doing. Presumptions about what the client does and what he might do are both likely to be important; sometimes current behavior, sometimes potential behavior is of greatest pertinence. This point of view is presented without a wish to become enmeshed in any controversy of structure versus function, or of the advisability or feasibility of separating the two. Function implies and defines structure; the latter is known through the former.

Relevant behavior may be found in that which is overt and that which is covert, that which is in consciousness and that which is unconscious or preconscious, the molar and the molecular. Things which the person may *do* include the entertainment, at various levels of consciousness, of goals, ideas, beliefs, or feelings; the exercise of various intellectual and social skills, and other means of manipulating the environment; and the many possible ego defensive maneuvers. Behaviors that are habitual or part of a life style would ordinarily be of greater import than occasional behaviors.

Although potential behavior may sometimes overshadow, in importance, actual behavior, often the two need to be jointly considered. Paranoid ideation may be a factor in potential assaultive conduct, but we may also be interested in the presence or absence of such thinking because it is needed to fix a diagnosis, determine feasibility for psychotherapy, or to estimate the client's ability to adjust to a certain environment. The psychologist can often predict potential behavior, such as improvement or retrogression, or socially significant actions when adequate indications are not otherwise available. Even though past behavior is often the most efficient predictor of future events, nevertheless, the psychologist can often point up unsuspected trends or tensions, the sort of stimuli that activate them, and perhaps even estimate the thresholds at which they are activated.

With these several considerations in mind, we may now being to think about the problem of organization. The very wording of this proposal indicates our bias of presentation in this book: personality ought to be contemplated as an organized whole, not as unorganized segments.

In this book the psychologist has been exhorted to humanize his reports, to think and write in simple operational terms, and to describe his client in functional language. In basic form, this mode of delivering personality data approximates the manner in which one layman describes another, without of course the loose methods of observing and reaching conclusions some laymen employ.

Lay evaluation is organized into functional unities that focus on behaviors. The layman concentrates, as the occasion demands, on areas of felt concern, such as an associate's intelligence, sincerity, friendliness, or "personality." He reaches conclusions rather directly—comes to the point and tells what sort of a person someone is. "He's the sort of feller you can trust. You can count on him when you need him. He'll go out of his way to help when you're in a jam." The narrator may then cite some empirical supporting evidence, or perhaps even intuitive knowledge. One can hardly be more succinct than the late President Lyndon Johnson who characterized a political rival as "a man who can't walk and chew gum at the same time." The layman never segmentalizes his subject into predetermined and fixed discrete areas like "intellect," "emotions," and "interpersonal relations." His lay listener might have difficulty in integrating such segments into some kind of a functional whole. Professional people sometimes have similar problems.

A segmentalized presentation of more or less static personality data may appear to be scientific and clinically functional because it suggests the existence of distinct, identifiable personality components that were isolated and measured, or otherwise evaluated. But we believe that personality is a functional interrelated unity, and we concur with those who believe that clinically important traits are largely specific, that a stimulus in a total situation is as relevant as the organism or its responses. An extreme point of view holds that general traits may be invalid abstractions of transactional behavior. But even if we think in terms of psychometrically defined general traits, the pesonality segments ordinarily discussed in reports do not correspond with personality variables so established. Nevertheless, segments seem to some workers a convenient way of thinking about a person. A report composed of information on various a priori established segments may seem crisp and "scientific." It is crisp. It is no more scientific than an integrated presentation.

The presentation of discrete segments to a report reader may be regarded as akin to presenting him with data having a certain degree of rawness. The whole is more than the sum of its parts, and the functionally integrated report has meaning which is not to be found in the separate information units with which the psychologist initially deals. It is logically the psychologist's duty to integrate his data, if we accept that his purpose is to present functional conclusions rather than mere elemental data. Assigning this duty to the psychologist is technically sound because he has a grasp of all of his findings, those that he judges should enter his report and those which should be omitted. He ought to be able to formulate more meaningful psychological conclusions than someone who has a less intimate grasp of the basic materials.

THEORETICAL CONSTRUCTS AND THE REPORT

The psychologist's task is to translate the raw material of his protocol into a meaningful, useful personality picture. This is the most difficult part of his evaluative duties. All of the various personality theories might be of some help here; the same is true of theories of assessment and experience with assessment modalities. In general, clinically derived theories, especially Freudian psychoanalysis and its more socially oriented modifications, are pertinent, since they are concerned with personality development and the major conditions of the maladjustment and readjustment processes. At the same time, psychoanalysis is not particularly conversant with the assessment of skills, with many aspects of rehabilitation, or with behavior therapies (but see p. 23). Other orientations, as for example learning or conditioning theories, are also adapted to help understand personality development, maladjustment, and readjustment. Increasingly, a phenomenological approach is recognized as very useful. This recognition stems both from the rise of humanistic psychology and from the now classical use of such perceptual tools as the Rorschach and the TAT.

As helpful as systematic views of personality can be, they bear no specific relationship to the interpretation of test responses. They can, in fact, become unduly injected into a case and lead both the unwary psychologist and his reader astray, away from the individual and in the direction of the generalities that characterize most persons. Tests can be interpreted in the framework of any number of personality theories. The Rorschach owes allegiance to no particular theory and is compatible with many. The Murray TAT can of course be interpreted in the light of the viewpoint on personality from which it emerged, but more often the TAT stories are assigned meanings in the light of contributions by Freud, Sullivan, Adler, Jung, or Rank. Responses to a psychometric procedure (e.g., the WAIS) are freely interpreted as contributions to personality understanding. Even the Szondi, which is intimately derived from a particular genetic view of personality, can be interpreted in terms which ignore its basic premise.

Intrepretation that closely follows a personality theory, for example, Freudian psychoanalysis, can be technically superb in terms of the accuracy of the insights offered, completeness and potency of presentation, and internal consistency, yet fall far short of the case requirements. A protocol thus interpreted is likely to give workers who are sophisticated in analytic theory an excellent understanding of such matters as basic drive structure, psychosexual status, and developmental factors. Unfortunately, an understanding of such matters may not be very helpful in working with a particular individual, whereas other personality information may be much more pertinent. Knowledge of early factors in the client's emotional development can be quite beside the point when the problem is one of attempting a community readjustment, or treating the individual with available modalities such as electric shock, occupational therapy, or antidepressants. Many modern analysts, as well as other psychotherapists, do not rely very much on information about the person's early life, preferring in many instances to deal with how he copes with contemporary problems.

THE CLIENT'S NEEDS AND THE REPORT

What would seem to be required is a realistic and eclectic point of view on what are the important personality variables commonly found in the people we evaluate. The topics of concern must be established on the basis of judged relevance for each individual case, not on the basis of the topics prominent in some personality theory, nor on classes of content thought to be regularly made available through the use of various tests. At the present stage of our development, this task may be accomplished independently by psychologists through both experience and theoretical orientation. Theory is sometimes to an extent implicit and based partly on personal factors in the psychologist, hence perhaps less alterable than it should be. But regardless of the reason, some workers will stress the role of hostility, the oedipal status, inferiority feelings, repression, or fixation at the oral level. An a priori list of variables acceptable to all would be extremely difficult to draw up, although systematic investigation might eventually succeed with this task.

The General Topics of the Report

Quite arbitrarily, we can draw up a useful list of tentative general personality topics that could provide the basic elements around which the psychologist might conceptualize his case presentation. These may be regarded as "handles" with which the psychologist can come to grips with his mission in the presence of the mass of material he elicits from his client. Although something might be written on almost every one of these topics for every person (a systematic approach to shotgun reporting!), usually a person can be meaningfully and effectively described in skeletal form by considering him in terms of just a few of them. In most instances, the case presentation can probably be conceptualized around perhaps three to six of these topics. Occasionally seven or eight might be required, but at other times, particularly when a pointed question is asked, even one or two might suffice. The report can then be rounded out with subcategories also taken from the list.

This list of topics cannot be offered as complete, nor are all topics mutually exclusive. Each psychologist may wish to add those personality topics he regards as generally pertinent.

Examples of General Personality Topics Around Which a Case Presentation May be Conceptualized

Achievement
Aggressiveness
Antisocial Tendencies
Anxieties
Aptitudes
Attitudes
Aversions
Awarenesses
Background Factors
Behavioral Problems
Biological Factors
Cognitive Functioning
Cognitive Skills
Cognitive Style
Competency
Conative Factors
Conflicts
Content of Consciousness
Defenses
Deficits
Developmental Factors
Diagnostic Considerations
Drives, Dynamics
Emotional Cathexes
Emotional Controls
Emotivity
Fixations
Flexibility
Frustrations
Goals
Hostility
Identity

Intellectual Controls
Intellectual Level
Interests
Interpersonal Relations
Interpersonal Skills
Life Style
Molar Surface Behavior
Needs
Outlook
Perception of Environment
Perception of Self
Personal Consequences of Behavior
Placement Prospects
Psychopathology
Rehabilitation Needs
Rehabilitation Prospects
Sentiments
Sex
Sex Identity
Sex Role
Significant Others
Situational Factors
Social Consequences of Behavior
Social Role
Social Stimulus Value
Social Structure
Special Assets
Subjective Feeling States
Symptoms
Treatment Prospects
Value System
Vocational Topics

The Concept of Case-Focusing

Related to the selection of general topics on which to report is another major but more specific aspect of the conceptualization of the report. This is the matter of selecting the appropriate focus of interpretation—the kind of conclusions to be derived from the raw data. Test manuals and textbooks, good as they may be, can suggest interpretations only in the general terms of the accepted meanings of such variables as test responses, scores, or quantitative patterns. The psychologist must adapt these general interpretive meanings to his specific case and mission. As he peruses the protocol and determines the central and pertinent personality topics with which he must deal, he simultaneously develops the interpretations (conclusions) in these topic areas as his mission requires.

There are several differences between interpretations made in general terms and *case-focused interpretations*. First, the case-focused interpretation is derived relative to a mission. We administer selected tests and search the elicited protocol for any information related to the evaluation goal. Such data are emphasized to the partial or total neglect of other material. Second, interpretations are made according to their implications for action. The psychologist bridges the gap between the general interpretation and the perceived needs of the mission; in effect, *his conclusions, with greater or lesser directness, are recommendations*. His interpretations tell the report readers as much as possible about the practical meaning gained by the psychologist's unique approach. Finally, in the case-focused interpretation the psychologist is not content with reaching conclusions solely on the basis of the restricted evaluation units (e.g., tests, subtests, scores, ratios, profiles, indexes) on which validity research has been done and for which published interpretation guides are available. Following sophisticated clinical practice, he appropriates whatever fortuitous data are available. Thus he may probe the meaning of verbalizations or of symbolic productions, interpret sequences or combinations of responses or scores in a manner not authorized or explicitly set forth by the test manual; he may consider meanings derived by comparing scores or responses on one test with those on another (the battery approach), or reach conclusions from any of the preceding in the light of, or in combination with, such information as that provided by anamnesis, behavior reported by others, or physical examination.

Let us consider a few brief examples showing the difference between general interpretation and case-focused interpretation. For meaningful, psychological work, general interpretations are incomplete interpretations which, too often, are of the Aunt Fanny sort. The mission of the psychologist is more closely related to knowing, for example, whether the client will act out than whether he is "hostile"; whether he requires treatment rather than whether he has "anxiety."

Here is a statement from a case report.

> The patient appears to be an immature, dependent individual whose passivity and feelings of insecurity leave him with little capacity to initiate decisive action.

There are four Aunt Fanny-type statements in this example: "immature," "dependent," "passivity," "feelings of insecurity." These four subconclusions contribute to a final conclusion, ". . . leave him with little capacity to initiate decisive action," which may or may not have specific meaning to the reader, depending partly on what other information he has about the patient. On the basis of interview information and impressions, and a social history, the referring clinician might not even know that the patient cannot initiate decisive action. Even if the conclusion is correct, this behavioral fact may not be apparent on the surface and may come as a complete surprise to the clinician. What is he to do with this conclusion? What does it mean in terms of the patient's condition? At best, if the person who has made the referral has corroborating information to the effect that the patient cannot initiate decisive action (which would reduce the value of the psychologist's contribution, since people who cannot initiate decisive action probably are dependent, immature, passive, and insecure anyway), he can integrate this with the psychologist's general findings and other data, and reach some pertinent understandings. The psychologist, on the other hand, has available much additional information (through tests and from other sources) that would permit him to make an even fuller integrative statement on the patient's psychological make-up. Instead, he seems to stay close to his tests, as if he might have interpreted them "blind." Had he been closer to his patient and drawn on all information available to him, he might have written something like this:

> The patient currently presents an apparent picture of self-assurance since he is socially deft, alert, and obviously knowledgeable. Nevertheless, an overprotected upbringing becomes apparent when he has to put forth directed and sustained effort such as evidently was required in his recent business venture which failed and preceded by a few weeks his admission with a diagnosis of depressive neurosis. His need to achieve "success" is mostly a matter of his family's aspiration for him and is not congruent with his inner needs. Thus we find a person who does not at a deep level aspire to adult standards for responsibility and achievement. He would rather receive than produce. Hence when he finds himself in a position of responsibility he becomes fearful of his ability to perform as expected. Tension, confusion, indecisiveness, and depression are the results, the patient alternating between different courses of action but unable to take definite steps.

Another general interpretive statement gleaned from a report reads:

> Tension, depression, aggression and sexual conflict are evident in the protocol.

One hundred percent Aunt Fanny!
Maybe the patient is something like this:

> This patient is deeply involved with a mother figure, and mixed feelings about this relationship seem to be associated with the symptoms for which the patient seeks help at the clinic. A dependent and overly close relationship with this parent has hampered his ability to assume a male role without conflict, and his mere urges to heterosexual expression cause him to feel anxious and tense, sometimes to a degree which incapacitates him for his everyday functioning. At the same time his sexual tensions and fantasy mean to him that he is going against his relationship with the mother, a feeling which ties in with other deep negative feelings which he has for her.

But this guess might be wrong. Possibly the next piece of fiction would be more descriptive of the patient who produced the protocol. Notice, incidentally, that an Aunt Fanny "sexual conflict" may fit both sexes.

> The client is in conflict over what are proper sex mores, the family and church teachings being on the one hand, and her liberated peer group standards and pressures being on the other. She initially complained to the counselor of an "inability to concentrate," and she does in fact seem to have a degree of tension which at times may hamper her studying. But she has always apparently become anxious when in conflict, and her present struggle to readjust to the standards of her new environment is hardly the basic cause of tension. What probably really brings her to counseling is a feeling that she is "letting down" her parents (a matter of truth at a fairly deep level where she does entertain rebellious urges). The implication this has to her for a vital relationship in her life has been causing her to feel unhappy.

And another illustration:

Thinking is syncretistic.

What does this mean for a particular patient? Perhaps that—

> Although the clinical impression suggests a quite good remission, psychological examination of the thinking processes indicates an active psychosis, the nature of which suggests that if the patient is now returned to the community he might repeat the behavior which led to his hospitalization. It is true that the patient has better emotional controls now, but his thinking causes him to reach some unlikely, sometimes bizarre ideas because he is prone to illogically relate unrelated ideas in a manner which can cause social difficulties. It might be well to delay discharge and have this patient's thought processes restudied in three weeks or a month.

These passages illustrate the relation of the case-focused approach to the mission and to implications for action. We need a final illustration to point up the role of the battery in the case-focused approach, particularly of the value of integrating data from diverse sources. We cannot afford unduly to restrict our approach and to put all of our diagnostic eggs in one basket.

Such, oddly enough, was the case with a psychology professor who happened to be a confirmed bachelor, and who for his single blessedness was routinely badgered by his colleagues. Eventually he tired of this and to demonstrate to his friends (and perhaps to convince himself) that his sole reason for being unmarried was the misfortune of not yet having met the "right" woman, he embarked upon a practical plan of action. He constructed a rating schedule consisting of twenty graphic scales, each of which could contribute from one to five points to the total score. Each scale was designed to assess a key dimension (by male consensus in our culture) of feminine charm and wifely quality. Though the procedure he followed in developing the schedule left something wanting in the way of rigor, his faculty associates agreed that it did have face validity as a basis for seeking a wife. The professor declared publicly that when he met a woman who attained a score of 90 he would propose marriage to her.

Shortly after this event, the professor transferred to a university in another part of the country and was not seen or heard from by his colleagues for several years. One September, however, the professor and a former associate met at a national scientific meeting. After the perfunctory amenities of greeting, the conversation went something like this:

"Married yet?"

"Nope."

"Guess you haven't met a woman who comes up to 90."

"As a matter of fact, I have. Met one in fact who came up to 96."

"So why didn't you marry her?"

"Didn't like her!"

THE PROCESS OF CONCEPTUALIZATION

In conceptualizing his presentation in terms of his mission, the psychologist might first imagine that he has been asked, "Tell me about this person." In responding to such a request he recognizes (1) that he must be selective of the information he reports, and (2) that he must meaningfully organize this information.

The first task takes cognizance of the frequent observation that the various aspects of a person's existence may be understood in terms of some kind of hierarchical order, and from this structure those traits which are of "central or dominating importance" may reliably be judged (Conrad,1932). As a result of psychological study, certain features suggest themselves as predominant in the person's psychoeconomics. In our clients we may identify organizing centers or central themes, which may relate to underlying tendencies or to modes of expression. Thus we become aware of the basic role of such issues as an inadequate self-concept, an attitude of interpersonal hostility, a need for achievement, a rigid control over emotional expression, tendencies to withdrawal, conflicts over sexual goals, or a pattern of achieving self-needs through the manipulation of others. A large number of such issues may be identified in any personality, although there is perhaps a relatively smaller number of recurring themes that accounts for many of the topics found to be apparently relevant in case studies.

The organization of the central themes into a report may, for discussion purposes, be regarded as involving several different tasks. What the psychologist

considers most important must be made to stand out, with the other material
assigned an auxiliary role for the sake of completeness. Importance is
gauged in terms of consequences, which might mean that the major emphasis is
not accorded to the most central feature in the person's psychoeconomics—
if this can be determined. Thus, a hospital psychologist, for example, must think
in such practical terms as whether his information will give the staff the sort
of understanding they need to relate more effectively to the patient.
The psychologist may have determined that dependency, hostility, and a poor
male sex identity are the central themes; he must decide on a hierarchy of
emphasis for these. But if depression and suicidal tendencies were also
identified, the practical imperativeness of this finding would dictate that
it be emphasized, even though sexual conflict was basic in undermining the
patient's adjustment.

There are as many means of supplying appropriate emphasis to content as
literary creativity will permit. For practical use, however, the more
common techniques will generally suffice. These include the order of presentation,
the skillful and appropriate use of adjectives, and the use of vivid illustrative
material. Less often the psychologist might resort to the use of underlining,
capitalization, dramatic presentation (such as is produced by a clipped
statement), or an exclamation point. Sometimes the occasion presents itself
when the psychologist can state in virtually so many words what is most
important: "This man is best understood through a description of his deep
dependency needs and his manner of attempting to gratify these."

The skillful use of repetition can also make for effective emphasis.
This is perhaps best accomplished by weaving the central theme through all or
a substantial part of the report, relating subsidiary themes to that which has
been selected as the main point for emphasis. The dependency theme alluded
to in the previous paragraph, for example, can be related to the other
prominent and clinically relevant personality themes. Suppose that there
are in the person strong but inexpressible urges, a tendency to perceive
the environment as threatening, feelings of inadequacy and depression, deep
anxieties about the adequacy of his maleness, and the objective appearance
of free anxiety. All of these may be more or less directly related to the crucial
dependency problem, and the dependency theme might be presented in a
number of contexts.

What this amounts to is that the psychologist should practice a mild form
of caricature. This was also the intent when the principle of selectivity of
content was advocated. We are charged with presenting a clinically useful
picture, not an exact photograph. Admittedly, by eliminating certain material
judged to be nonrelevant to the purpose we produce a distortion of the whole
personality; yet we might as well accept the fact that we cannot present an
undistorted picture of the personality—its full content is simply not available to
us, and we may not be entirely accurate in what we do know. The shotgun

report, too, deletes information, but its errors are more serious because its bulk can prevent the reader from recognizing the relative importance of the various topics, and so cause him to produce his own distorted image. Test-by-test reporting, segmentalized reporting, and traditional, non-case-focused reports, for various reasons, have similar effects.

Along with seeing the case in terms of its needed emphases, the psychologist must consider the detailed attributes of the central themes to be understood and presented. Each basic theme must be seen in terms of its role in the person's economy, its unique components, its social import, and associated personality information (for example, the relationship of a central theme of inferiority feelings to a subsidiary theme of deficiencies in heterosexual functioning). It is these that make the central themes take on the action characteristic of life.

Once he understands his client and the basic tactics of case presentation in terms of the overall guiding principles discussed here, the psychologist is ready to outline his report—preferably on paper, although this might not be necessary for some seasoned psychologists. The first step in this task is to select from a population of personality topics, such as that presented in the list on page 114, those that comprise the central features of the case. (For purposes of simplifying the present exemplification, let us assume that this listing is identical to one the reader might find suitable.)

Outlining a Report

Here is an example of how a case may be outlined, together with the report that emerges. The report will serve to initiate a discussion of the often troubling problem of intraparagraph and interparagraph organization.
The client, a young man in his twenties, had twice in recent months come into difficulties which led to his arrest, the first time for "bookie" activities and the second time for threatening his parents with a gun after consuming "12 or 14 beers." The psychiatrist who examined the client on direction of the court referred the case to us, with the request that we probe the meaning of the antisocial tendencies.

We determined that the client had a basic conflict centering about passivity and dependency, these being associated with what the client perceived as a harsh father, and hence a (now generalized) need to rebel was developed. No fewer than four clinically relevant defenses were erected against this conflict, (1) a denial of personal inadequacy, (2) a denial of real events, which precludes effective or constructive action, (3) a renunciation of personal goals so as to gain support (and thus perhaps to be maneuvered by "bad company"), and (4) a hostile and unrealistic fantasy life. The typical view he presented to others and the difficulties he experienced in cognitive functioning round out this picture.

The core personality topic outline might go like this:

    I.   Conflicts
    II. Social Stimulus Value
    III. Cognitive Functioning
    IV. Defenses (1)
    V.   Defenses (2)
    VI. Defenses (3)
    VII. Defenses (4)

This preliminary outline form is both general and incomplete. Yet it presents an overall structure for the report, and the topic headings might well form the bases for paragraphs. In practice we would now simply translate these headings into more specific behavior referents, and elaborate on the content of the paragraphs. Let us here, however, in order to show how a list of personality topics guides in the reporting of subcategories too, add the step of including these general topics.

These additional topics (or subtopics) might be listed as:

Attitudes	Interpersonal Skills
Awarenesses	Needs
Cognitive Skills	Outlook
Conative Factors	Perception of Environment
Content of Consciousness	Perception of Self
Deficit	Personal Consequences of Behavior
Drives, Dynamics	Psychopathology
Emotional Cathexes	Subjective Feeling States
Emotional Controls	Social Consequences of Behavior
Frustrations	Social Role
Goals	Value System
Interpersonal Relations	

The outline then becomes

    I.   Conflicts
         A. Self-Perception
         B. Goals
         C. Frustrations
         D. Interpersonal Relations
         E. Perception of Environment
         F. Drives, Dynamics
         G. Emotional Cathexes
         H. Emotional Controls
    II. Social Stimulus Value
         A. Cognitive Skills
         B. Conative Factors
         C. Goals
         D. Social Role
    III. Cognitive Functioning
         A. Deficit
         B. Psychopathology

    IV. Defenses (1)
        A. Self-Perception
        B. Needs
        C. Conflicts
    V. Defenses (2)
        A. Subjective Feeling States
        B. Attitudes
        C. Deficits
        D. Personal Consequences of Behavior
        E. Awareness
        F. Subjective Feeling States
        G. Awarenesses
        H. Social Stimulus Value
        I. Social Consequences of Behavior
    VI. Defenses (3)
        A. Interpersonal Relations
        B. Needs
        C. Interpersonal Skills
        D. Emotional Controls
    VII. Defenses (4)
        A. Content of Consciousness
        B. Needs
        C. Values
        D. Needs
        E. Social Consequences of Action

. . . which now, in more lifelike terms, still highly detailed for teaching purposes, becomes

    I. Conflict centering about dependency and passivity
        A. Feelings of inadequacy
        B. Frustrated personal goals (dependency and passivity)
        C. Faulty, unsatisfying relationship with father
        D. Father seen as cold, rejecting, punishing
        E. Rebellious tendencies which are generalized
        F. Control over negative impulses out of fear
    II. How others see patient
        A. Intellectual level and skills
        B. Lack of will to function at optimum
        C. Fluctuating goal for self-achievement
        D. Social irresponsibility
    III. Cognitive functioning
        A. Deficiencies under stress
        B. Psychopathological aspects of deficiencies
    IV. Denial of felt inadequacy
        A. Negative view of self
        B. Need to feel "like everybody else"
        C. Conflict over adequacy as a male
    V. Denial and non-experience of pertinent realities
        A. Partial avoidance of depressed feelings
        B. Naive attitude
        C. Inability adequately to assess his behavior

       D. Inability to correct own behavior
       E. Inability to understand problems
       F. Depressive tendencies
       G. Lack of full experience of depression
       H. Social masking of depressed feelings
       I. Relation of inner feelings to negative social behavior
  VI. Social maneuvers to gain acceptance
       A. Receptive orientation
       B. Need for support
       C. Techniques of gaining support
       D. Control of negative impulses to retain support
 VII. Fantasy as a basic defense
       A. Value of fantasy
       B. Needs as reflected in fantasy
       C. Deficiency of social values
       D. Need to appear in socially favorable light
       E. Fantasy content and deficiency of social values as a basis for unlawful activity

. . . and then, initiated by an opening summary or overview, is translated into the body of a report:

    This man is most readily understood in terms of his unusually passive, dependent approach to life and his attempts to overcome the deeply unhappy state brought about by this personality limitation.
    Mr. A does not feel very adequate as a person, an attitude which is developed through experiencing a continual sense of failure in terms of his own goals, and which apparently is reinforced by others. In fact, his relations with his father very likely are the basic reason for such feeling. This person is seen by the patient as cold, rejecting, punishing, and unapproachable. He has an urge to rebel and fight against this person—an urge which has been generalized to all society, but he is afraid to give vent to his impulses. Whatever emotional support he does get (got) seems to be from the mother.
    As others see him, he seems to have the essential capacity to do well if only he would try. He scores at the average level on a test of intelligence (IQ: 106), he is able to learn readily, when he wants to, and on occasion can perform unusually fast and effectively. Yet he does not typically follow through on this advantage. His willingness, sometimes even his desire, to do well fluctuates, so that in the long run he could not be regarded as a constructive or responsible person.
    Other personality deficiencies also compromise his functioning. Under stress or when faced with difficult problems he becomes blocked, confused and indecisive. His thinking does not show sufficient flexibility to meet such situations so that he would be regarded as inadaptable and unspontaneous.
    Mr. A's felt inadequacy causes him to feel that he is not as good as others. By way of reassuring himself on this matter he frequently during examination makes remarks that he is "like everybody else." The feeling that he is inferior includes also the sexual area where he is quite confused about his maleness. It is likely that one or more sex problems contribute to his sense of failure, although, quite understandably, he denies this and indicates a satisfactory sex life "like everybody else."

He hardly experiences the full effect of his failures, however. He protects himself by denying many events of reality, by keeping many facts about himself and others unconscious, by a general attitude of "not knowing"— an attitude of naiveness. He can hardly take corrective action about himself because he does not understand himself or his actions, or recognize the nature of his problems. Oddly enough, as already stated, this is an unhappy person, but he does not adequately recognize this fact nor does he appear to others as depressed. Yet on occasion this might be a factor in his behavior which could be personally or socially unfortunate.

This man's insecurity about himself forces him into a receptive orientation to other people. He must have friends to provide support. To achieve this he presents himself in a positive, correct light, tries to say the "right" things and even to be ingratiating and obsequious. It is important that he create the "right" effect and may resort to dramatic behavior to bring this about. "Friends" are so important to him that he sometimes must take abuse in order to hold them. He must always hold back hostile expression.

But it is perhaps in fantasy where the greatest satisfaction is derived. He dreams of being a "success" (his term)—accumulating enough money by the age of 35 so he can retire and effortlessly enjoy the comforts of the world. In his fantasy he is independent of authority, can openly express the aggression he ordinarily cannot, and flout society. He has no positive feelings about social rules (although he may profess to), but is concerned when apprehended for misconduct, possibly less for the real punishment than for how it "looks" to be known for doing what he is afraid to do. It is little wonder then that he is easy prey for an "easy money" scheme.

The reader will note that the sections of the outline and the paragraphs in the report contain heterogeneous and occasionally repeated content. This is intentional. A report consisting of homogeneous paragraphs would be a form of segmentalized report (though perhaps not as artificial as the kind of segmentalized reports commented on in this book), and subject to some of the same censure. What the psychologist should try to do is relate in his report those behaviors that occur together in the functioning context of the person. If sex conflicts hamper intellectual functioning, these related facts should be mentioned as closely together as they are in this sentence, not as unconnected statements occurring in different and possibly widely separated paragraphs. In a good report, the beginning of a paragraph commonly announces the integrated theme of the topics that compose it.

Arranging Findings in a Report

There is a final and most important consideration pertaining to effective organization. How are the component findings to be arranged in a report? How, for example, was the scheme for the above report developed?

First consider the intraparagraph organization. The intention was to take the main integrated themes emerging in response to the imaginary request to "Tell me about this person"—the brief statement of the psychologist's findings that precedes the outline (p. 120). Thus each of the four basic methods of defense the client uses has some meaningfully interrelated components. Consider the derivation of the fifth paragraph of the report. That the client feels inadequate was one of the principal conclusions of the psychologist. In fact, the client's repeated statement that he is "like everybody else" strengthens this conclusion and also suggests how he tries to adopt an attitude to deny his feeling of inadequacy. The psychologist also had strong reasons to reach the conclusion that the client had several prominent sex conflicts associated with his feelings of inadequacy—a conclusion perhaps strengthened by the client's comment (to a sentence completion item) that he has a sex life that is "like everybody else." (Notice, incidentally, the emphasis to be gained by repeating this expression closely together in different but related contexts. The topics in the fifth paragraph obviously belong together.)

Or look at the third paragraph. From observations of samples of the client's intellectual functioning, it was apparent to the psychologist that he would impress others well in this respect, at least as regards capacity. Yet it was also clear by the client's performance on a number of tests that there was a fluctuating will and a consequent lack of goal-directedness and responsibility. It was further noted that he meets many of his problems through fantasy, but this possible way of elaborating on the theme of irresponsibility and its social effects was reserved for the emphasis that can be brought about by treating a topic in a final paragraph. In the third paragraph, however, it was thought appropriate to contrast his capacity with his output, since this discrepancy suggests that people would be critical of him, an important finding in view of what rejection means to the client. The theme was not "pushed" more strongly only because the conclusion was not judged to be sufficiently firm. It it were, it could easily have been developed in this paragraph.

There is one simple rule for deciding on the contents of a paragraph: functional relatedness (what relatedness is there in the other paragraphs in the report on Mr. A?). This criterion permits the intentional repetition of items of content in different paragraphs. Beyond this, the psychologist has to decide how to arrange the several items in the paragraph and how to word his thoughts for effectiveness. The limiting factor in learning this skill is probably the basic prose style of the psychologist. Nevertheless, much of the ingenuity needed for this skill can be acquired. Perhaps most important are the terms in which the psychologist thinks. If he is prone to think that his task is to convey his "findings" that the patient has anxiety, hostility, and narcissistic wounds, this is probably precisely what he will convey to his reader. But if he understands his case in terms of his practical mission, he is likely to conceptualize both his understanding and his mode of expression in terms of how his readers will relate what he has written to their own missions.

The tyro can learn how to make a paragraph hang together by studying samples of effective clinical writing. Supervisors are often in a position to make relevant suggestions in training conferences based on live case material. There are any number of writing techniques that can be adapted for specific effect. For example, in paragraph three the method of contrast was used. The client's capacity was contrasted with his productivity because of the social meaning and implications such a discrepancy may have. Some of the techniques that aid in interparagraph organization might also be useful.

The organization of paragraphs in a report is possibly more complex than the organization of conclusions within a paragraph, because the report is a larger conceptual unit. Moreover, the organization of each report must have its own rationale, though certainly other reports may have a similar rationale and be organized along similar lines. How do we arrive at a rationale for organizing a report? How, for example, was the rationale for the report on Mr. A. arrived at?

First, Mr. A was understood in terms of an approach to life (central personality theme) that is not socially adaptive and leads to some personally unsatisfying results. The ways in which he tries to overcome some of the effects of his basic personality orientation bear rather directly on the reason for his being referred to us. By stating the central problem the client may quickly be introduced to the reader in general terms, with the understanding that the necessary details will follow.

The top priority then became the further development of the theme introduced in the first paragraph, hence the need to know about his feelings of inadequacy. This topic led naturally to a discussion of what the client is "really" like in contrast to his misperception of himself. However, he is also objectively seen to have shortcomings, so the deficiencies mentioned in the fourth paragraph supplement those commented on in the third. So far, we have presented the logically related topics of the client's perception of himself and an external evaluation of some of his qualities. All of this was thought to be pertinent to the problem for which he was referred.

The next four paragraphs are logically interrelated, since they serially disclose how he copes with his feelings about himself. First, in paragraph five, is a discussion of the basic manner by which he tries not to feel inadequate. The theme is amplified in the sixth paragraph, which suggests a very wide scope of denial, and the effect this might have. The seventh paragraph shows a social maneuver he uses as a defense for the same basic problem. The final paragraph suggests an additional defense for this problem, that of a fantasy life that seems to be closely associated with his long-term antisocial activities (being a "bookie").

The overall guiding principle was to present the man in terms of his personality as this pertains to his antisocial activities. Nevertheless, the relationship between what is described in these paragraphs and his social difficulties is not mentioned in every instance. It would be logical enough to do so, but a different scheme was used in preference to cluttering the report with what in this case would be speculations. Instead, the speculations were gathered together as a "speculative note" that was appended to the body of the report. Its purpose was to attempt to relate, more directly than responsible interpretation practices permit, the basic personality of the man to his unwanted behaviors.

Speculative Note

The client's antisocial behavior appears to be related to the personality problems noted here, and in his method of coping with these. His negative attitude to authority (father), of course, would seem to be a basic ingredient. His need for support is another factor, and the support of a group of persons on the other side of the law might be as meaningful as support from another source. As we have seen, he will go out of his way (engaging in illegal activities?) to retain his "friends." His fantasy life of wealth and leisure also would seem to make unlawful activities appealing. Finally, his intellectual inefficiencies and his inadaptability might tend to give trouble in more straightforward enterprises. He does not genuinely feel he is wrong.

Concerning the gun incident, the client seemed to be trying to indicate to the examining physician that the weapon was used to try forcibly to extract sympathy and support that he could not get by passive means. The gun evidently made him feel powerful and the reasoning was childish and incomplete. Apparently the act was impulsive. The client admits to consuming 12 or 14 beers before the event and this probably loosened his usually tight control over direct hostile expression. Further acts either against himself or against others cannot be ruled out, although no specific or immediate danger is foreseen.

There are many possible schemes suitable for organizing reports. The total number is probably limited only by the psychologist's ingenuity and his variety of case material. The following suggestions pertain to some elementary organizing schemes. In many instances one of these will not be a sufficient scheme for a whole report; several strategies will have to be combined.

Regardless of the presentation scheme, an overview statement is commonly in order. In any event, a clear focus and objective must always be established in the light of the available material and its significance. Sometimes it will be most effective to present a major conclusion at the beginning (a purpose often served by an overview) and then make supporting information available. At other times, the psychologist may be able to build up to the major conclusion and present it more forcefully at the end of the report. It is difficult to generalize. Most often, when the psychologist is asked to contribute a diagnosis, he may consider this problem toward the conclusion of his report, after the relevant evidence presumably has been presented. But a diagnosis may be offered at the beginning of a report for a good reason:

"This is a severely schizophrenic patient whose homicidal fantasies and inability to control his behavior could pose a serious threat to the community."

1. The simplest approach to report organization is possible when it is necessary to deal only with a limited segment of behavior, such as might be the case when servicing a highly specific consultation request. Thus, when dealing with intellectual efficiency, the report considers serially the several pertinent aspects of this problem. Or if the problem is one of deterioration, as for example in a brain syndrome, it is necessary only to cite the related data contributing to the major conclusion, e.g., that deterioration is present. Probably the relative seriousness of the signs, such as memory defect, inability to shift concepts, concreteness, confabulation, loss of mental control, confusion, and loss of orientation, will suggest a meaningful order of presentation and appropriate data groupings, e.g., memory defect and confabulation would probably be closely linked.

2. With more complex material, a quite simple, yet effective approach, is to present a general opening statement, an overview, or an introductory statement, followed by the necessary elaborations and whatever other pertinent information is required to round out the personality study. A report might start: "The dominant emphasis in Ms. B's life is manipulating others in order to realize a set of strong ambitions." The nature of these ambitions, why they are important to her, and her techniques of manipulation might then be commented upon. Finally, whatever else is important, such as capacity (e.g., intellectual or social), situational frustrations, adaptability, or the effects of failure, could be woven into the theme.

3. Some reports might be essentially a buildup to a diagnosis or some major conclusion. What is required is that the psychologist present bits of evidence step by step, as these contribute to a final conclusion. A tightly reasoned report of this sort might be in order particularly when the conclusion is of far-reaching significance. Examples would occur when a diagnosis is an essential ingredient in a court decision, or when contemplated action like commitment to or release from a hospital might hinge on the psychologist's findings. Such an organization might be in order when the psychologist feels he must convincingly present findings that are not at all apparent. Quite frequently, for example, clinical diagnosis may point to neurosis while psychological indicators suggest psychosis.

4. A cause and effect presentation can be useful when concern is with some symptom whose basis needs to be understood. Physical symptoms which are medically thought to be psychogenic are a common instance. This approach is also particularly valuable when a social symptom, like misbehavior in school or criminal behavior, needs to be understood and identified with a set of dynamics or with pathology, such as a brain syndrome. It may be best at times to first explore the nature of the unwanted symptom and then to deal with its causes. At other times it may be appropriate to deal with

the pertinent underlying psychological material and show how this relates to the issue of concern.

5. In many instances the order of presentation might be from periphery to center or from center to periphery, and the most effective approach can be a subjective matter. Frequently it is helpful to contrast the surface picture with what is not apparent. Reasons for doing this might be (*a*) to alert others to unsuspected personality features; (*b*) to contribute understanding as to why a person who is without evident pathology gets into difficulties; or (*c*) to contrast a superficial picture or facade with what the person is "really" like.

6. Sometimes it is appropriate to emphasize the subjective view of the individual if the writer feels it is important to understand a situation(s) as he does. Contrasting the subjective picture with the external viewpoint can often contribute valuable perspective to a case. When the fantasy life, orientation, or perception of environment is particularly important, the value of this approach becomes evident.

7. Contrast can be an appropriate organizing focus of a report. The nature of a conflict may be brought out quite effectively by contrasting its elements, for example, incompatible goals. Contrast can also be functional when different layers of behavior need to be understood in relation to one another. An illustration of this might be severely hostile attitudes sublimated in one who fights for social justice. This technique is also called for when the findings of a current examination are compared wtih those of a previous examination. The writer sets forth the important similarities and differences uncovered in the two examinations and whatever significance these might have.

Illustrations of organizational schemes are presented in Chapter 7.

EXEMPLIFICATION: CONCEPTUALIZING A PSYCHOLOGICAL REPORT

We are now ready to apply all of the foregoing to some additional live case material, starting with the consultation request and proceeding through the administration of a battery, the case-focused interpretation, and the conceptualization of the report.

Background

The patient is a fifty-year-old single man, a high school graduate, who had suffered his first break, diagnosed as schizophrenia, some twenty-one years earlier. Following remission he had worked at several sales jobs, and as a laborer. He experienced another schizophrenic break five years prior to being seen by the author, and had been hospitalized continuously since that time.

Following the acute period, about which he has only the vaguest memory, the patient made a good hospital adjustment. He is liked by the staff and engages in several hospital activities.

Consultation with a psychologist was sought for the purpose of assessing his current psychological resources, and with specific interest in any possible rehabilitation potential he might have.

Clinical Behavior

During his contact with the psychologist the patient showed as prominent characteristics courtesy, correctness, and superior, though pedantic, language usage, that suggested a strong intellectual orientation. He also seemed to be full of self-doubt and indecisiveness. For example, he frequently spoke of his desire to leave the hospital and get a job, but then he would follow these expressions of desire with doubts about his ability, his readiness, his age, and the employment situation.

Test Battery

MMPI; Rorschach; TAT; Sacks Sentence Completions; Bender Gestalt; WAIS.

Manner of Presenting Test Protocols

The test protocol for each test is preceded by a statement as to the primary reasons why the test was used. Then the test information is presented and followed by some case-focused interpretive comments. This procedure does not imply a test-by-test interpretation, but it is a matter of convenience here to present interpretations contiguously with the test products from which they are largely derived. Each test is interpreted, however, with an awareness of the test products of the entire battery (including clinical observations) and other pertinent material. After eliciting the basic information units, these are integrated into a psychological report.

MMPI

The MMPI was selected primarily to disclose basic personality trends, including the strength of pathological dispositions.

The most conspicuous features of the profile are a high "cannot say" score (158) and an L of 8. The remaining two validity scales are within normal limits. The clinical scales and Scale O (Si) are between T scores of 30 and 70, with the exception that Scale 9 (Ma) is at 20. This latter contrasts with Scale 2 (D) at 60, Scale 3 (Hy) at 57, and Scale 1 (Hs) at 47. The remaining scales hover around 40 with Scale 8 (Sc) low at 35.

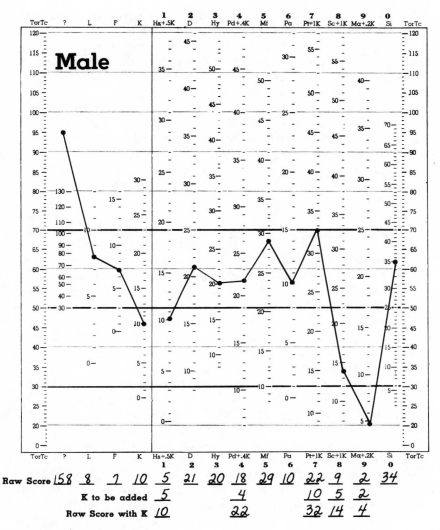

TorTc	?	L	F	K	1 Hs+.5K	2 D	3 Hy	4 Pd+.4K	5 Mf	6 Pa	7 Pt+1K	8 Sc+1K	9 Ma+.2K	0 Si
Raw Score	158	8	7	10	5	21	20	18	29	10	22	9	2	34
K to be added					5			4			10	5	2	
Raw Score with K					10			22			32	14	4	

FIG. 1 MMPI Scales

Some of the suggestive MMPI responses (including "?" responses) were then
used as a basis for interview. Elicited in this manner were statements by the
patient to the effect that he often feels anxious, unhappy, worrisome, and unsure

of himself. The latter point was unusually prominent, the patient vacillating on his responses, probing various possible meanings for each item, and often ending in a morass of confusion. Unproductive philosophical ruminations were frequent. Asked whether he cries easily, he developed a discourse on the possible meanings of "easily," uncertainty about the frequency of this behavior in others, variations at different times of his life, changing circumstances of life which would change the frequency of crying, and how does one judge when crying actually occurs (?). When asked for further information on the items relating to sex, the patient was somewhat uneasy. Though quite a handsome man, he indicated he had never had any dates or other close contacts with women, and questioned whether it was really right to expect that everyone should live the same way. He then added that any sort of sex has long ceased to be a part of his life; it is not necessary.

Interpretive Comments

The outstanding feature is the high "cannot say" score. In view of the patient's indecision, rumination, vacillation, and the frank statements of uncertainty he expresses when asked for more information relating to his responses, it seems that his attempt to deal with problems through exhaustive mental control robs him of spontaneity and makes him ineffectual, particularly when real decisions are called for. So pervasive is this characteristic that it is observed both when he has to make up his mind about personal matters, and when he has to recognize his position on issues having no apparent consequences to the self. The high "?" score has the effect of decreasing the absolute elevation of the clinical scales. But the fact that Scale 2 is highest, and contrasts with an abnormally low Scale 9, suggests a depressive component. What does this mean in terms of the mission? The case record does not mention depression and he does not appear to the psychologist to be depressed. To be sure, he apparently does experience unhappiness ("I wish I could be as happy as others seem to be"), but what may be more relevant to our purpose would be the practical effect of some sort of depressive equivalent. Here we may think again of a decrease of spontaneity (which does seem apparent clinically), and especially of a low opinion of himself, a lack of self-confidence which is part of the basis for his ruminations and indecisiveness.

The elevated L scale apparently does not relate to attempts at deliberate falsification of the protocol. The man seems to exude sincerity throughout the contact as he strives for precision, or really overprecision. Elsewhere, he gives the impression of rigidity and high moral standards of overconventionality, of an unrealistic and unbalanced orientation which almost makes him too good for this world. One wonders how this might reduce his effectiveness in the give-and-take of active interaction in the competitive existence "on the outside."

Clinically the patient shows no evidence of his earlier schizophrenia, and the low value of Scale 8 suggests further that underlying schizophrenic conflicts and solutions are not a problem. There are, however, neurotic-type conflicts apparently beyond those already mentioned, such as worrying, perhaps even tendencies to somatization (Scale 3 would probably be significantly higher were it not for the large number of "?" responses). But the important conclusion is that the earlier psychotic problem and earlier problems of adjustment (for example, in the sex area, where he hints he found some sort of outlet), are now of little more than historical value. Rather, he may be crippled by neurotic-type defenses, and hence the psychologist's answer on the matter of rehabilitation must incorporate a strong note of caution.

Rorschach

The Rorschach was used to study projectively the general personality, including pathological behaviors, and with heavy emphasis on his efficiency, effectiveness, and resourcefulness.

Card I. Reaction Time: 2"

1. Well, that one looks like a bat. What does it indicate? Well, a bat. Only that the outline looks a little like it. (E.: Some people see more than one thing on these cards). No. That's it.

Score: WF+AP

Card II. First Comment: 15"

Well, doesn't look like anything to me.
    If I turn it up this way it might look something like a flower, but it doesn't look like anything to me. It does have coloring similar to some growing plants that look something like the black tulip. The coloring. I don't know.

Score: Rejection, color description

Card III. First Comment: 20"

Well, that doesn't look like anything to me—anything I've experienced. It has coloring something like what I've described in the previous one, but I don't know what it is. Well, to me it doesn't look like anything that has come to my experience so far.

Score: Rejection, color description

Card IV. First Comment: 13"

That one has a similarity to the first one, but I don't know. Just a symmetrical outline. No similarity to anything—although I saw some pelts at one time. Might look like that. No, I don't know.

Score: Rejection, card description

Card V. First Comment: 10″

Same thing again. I don't see anything there except that it's symmetrical on both sides. Just ink.

Score: Rejection, card description

Card VI. Reaction Time: 50″

Well, I don't know. Couldn't be any geographical outline. I don't know what it is. Doesn't ring any bell.
1. It could be the pelt of an animal.
   Inquiry: (Indicates W). I guess mostly the shape.
   (E.: Anything else?) I don't know. I guess the shape.

Score: WF+AobjP

Card VII. First Comment: 15″

I get nothing from that one. No, I just don't make anything of that. O.K.? Except that these two dark blots are similar.

Score: Rejection, card description

Card VII. Reaction Time: 6″

1. Well, that's similar to a flower, a growing thing. Has color similar to an orchid. Of course the shape isn't very similar to that of an orchid, but the coloring is. That's all I get out of that.
   Inquiry: (Indicates D2).

Score: DCFBot

Card IX. First Comment: 4″

Again we have coloring, but outside of that doesn't ring a bell. O.K.?

Score: Rejection, color comment

Card X. First Comment: 12″

Well, to me the general outline of the whole thing—doesn't mean anything, but the coloring is similar to what you see in plants.

Score: Rejection, color description

Interpretive Comments

This protocol, while not yielding enough in the way of scores to make tabulation worthwhile, nevertheless gives some information most pertinent to the mission. The patient's ineffectiveness, his inability to cope with demands is more than obvious. Although an individual of superior intellectual endowment (WAIS, verbalizations as on the TAT and the Sacks Sentence Completions), his ability to reach practical solutions is inferior to that of most people. This shortcoming bothers him very much, and he dependently seeks reassurance. The skeleton of a high intellect and broad interests are now of little practical meaning. There is instead cause for concern in his experiencing of strong emotional pressure with which he tries to deal intellectually, but he often salvages some stability by default of responsibility. One would hesitate to demand much of him.

TAT

The TAT was used primarily to try to elicit the goals of this patient, other pertinent needs as they relate to his psychological status and rehabilitation prospects, the stresses he experiences, and how he may be inclined to handle these. The TAT was also thought important as a means of assessing an aspect of his intellectual resourcefulness, specifically his ability to organize words and thoughts effectively. He had previously required such ability in his work, and might need it again.

Card 1. Oh, well. Here we have a little boy—attentive on a violin and bow placed in front of him. He's very much enraptured. He seems in deep thought in being concentrated on the violin. I imagine he's an incipient learner—a student of the violin. He has an artistic taste. Looks as if he might have been well cared for. (How does it turn out?) Well, I imagine he's going to do some practicing.

Card 2. The picture depicts a rural scene of a farmer and a work animal facing a plowed field which may have been recently finished; standing by on a hillock and leaning or resting upon an upright tree is a woman which is part of the rural environs apparently. In the foreground is a woman who may be younger than the other who is carrying a couple of books.

Card 3 BM. This picture seems to be one of discouragement. The figure which is seated on the floor with its back to the viewer seems to be the picture of grief or some disappointment or discouragement.

Card 4. Apparently a most attractive young woman whose general make-up appears to be as sleek as a piece of sealskin is trying to embrace a rather ruggedly handsome young man. The whole attitude suggests supplication and a rather questing or searching look covers her features and seems to be suggested in the whole poise of her body while he, on the other hand, is turned away in complete negation or as if not wishing to heed her.

Card 6 BM. The location which appears to be a woman's dwelling house shows an elderly lady wearing an expression of somewhat rather poignant surprise and wonderment. She holds her hands clasped before her and holding what may be a handkerchief. The quite noticeably younger and taller man who is conservatively attired in what appears to be dark and conservative apparel, stands hat in hand, his mien wearing a look of somewhat serious expression as if he had just been the bearer of somewhat recent and somewhat astounding news.

Card 7 BM. In the picture are two men, one older than the other. The older man appears to have rather regular features and apparently has a mustache and may be intent on or may have been in intent conversation with the younger man whose features seem to be more aquiline than the younger man's.

Card 13 MF. This scene is a sleeping room with a rather dark background. Lying on a cot against a wall is the sleeping figure of a woman perhaps in illness or death, for standing feet wide apart and back to the figure a man stands with the forearm of his right arm covering his eyes as if to hide his despair or grief.

Card 18 GF. The scene appears to be at the foot of a staircase. A woman who has rather rugged features (her cheekbones seem to be rather high) seems to be embracing or examining another figure, that of a woman which is turned toward the viewer of the scene. It may be that a mishap has occurred such as the figure with side and back turned toward us has fallen downstairs.

Interpretive Comments

The patient obviously retains his excellent command of words, but there is a "tightness," or stiffness and lack of spontaneity or significant meaningfulness to his stories. Some confusion or loss in the train of thought is also sometimes observed. He is overly cautious, stays close to home base, and is not very adventuresome, though his earlier ambition and pedantically flavored intellectual achievement is evident. He attempts to give the scenes organization more than he tries to develop plots—a seeking for stability and structure—very much like what he does on the Rorschach when he comments on symmetry and other relationships within the blots. A depressive trend may be inferred from his lack of self-confidence, which does not permit him to do more with the stimuli, and rather directly by his story to 3 BM. Even though his ability to function is lacking, he remains alert and perceptive.

Sentence Completion Test

A Sacks Sentence Completion Test[2] was used because it systematically samples the patient's feelings about significant areas of life as these relate to the referral problem. It was hoped especially to learn something of his goals, work attitudes, self-confidence, and feelings about others.

> I feel that a real friend . . . is one that sticks by you through adversity.
> When the odds are against me . . . I don't know how to answer that. Sounds as if—I guess rather than run away, stay there. Guess you might as well quit. Have to find a solution.
> I would do anything to forget the time I . . . can't think of anything.
> If I were in charge . . . you mean of some group? We would start at the beginning.
> To me the future looks . . . well—fairly serene you might say.
> The men over me . . . are helpful, considerate, kind.
> I know it is silly but I am afraid of . . . Oh some of us are afraid of lots of things—got reason to be. Anybody'd be afraid of a rattlesnake. It's not silly. I'm afraid of heights. That might be silly.
> My father hardly ever . . . well, I never see him. Been gone a good many years.
> When I was a child I enjoyed . . . ice skating. How's that?

---

[2] Reproduced with the courtesy of Dr. Joseph M. Sacks.

What I want is a woman who . . . I never thought much about women. Oh, I'd rather not. Haven't thought of it in a long time. Most men want women who are companions, homemakers, I guess.

In my married life . . . you know I'm not married.

When I am at home with my family . . . I have a slight nucleus of a family.

At work I get along best with . . . I get along with almost everybody.

My mother . . . well, I got along with her all right.

Most of all, I want to . . . learn a satisfying vocation or skill.

I don't like people who . . . talk about themselves too much, although it's not such a fault.

I believe that I have the ability to . . . well, it certainly isn't drawing—Oh, to do usual, ordinary everyday tasks.

My greatest fault is . . . I smoke too much.

If people work for me . . . I usually work for other people.

Ten years from now, I . . . don't know what to expect. I was hoping to be home.

In school, my teachers . . . well, I found 'em most pleasant.

Most of my friends don't know that I am afraid of . . . I don't know if they don't know what I am afraid of.

If my father would only . . . I told you my father was dead. I can't think of much.

I was happiest when . . . I was in my twenties, you might say. Well, I'm fairly happy at the moment.

I think most girls like . . . Oh, I don't know. I haven't had much experience. Like automobiles would be a safe answer—like clothes.

I think a wife should . . . I don't know, I never had a wife.

When my family gets together . . .used to get together. We usually have dinner together.

Those I work with . . . are generally average Americans, you might say.

My mother and I . . . I told you my mother is dead.

I could be happy if . . . Oh, all could be happy under certain circumstances—food, rest, shelter.

Most people I know . . . go to business or work everyday.

I failed when . . . I tried to accomplish tasks in which I hadn't had any training.

At times, I have felt ashamed . . . you think one should feel ashamed for having been in a mental hospital?

The people who work for me . . . none.

Some day I . . . expect to see my brother and sister again—how's that?

When I see the boss coming . . . I just go on with what I'm doing.

I wish I could lose the fear of . . . I don't like to be in strange places and away from people I know. I suppose most of us are afraid of the unknown.

Compared with my mother, my dad . . . was—physical appearance of a father—dark, mother light—father stern—mother not so stern—stern enough.

When I was younger . . . we think the world is our oyster. Let me think of something else. Used to enjoy taking long walks in the country—skiing.

I believe most women . . . I don't know anything about women. I read that most women like clothes.

When I have sex relations . . . I don't have sex relations.

When there is a quarrel in my family . . . well, I suppose every family has had quarrels. Mine hasn't had many.

I like working with people who . . . are friendly and happy.

My mother thinks that my father . . . was the finest man she ever met.

What I want most is . . . Oh—a position or job with security—not a particularly exalted position—with people I've known for years.

When I'm not around, my friends . . . I don't know about my friends when I'm not around.

Compared with others, I . . . am fairly slow, let's say.

The worst thing I ever did . . I'm trying to think of it, I got drunk once. Did you ever get drunk? I slapped my sister once.

In giving orders to others, I . . . I've never given orders to others.

When I am older . . . I hope to be retired.

I can work best when my supervisor . . . will give me a little assistance when I'm on something new.

My fears sometimes force me to . . . Oh, I don't know, be cautious.

My father and I . . . well, let me see—we were pretty good friends I guess. He was pretty stern with me.

I remember when . . . Oh, when I just started school.

When I think of women . . . Well, I never think of women very much. What do they mean by that? There are always women around.

My sex life . . . I don't have any sex life.

When I was a child, my family . . . consisted of 6 persons, we might say.

People who work with me usually . . . find no problem with me.

I like my mother but . . . I told you she is dead.

What I want out of life . . . good health.

Interpretive Comments

This test again discloses a person who in most areas in conventional, his needs to comply apparently linked with a need for approval. Perhaps the vocational motivation and desire for social responsibility and productivity which he expresses are a reflection of this orientation. We also see again his mixed feelings, rumination, dependency needs, a fear of the unknown, and especially a fear of change in routine. This socially oriented person may also be characterized as short on perseverance, as being impatient and having the urge, if not the ready ability, to act out. The present depth of some of his aspirations is questioned, and the cognitive slippage evident in the protocol suggests that such aspirations are not realistic.

Bender Gestalt

This test was selected primarily to observe how the patient would approach a task, to note any possible signs of disorganization or organicity, and for any fortuitous personality information that may be inferred from the reproductions.

Interpretive Comments

This test suggests a lack of gross disorganization or of organic damage, but poor planfulness, particularly for so pedantic an individual. There is also evidence

of a striving quality (from his verbalizations) and a dissatisfaction with a
product which does not come up to his high standards. In view of the
shortcomings which he demonstrates in life, and on other tests of this battery,
we may infer the conflict that is brought about when he actively manipulates
the environment, hence his need not to be very bold.

WAIS

This test was used primarily to study the integrity and current effectiveness of
intellectual functioning rather than to determine the intellectual level per se.
The test was also thought to be a possibly important indication of the
patient's overall personality integrity.

Interpretive Comments

There is little doubt about the intellectual endowment of this patient, and his
ability to impress by his vocabulary, word usage, and knowledge of events.
Yet a mechanical, pedantic quality is evident, and his psychometric score seems
more related to history than to potentiality for application.

His intellectual achievement is more a matter of previous prominence and
the core of what survives of his personality. It is obvious that his functioning is
inadequate, that he needs much structure, is confused in new situations,
and confuses related ideas and events. He is too unsure of himself. He cannot
carry on independent effort long. His awareness of these shortcomings has
a damaging impact upon the impression he has of himself.

An outline based on the several case-focused interpretations may now be
prepared. Such an outline, for reasons of pertinence, omits or underplays
topics that are quite obvious in the present protocol and are commonly
given prominence in psychological reports. Matters of hostility and sexuality,
for example, pertinent to the personality but not to the reason for referral,
tend to be overlooked or minimized. In fact, the patient's sexual history
comes in for a good deal of attention in the case folder, and one of the
psychologist's contributions is to point out that, while this topic may be
interesting, it is not a matter for present consideration.

The interpretive material suggests three prominent themes relevant to
this consultation. They are cognitive functioning (or cognitive integrity, not
cognitive skills), a strong surviving personality need (that of dependency,
which takes on added significance at the present time), and his
defensive structure. These topics, together with an overview—which in this
instance would be essentially a summary of the patient's current status—
constitute the basis for the report.

TABLE OF SCALED SCORE EQUIVALENTS*

RAW SCORE

Scaled Score	Information	Comprehension	Arithmetic	Similarities	Digit Span	Vocabulary	Digit Symbol	Picture Completion	Block Design	Picture Arrangement	Object Assembly	Scaled Score
19	29	27-28		26	17	78-80	87-90	21				19
18	28	26		25		76-77	83-86					18
17	27	25	18	24		74-75	79-82	20				17
16	26	24	17		16	71-73	76-78		48			16
15	25-26	23	16	23	15	67-70	72-75		47			15
14		22	15	(22)	14	(63-66)	69-71	(19)	46			14
13	(23-24)	(21)	14	21		59-62	66-68	18	44-45	36	44	13
12	21-22	20	13	19-20	13	54-58	62-65	17	42-43	35	43	12
11	19-20	19	12	17-18	12	47-53	58-61	15-16	(39-41)	34	42	11
10	17-18	17-18	(11)	15-16	(10)	40-46	52-57	14	35-38	(26-27)	41	10
9	15-16	15-16	10	13-14		32-39	47-51	12-13	31-34	23-25	40	9
8	13-14	14	9	11-12		26-31	(41-46)	10-11	28-30	20-22	(36-37)	8
7	11-12	12-13	7-8	9-10	9	22-25	35-40	8-9	25-27	18-19	31-33	7
6	9-10	10-11	6	7-8	8	18-21	29-34	6-7	21-24	15-17	28-30	6
5	7-8	8-9	5	5-6		14-17	23-28	5	17-20	12-14	25-27	5
4	5-6	6-7	4	4	7	11-13	18-22	4	13-16	9-11	22-24	4
3	4	5	3	3		10	15-17	3	10-12	8	19-21	3
2	3	4	2	2	6	9	13-14	2	6-9	7	15-18	2
1	2	3	1	1	4-5	8	12	1	3-5	6	11-14	1
0	0	0-2	0	0	0-3	0-7	0-11	0	2	5	8-10	0
	0		0					0	0-1	0-4	5-7	
											3-4	
											0-2	

SUMMARY

TEST	Raw Score	Scaled Score
Information	23	14
Comprehension	21	13
Arithmetic	11	10
Similarities	22	15
Digit Span	10	9
Vocabulary	64	14
Verbal Score	44	75
Digit Symbol	44	8
Picture Completion	19	14
Block Design	41	12
Picture Arrangement	26	11
Object Assembly	37	12
Performance Score		57
Total Score		

VERBAL SCORE 75 IQ 112
PERFORMANCE SCORE 57 IQ 121
FULL SCALE SCORE 132 IQ 120

FIG. 2 WAIS Scales

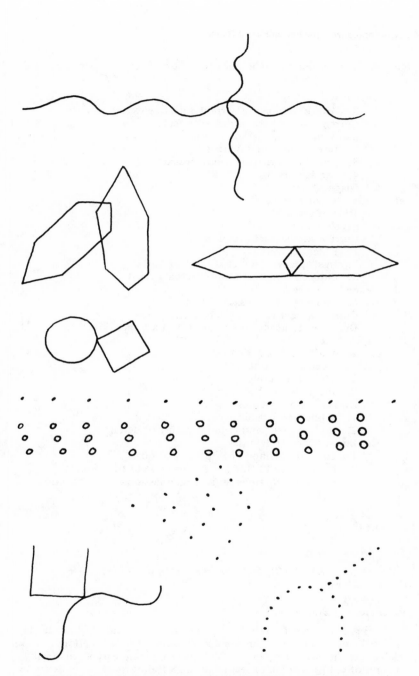

FIG. 3 Patient's Reproductions, Bender Visual Motor Gestalt Test

A fairly detailed outline to guide the preparation of such a report may read:

  I. *Overview*
   A. The role of defense in current adjustment
   B. Current role of basic personality factors
     1. Achievement
     2. Intellectual development
     3. Defensive structure (obsessive-compulsive)
     4. Sex factors
   C. Diagnostic status
 II. *Cognitive functioning*
   A. Role of intellect
   B. Psychometric level
   C. Current intellectual adequacy
     1. Pedantic overlay
     2. Inadequacy of directed thinking
     3. Subjective import of intellectual deficit
III. *Dependency needs*
   A. Dependency as lifelong problem
   B. Current accentuation of dependency needs
   C. Dependency needs mitigating against a responsible role
 IV. *Defensive picture*
   A. Reduction in life activities
     1. Decreased spontaneity
     2. Stereotyped relationships
     3. Indecision rather than action
   B. Evaluation of defenses
     1. Maintenance value
     2. Rigid, brittle, and tenuous nature of defenses
   C. Implications of defenses
     1. Lack of likelihood of further psychosis
     2. Potentiality for further compromise of functioning
     3. Recommendations re: referral question—need for caution and planning

The report then reads:

Tests Administered

Rorschach; TAT; WAIS; Sacks Sentence Completions; Bender Gestalt; MMPI.

Psychological Evaluation

Mr. B is best understood today by observing the nature of the adjustment process he utilizes to maintain some level of responsible function, however inadequate this may be by usual standards. Dominant earlier personality features of the patient are of secondary importance now, or are useful to consider only as they give perspective to the case. In particular, a strong emphasis on achievement, on intellectual development, on conformity, on exactness and dependability (what would be called an obsessive-compulsive type of personality structure) have likely served to offer him some protection from early conflicts and later were probably factors associated with his personality disintegration. Similarly, a sexual orientation, based on very deep sex conflict, is reflected in an apparent lifelong absence of heterosexual experience with possible periods of other forms of sexual activity. The more usual symptoms of an active psychosis, such as characterized the patient several years ago, are not particularly evident now, due at least in part to a severe debilitating inhibition and restriction of life activities more or less in all areas of personality expression.

The patient relates best on an intellectual level, utilizing as well as he can the residuals of a superior mental endowment. Psychometrically he currently scores at the superior level of intelligence (Full Scale IQ: 120, Vocabulary Level: 126), but this is reflective only of former intellectual capacity and of the role intelligence once played in his life at the expense of a more rounded personality development. His psychometric score is not at all indicative of current intellectual adequacy and, in fact, an examination of his mental functioning provides an understanding of those aspects of his disturbed psychological status which are of the most practical significance. Once the observer is no longer impressed by the patient's vocabulary and superior but pedantic word usage, very severe flaws are noted in his functioning. In the patient's own terminology, which he frequently verbalizes as an overall expression of concern about his decline as a functioning personality , he has "retrogressed." We see now a person who has difficulty in giving sustained thought to a task or to a problem, but who is inclined rather to ruminate aimlessly and ineffectually. He vacillates between different solutions or courses of action, but in the end remains indecisive, unsure, baffled. He is unsure of himself, particularly when faced with novel situations or when the setting (physical, social, or otherwise) is altered. But even under familiar circumstances he is likely to become confused and to have difficulty in separating related events and ideas.

This compromise of intellectual function, which has always been his strong point, accents the significance of what are no doubt life-long exaggerated dependency needs. His acquired intellectual inadequacy has heightened his need for external support and for environmental dependability and stability. He is not able to take on any significant degree of responsibility, probably no more than he has now in his role as a patient with grounds privileges. Changes in routine or in requirements could have unfortunate consequences.

From an overall viewpoint then, the patient is defending what functional integrity he has by a drastic reduction in life activities, a lessening of spontaneity, and the maintenance of control through restricting relationships essentially to stereotyped intellectual contacts; and internally, through ruminative vacillations and indecision in place of action; This defensive operation maintains him at a level of adjustment that is now probably optimal for him, but at the same time it is a defense that is rigid, brittle, and always tenuous. He now seems sufficiently distant from his basic conflicts and earlier pathological defenses so that it does not appear likely that a break of his defenses would precipitate an overt psychosis. It is almost certain, however, that even though he is motivated toward rehabilitation, increasing his responsibility or making significant changes in his living circumstances would bring about a state of severe anxiety and compromise even further his effectiveness as a functioning person. Any change in circumstances for him then would have to be approached with caution and require careful planning and preparation.

part two

PSYCHOLOGICAL REPORT WRITING PRACTICUM

CHAPTER SIX

A Workshop
on
Psychological Reports

The basic approach of this book is one of self-examination. In this chapter we are ready to apply the principles that emerged from our examination of the report writing process to samples of live case material. Learning to be an effective psychologist is largely up to the individual, and psychologists in training must build upon their own idiosyncratic strengths and be ever watchful of their known weaknesses.

The material presented here is in the nature of a workshop on psychological reports. It is built around reports and excerpts from reports that should have instructional value in the writing of reports. This content was gathered from case folders over a period of time, and is presented along with comments based on the principles and conclusions of this book.

Most of these reports were written by students, hence in general they are a better source of instructional material than the products of practicing psychologists. Nevertheless, experienced persons often have the same difficulties as tyros. Some of the reports, particularly those written in test-by-test fashion were selected to demonstrate an approach that is, fortunately, much less popular than it was some years ago. Several of the reports are of the shotgun type, harking back to a time when it was common to encourage students to include as much as possible in their reports in order to demonstrate their interpretive competence. Although this teaching method is still in use, we strongly encourage supervisors to teach the writing of case-focused reports. The student can demonstrate his interpretive skills in conferences with his supervisor, and his overall qualifications as a psychologist in his case-focused reports.

The approach is informal, and the critique is similar to what might transpire in a supervisory conference. For self-instruction or assigned instruction, it may be profitable for the student to apply the principles of the preceding chapters to the following selections or to samples of his own reports. It is well to be aware, while doing such exercises, that some of the reports can be variously criticized, according to one's point of view. Thus a selection might merit the labels "academic," "theoretical," and "cold and impersonal" at the same time. Some readers will be more inclined to describe a piece of writing by one of these terms, some by another.

In most instances, the reasons for referral of the cases which resulted in the following passages are not known. Most of the referrals were probably general. The overinclusiveness that is typical in the ensuing reports probably would not be much altered were the referrals specific, however.
Unnecessary content is a major characteristic of many traditional reports.

CASES AND COMMENTS

Workshop Case 1

The first exhibit is presented to illustrate a number of principles. It was selected also because of its uniqueness, and for the question it poses: Can flexibility be overdone?

Behavior During the Examination

The patient, John C., appeared to be very alert and in good contact with his surroundings. He claimed that he was in the hospital because of his wife's threat to leave him if he did not come here and cure his chronic alcoholism. He also felt that his children would be hurt. The obvious omission in his statements is a reference to himself as having anything to do with his being in the hospital or acknowledging his desire to get well for his own sake. But the omission is understandable if we make the following assumptions: (1) He does not want to acknowledge any responsibility for himself; and (2) his problem is really his wife's problem. In support of these assumptions consider the following incident which occurred at the very beginning of the testing session between the patient and the examiner.
The examiner brought an ashtray into the room. There may have been some question as to its decorative value but there really were no grounds for questioning its use as a supplement to smoking. Nevertheless, the

patient asked, very timidly, if he could smoke. Now, if he knew the answer to his own question which was made all too obvious by the ashtray that the examiner had *just* brought in and placed before him, why did he ask it? Again, his behavior makes perfectly good sense if we assume that (1) he wanted the examiner to give him explicit permission for smoking, thus setting up the examiner in a judgmental role; (2) he wanted to appear inept and helpless in the situation, hoping that the examiner would then be inclined to intervene and direct him since he "obviously" could not direct himself with any measure of success if he were inept and helpless; (3) he was so self-absorbed that he was not attending to the situation and the ashtray was not in his perceptual field. However, since the question, "Can I smoke?", followed *immediately* upon the presentation of the ashtray, we may reject this assumption as not doing justice to the facts. Thus, there is a striking parallel between his expressed relation to his wife and the relationship he tried to establish with the examiner. In both cases he is told what to do ("Go to the hospital." "You can smoke."), and he disclaims responsibility for both ("I am in the hospital because of my wife." "I smoke because I have your permission.").

Consider another example in which two items of the patient's behavior which followed each other in close temporal succession *appear* absurd because they are mutually exclusive. The patient let the examiner know that he was enjoying the tests and that he found them very interesting. (We will disregard, for the moment, the rote fashion of his verbalization.) As often as he let the examiner know this, which was several times, he just as often followed it with an inquiry as to how many more tests there were left, leaving very little doubt in the examiner's mind that the patient wanted to leave and was trying to find out how much longer it would be before his "enjoyment" would be terminated. Again, certain assumptions make good sense out of what is, prima facie, an absurdity. These assumptions are that: (1) He would not permit himself to be interested in or to enjoy what he was doing, the product of a pathological predilection for discomfiture. Thus, he could not even say he was interested in what he was doing with any real conviction in his voice. But, this certainly does not explain why he should ever mention his "interest" and "enjoyment" to begin with. This brings us to the second assumption which ties together many loose ends: (2) The patient did not really mean he was interested at all as his voice, for one thing, indicated. His subsequent behavior (asking the examiner how much more time the testing would consume) gave the lie more certainty than ever to his preceding words ("I am enjoying this"). So why did he say he was enjoying the testing? He said it strictly for the consumption of the examiner. The patient's modus operandi vis-à-vis the examiner was to act the role of a "good' testee thus entitling himself to the examiner's charity in return. "Surely the examiner will be pleased with me and relax his gimlet eye if I flatter him as a purveyor of good things." This role, we may note, was part and parcel of a pervasive obsequiousness and servility that ran through all of the patient's behavior. Possibly, at a more dynamic level, we are observing a rigid reaction formation against hostility which has lost even its pseudo-adaptive quality and culminated in a sticky sweetness which is emotionally inappropriate to the situation.

Test findings

The patient's intellectual functioning is in the normal range (Full Scale IQ 97). His almost total failure on the Arithmetic Subtest of the Wechsler-

Bellevue suggests a severe defect in concentration. His Performance Subtests are generally better than his Verbal, suggesting an intelligence potential in the bright normal range. An overall educational retardation is suggested if, in addition to the low Verbal and Arithmetic scores (the latter score is, of course, too low to be *only* a matter of educational retardation), one makes a qualitative evaluation of the Information Subtest where the patient shows an inability to even closely approximate the population of the United States or the distance from New York to Paris.

Personality-wise, the patient is unable to relate to people. The intimacy implied in such relationships brings the danger of his experiencing hostile impulses toward the objects of his "affection." Thus, he relates to women, whom he conceives of as mother figures, by provoking them, thus externalizing (projecting) his hostility and setting up the situation so that the hostility is directed back at him. This seems to serve the triple purpose of (1) distorting the outer world as a hostile place and reversing the source of the hostility so that the net effect is for him to disown (repress) his own hostility, yet still define his relationships within a hostile context; (2) punishing himself to serve an expiatory need based on his own completely unacceptable hostile impulses; (3) forcing other people to take an interest in him, thus temporarily putting his isolation in abeyance and making his own need for human contact seem to be the need of the other person. His chronic alcoholism in this context seems to be an attempt to be taken in hand and punished for his derelictions toward his wife and family. His social naiveté allows him to think that an apology for wrongdoing ("wrongdoing" is used here not in its moral sense but to define something the patient does which he may depend upon to provoke somebody) will bring everything back to its ante-bellum status. The "peace" is maintained until, unable to bear his isolation and loneliness, and unable to relate to people because of his hostile feelings (exaggerated all the more when he realizes his need for them) he commits a social crime, i.e., infidelity or irresponsible alcoholism, to hurt his family. The crime naturally forces the intervention of some other people to take him in hand (usually the wife in her maternal role).

The dynamics of this particular patient's pathology seem more clear-cut than is usually the case. He was placed in a home by his mother as an infant. She could not maintain him because her husband was an alcoholic and made the marital relationship impossible to endure. He did not see his mother again until, as a grown man, he accidentally located her. In all probability the mother rejected the infant not because she could not maintain the expense, but because she looked upon the child as part and parcel of the hated husband. Thus, traumatic rejection experiences in the patient's background have severely warped his whole personality development. Affectionally deprived in a most basic way, he can find affection only by twisting his human relationships in such a way that he "finds" rejection everywhere. Is this also a way of finding his parents everywhere? In the most naively impossible way he tries to gain acceptance by being apologetic, an acceptance which is doomed to be very short-lived since it amounts to nothing but an uneasy truce with none of the relevant issues even hinted at. Thus he may be assured that the rejection will be forthcoming again, symbolically reconstituting the basic relation to the rejecting parents, the paradigm of all his relationships.

A therapeutic approach which has, in this type of case, succeeded, is the so-called relationship-therapy in the style of Jessie Taft or of the Rankian

School. The basic premise and whole modus operandi of such therapies are focused on just such a barrier to establishing interpersonal relationships on a realistic basis as the patient has to break through.

Summary

The patient, John C., is a 35-year-old man. Intellectually he functions in the normal range with a bright normal potential which is not reached because of a severe concentration defect and what appears to be an overall educational retardation. The patient's pathology seems focused around a severe disturbance in interpersonal relationships based on traumatic rejection experiences in infancy. Rigid reaction formations against his tremendous hostility toward people, conceived of as essentially rejecting, prevent the possibility of any but the most pseudo-adaptive adjustment.
Feeling intensely lonely and isolated, his need for people grows more urgent, as does his hostility toward them because he is so completely dependent on them. However, unable to acknowledge this need, he forces other people, primarily his family, to intervene in his life by committing some social misdemeanor (infidelity or alcoholism). Rejection experiences are compulsively sought after as a way of symbolically reconstituting the basic relationship to the rejecting parents, the paradigm for all his relationships. His attempt to break this relationship by a childish apology, usually to his wife conceived of in a maternal role, is as naive and shallow as it is abortive and unworkable. Yet he persists in maintaining a Pollyannish optimism. Thus, with his pathology firmly secured, he goes his self-defeating way.

Diagnostic Impression

Chronic Alcoholism in an emotionally unstable personality.

Just glancing at this report, one may wonder if it is too long. On reading it, one may be sure that it is. The relationship of length to usable content is disproportionate. Too much space is devoted to building a case, as opposed to presenting pertinent conclusions. In fact, what are the pertinent conclusions?

This question cannot be fully answered without knowing the reason for referral, which unfortunately is not available. We do know, however, that the person is in a hospital and is regarded as an alcoholic, at least by his wife. What then might have been the basis for referral? What might have been the psychologist's evaluation goal? What might he have contributed to the case? We can't be sure, of course, but a contribution to the diagnosis could be of importance. That is, is the presenting symptom secondary to some other condition—possibly a condition that might be treatable? Perhaps knowing the role alcohol plays in the patient's economy could be a therapeutic lead. Or it might be useful to know something of the patient's "ego strength," or of his motivation for therapy.

How well does the psychologist approximate goals like these? As to diagnosis, he is impressed that this is a case of alcoholism; this is a contribution of sorts in that he implies the absence of a number of other conditions, such as schizophrenia, depressive neurosis, or anxiety neurosis. He does, however, link the patient's drinking with an "emotionally unstable personality."

This diagnosis, no longer current, applies when ". . . the individual reacts with excitability and ineffectiveness when confronted by minor stress. His judgment may be undependable under stress, and his relationship to other people is continuously fraught with fluctuating emotional attitudes, because of strong and poorly controlled hostility, guilt, and anxiety" (American Psychiatric Association, *Diagnostic and Statistical Manual, Mental Disorders*, 1952). The accuracy of the diagnosis can hardly be challenged at this time, but the reader of the report has no warning that it is coming. The conclusion is in no way supported, and we in fact think that the text better supports another diagnosis (passive-aggressive personality?).

The psychologist does considerably better in defining the role of the symptom in the person's economy, and, if accurate, this information might be of value to a therapist. Unfortunately, we do not know if the man would be a good candidate for psychotherapy. The psychologist recommends a special kind of therapy, but the early part of the report suggests that the individual does not recognize that he has a problem, and that there is no motivation to change. On the other hand, the report would seem to indicate that the symptom is an aspect of the person's basic psychic structure. Quite apart from our general awareness of the difficulty of controlling alcoholism even through skilled, intensive psychotherapy, the successful treatment of the man through "relationship therapy" has to be questioned. Apparently the psychologist himself is skeptical, and seems to hedge here. He speaks of success "in this type of case," but does not prophesy success in the case of John C.

Looking at the case in overall perspective again, it is very well written. The composition is quite good and the report reads smoothly. The organization is grammatically logical, in a sense, yet there is no apparent development of major conclusions in the interest of effectiveness. Intelligence is given priority in the discussion, although how the patient's intellectual level or his intellectual defects are related to anything relevant is not apparent.

The flavor of the writing is captured by words like pompous, exhibitionistic, authoritative, erudite, and academic. Notice the deftness with which apparently insignificant events are made to yield their full portentousness. The reader should feel that he is being instructed in a method of clinical analysis as well as being informed. Most readers would probably also feel that the foreign expressions used in the report are a bit too show-offy for a clinical document, and the contribution about Jessie Taft and the Rankian School almost certainly is so. The reader might condemn himself for not being so smart as the psychologist, unless he concludes that the psychologist is now studying— or has recently studied—the various schools of psychotherapy. If the reader understands the matter this way, he may feel the comment to be gratuitous, and more appropriate in a term paper.

The report seems to have been written by a prosecuting attorney who sees the patient, a not very honest fellow, as always up to some nefarious end. But he won't "get away" with anything. The manner of expression contributes more to this impression than does the content. How much of the jockeying for position and trying to outmaneuver the other fellow belongs to the patient and how much to the psychologist is hard to tell. This question might be easily answered, of course, if we had available other sample reports by the same psychologist. Nevertheless, how the psychologist feels about his patient is evident in talk of a "modus operandi," of receiving the "examiner's charity," and of behavior which "gave the lie." "Now I've got you, you son of a bitch," is the way Berne (1964) puts it. The patient is seen as a manipulator and a leech.

The report would seem to be patient-centered in the sense that the discussion is about the patient and only minimally (as reports go) about tests and test products, and the common Aunt Fanny stereotypy does not occur. Yet the feeling is strong that the psychologist is really more interested in juggling ideas than in meaningfully describing the patient. From the hundreds of words appearing under the title "Behavior During the Examination," we know with a good degree of confidence that "the patient appeared to be very alert and in good contact with his surroundings" (no doubt already observed by the staff), the patient's view of his hospitalization, that the patient asked for permission to smoke after an ash tray was placed before him (and presumably also before the psychologist), that the patient indicated enjoyment of testing but behaved otherwise, and that the patient's behavior involved obsequiousness and servility. With a lesser degree of confidence we learn something more about the patient, mostly on a dynamic level. With at least the same degree of confidence, we could possibly know more about the psychologist than about the patient from this passage.

The responsibility with which interpretations are made here is a matter of great concern. Near the end of the report we learn, with eager anticipation, of how clear-cut the dynamics are. Then we find that the mother placed the patient in a home while he was an infant, an event which the psychologist unhesitatingly calls a "rejection" (we would need more evidence than presented here to be able to conclude that *the patient* felt rejected). Then the psychologist guesses that the mother, "in all probability," "rejected" the infant because she saw him as "part and parcel of the hated husband." There is no reason given why this guess was made, and there is no evidence offered that the patient's mother hated her husband, certainly not to such an extent that she also did not want their child. The fact (?) that the husband's drinking made it impossible for the marriage to endure does not necessarily indicate hatred. The mother may have had feelings of ambivalence, or possibly even some feelings of love for the man with whom she could not live. People are that way. Nevertheless, the psychologist accepts all of this without feeling the need to offer a bit of evidence, if he has it (the report writer does not impress one as being a devotee of parsimony), to make such far-reaching conclusions appear plausible, and relate them to the patient's way of life as he (the psychologist) understands it—apparently to no small extent in terms of his personal and class values. Thus, unsupported events are brought together to develop one speculation;

this is then accepted as a premise and another speculation built on it.
The purpose of this is not certain, since the patient's "dynamics" as described
are not clearly linked to the presenting problem (presumably alcoholism).
We are told that his mode of life is symbolically to relive the rejection by his
parents, but in the previous paragraph we find the symptom related to hostility
and a means of getting himself taken care of (the opposite of seeking
rejection). Quite evidently, this psychologist does not appreciate the difficulty
of relating current behaviors to their distant causes, even when there seems
to be an evidential link.

The responsibility of interpretation is also particularly suspect in the first
sections of the report. The psychologist arbitrarily restricts the possible
interpretations of the patient's behavior, and then selects the ones which seem
most reasonable *to him*. We can only wonder to what extent his obviously
ill perception of the patient guides his interpretations.

Workshop Cases 2 and 3

Presented next are the opening sections of two different psychological reports.
They have different headings suggesting different content or different
content emphasis, thus pointing out the variation in approach to introductory
report content.

Behavioral Note

This 46-year-old white male with two years of high school education
was tested on March 21, 28, and 29. He had, six years previously, received
some psychological tests at _____ Hospital.

The patient is a neat-appearing, lean individual with a drawn look
on his face. He talks slowly but profusely. His affect is flattened and his
bearing indicates quiet suspicion and a superior accepting condescension.
His attitude is one of "suffering the arrows of indignity" which are
thrown at him here in the hospital (such as psychological testing). He tries
to convey the impression that he is different from the other patients,
is quite intellectually superior to them, and is of an entirely different and
sensitive nature. This comes out in slightly depressive, self-pitying feelings
combined with intellectual pretentiousness and negativism. On the
Rorschach, for example, the patient complains of the ambiguity of the
blots, saying that the task is difficult for him because of his "analytic mind
and training."

He talks freely and openly, almost glibly, about his drinking and about
how the cure rests solely on himself. One gets the immediate impression that
insight is involved here, and perhaps to an extent it is. With further talking,
however, the feeling arises that this free, enlightened talk of "alcoholism" is
primarily an intellectual defense, almost an intellectual rationalization for
drinking. Responsibility, in some ways, can be thrown onto outside factors
by glibly saying, "I am an alcoholic," and implying that this is "beyond
my psychological control."

Attitude and Test Behavior

From the beginning the patient showed disdain. He studiously ignored the examiner and conveyed the impression that the testing situation was beneath him, but that, nevertheless, he would condescend to be tested. He displayed a piqued, churlish attitude and was openly derisive. Much of his test behavior, however, was quite inconsistent with this posture. He complied readily with most of the requests, and, at times, even reached out to meet the examiner part way. There were decided fluctuations in the tone of voice that he used. He would shift back and forth from snappy, derisive negativism to cooperation and even attempts to present himself as being reasonable and friendly.

During testing, he at first attempted to give the impression of superior knowledge and ability in elaborating beyond the requirements of questions. As items became slightly more difficult, however, he became aggressively defensive, attacking the value of testing and insisting that the questions were unclear and, therefore, not sensible. At these times he requested further structuring of questions. As the difficulty of the tasks increased he began to show signs of tension such as taking off his glasses, pressing his fingers to bridge of nose and temples, and breathing heavily. During these times he would often simply and quickly say "I don't know" without any visible effort to search for ways of handling the task. These admissions of failure were usually expressed in a weak, helpless, almost inaudible voice. He quite clearly tends to externalize blame for his difficulties and to avoid difficult situations using deprecation of other individuals or systems as a rationalization for such avoidance.

Both of these sections were written about the same patient by different psychologists, with an interval between examinations of about four years. What would primarily seem to be illustrated is the lack of agreement on what sort of textual content (if any) ought to precede the presentation of conclusions.

In the first passage some identifying information, no doubt available elsewhere, appears without apparent orienting value. The dates of testing could (in fact did) appear elsewhere on the report, according to the standard practice of the clinic. The statement that the patient had previously been examined is perhaps meaningful, but its significance is for the psychologist to determine, not the reader. The reason for the information about the patient's appearance given in the second paragraph is uncertain.

In the first passage the psychologist chose to write about what is apparently the presenting problem—alcoholism. In so doing he reaches a major conclusion, possibly the major finding of the evaluation procedure, to the effect that the patient does not accept responsibility for himself. Interestingly, the independent finding of psychologist number two is congruent with that of his colleague, although not as case-focused, i.e., he does not deal with the patient's presenting problem of alcoholism. Workshop case 2 based on test performance rather than on direct conversation with the patient about his behavior problem, might not be as readily related by the report reader to the patient's pathology. To do so he would have to take responsibility for making the inference that the patient's manner during examination gives understanding about the drinking problem. Therefore, the interpretation is less complete.

The first passage, containing abundant raw data, is written so that it is easy to pick out the essential conclusions—that the patient is pretentious, particularly in the intellectual sphere where he has a need to feel superior, that he is a sensitive person who feels wronged by others, thus explaining both depressive trends and the self-pitying behavior which he shows. With somewhat greater difficulty this material can also be extracted from the second passage (it is all there) which also points up, in the context of the examination, (uninterpreted) behavior fluctuations and external signs of anxiety.

Though the two psychologists present different raw data and to some extent write about different things, they do show congruence of basic impressions, although at different levels of generality. Both psychologists, however, could have integrated these conclusions with other findings to create a more effective, shorter, and less repetitious report. The basic conclusions derived from "test behavior" or "clinical behavior" are the domain of the psychologist, and should be presented and thoroughly mixed with his "test findings." Presenting "test findings" as the *sine qua non* of the report, not to be contaminated with other data and conclusions of the psychologist (or with material from other sources), only tends to perpetuate the belief held in some quarters that psychological evaluation (or "psychological testing," according to this point of view) is a laboratory procedure.

Workshop Case 4

The following text reads very much like a laboratory report.

Test Results—WAIS:

Verbal IQ.	114.	Full Scale IQ	. . . . 119.
Perf. IQ	121.	Classified—Bright Normal.	

The patient is presently functioning at a Bright Normal level of intelligence (IQ 119) demonstrating a Bright Normal capacity on the verbal scale and a superior capacity on the performance scale. There was a considerable amount of scatter on the verbal scale. On the performance scale, however, scatter was minimal. There was some intra-test variability. The patient's concentration and voluntary effort was good but capacity for abstraction and psycho-motor speed was inefficient. The test did show anxiety and depressive trends as well as some schizophrenic indications.

Draw-a-Person

The results of this test indicated that the patient manifested some degree of uncertainty in handling reality situations, and that his world is but vaguely perceived. Orality, anxiety, infantile aggression and dependence and guilt feelings are also present. There are some indications that the patient is attempting to compensate for an inadequate sexuality.

Rorschach

The tests show orality, anxiety, infantile aggression, and dependence and guilt feelings are also present. Color usage exceeds human movement, responses, and the F percent is high (72). He no doubt converts tension into psychosomatic complaints.

Bender Gestalt

No severe pathological indications. There is evidence, however, of infantilism and regression.

Szondi

There is an open demand for love and affection. The patient is openly accepting his emotional outbursts. He is fond of pleasure and ease and accepts things from people.

Babcock Memory Paragraph

The memory paragraph was greatly rearranged, distorted, and poorly recalled. The patient's memory is not functioning freely and efficiently; there is a definite indication of pathology.

Projective Sentence Completion

The patient balked a great deal in doing this test. He repeatedly asked if he had to fill in all of the sentences and stated that many did not refer to him. He took an unusually long time to complete the test. The results indicated insecurity, evasiveness, anxiety, dependency on mother and ambivalence toward her. The possibility of latent homosexuality was also indicated.

Word Association

Many clang associations and close reactions were given indicating a lack of flexibility of thought processes. A poor psychosexual adjustment was indicated. A good deal of orality was present. On the whole, the responses were of a regressive, infantile nature suggesting a schizophrenic process.

Object Sorting

There were many rejects, narrow, and split narrow groupings as well as many concrete and fabulatory explanations. Capacity for abstract thinking seemed to be impaired. The results indicate a schizophrenic process.

Such test-by-test reporting with a lack of integrated conclusions and only feeble, manual-type interpretations parallels the laboratory technician's report. Instead of WAIS, Draw-a-Person, and Bender Gestalt, we might have: Urinalysis, Hematology, and Serology. Instead of the sort of data which appear here we can imagine under these several laboratory headings: Color-appearance—clear amber; Reaction—acid; Specific gravity—1.020; Albumin—neg.; Sugar—neg.;

W.B.C.—8,000; Neutrophils—55; Lymphocytes—42; Eosinophils—2; Basophils—1; Hemoglobin—12.8; Hematocrit—42; Kahn—neg.; Wasserman—neg. These are meaningful bits of information, not for the laboratory technician who obtained them, but for one specifically trained to interpret and apply them.

From this point of view, consider, ". . . a Bright Normal capacity on the verbal scale and a superior capacity on the performance scale. There was a considerable amount of scatter on the verbal scale," or "orality, anxiety, infantile aggression, and dependence and guilt feelings are also present," or "There were many rejects, narrow, and split narrow groupings as well as many concrete and fabulatory explanations." Would it not seem apparent that the writer feels less capable of interpreting this material than the team members for whom it is intended? Or does the psychologist endow this material with an obviousness of meaning?

There is much test jargon ("rejects," "narrow and split narrow groupings," "concrete and fabulatory explanations") and some theory-derived language (e.g., orality and latent homosexuality). Are we to assume that the readers of the report know as much about these things as does the physician about basophils, the hematocrit, or the white blood cell count?

Perhaps the writer did not fully think so, for throughout the report there are *little* interpretations, jumps from raw data to partially interpreted data that are in the nature of general, unintegrated conclusions. For example, "The patient's memory is not functioning freely and efficiently . . . ," "The results indicated insecurity, evasiveness, anxiety, dependency on mother and ambivalence toward her." We can only wonder if such material meets the needs of the team, or if the psychologist felt he had a mission other than to report what the tests yield. What is the psychologist's concept of his role? There is throughout a tendency to attribute the conclusions offered to the tests rather than to the psychologist. If errors have been made they presumably are the fault of the tests. In any event, let us feel sorry for the report reader because he *cannot*, no matter how bright or learned he may be, interpret much of the content. Who knows, for example, in the context of the information given, the meaning of ". . . a considerable amount of scatter on the verbal scale" while on the performance scale "scatter was minimal." The further contribution that "There was some intra-test variability" would not seem to help.

The report is saturated with Aunt Fanny statements. Most of us, in our more candid moments, will admit to "anxiety," "dependence and guilt feelings," "orality," "insecurity," perhaps even to "dependency on mother and ambivalence to her," and to having "some degree of uncertainty in handling reality situations" (although use of the word "reality" makes the statement appear sinister). Nevertheless, much of the material may sound impressive, if not meaningful, to a nonpsychologist. But we should perhaps feel ashamed to write that "He is fond of pleasure and ease and accepts things from people" because this is probably true of the reader of the report and he may feel there is something wrong with him because of this. It is also perhaps going too far to write "The *possibility* of latent homosexuality was also indicated (italics supplied)." Not only may we not be enlightened to learn that the patient has latent homosexuality (because *it* is supposed to be well nigh ubiquitous—though *it* has no meaningful, or highly consensual, frame of reference), we should be quite surprised to learn that even the possibility of such is excluded!

But however critical we may be of this non-case-focused report, it is probably largely accurate. With the exception of a few statements (e.g., intellectual level, mention of pathological indications, and a diagnostic impression), the report is not specific enough to be wrong. Some of the statements are not transferable into demonstrable behavioral referents. What we need to alert ourselves for are the specific statements when they do occur, since it is only then that we may check for irresponsible interpretations. The psychologist is able to learn from the Rorschach that the patient "no doubt" converts tension into psychosomatic complaints. Other team members will either challenge the right of the psychologist to express this opinion, or get an erroneous view of the prowess of the Rorschach.

Workshop Case 5

Here is another test-by-test report.

WAIS

The patient is presently functioning in the Average range of intelligence, with a full-scale WAIS IQ of 102. This measure is, however, clearly not optimal. He refused to do either the Digit Span or Arithmetic subtests, saying, "You can't touch the darn numbers, Bill." The influence of impairing factors is also seen in inconsistent function. The patient's optimal capacity is most probably in the Superior range. His tendency toward pedantry, and a careful attention to minute details indicates compulsive features in the personality. Many verbalizations are rather bizarre, and test performance in general reflects marked deterioration.

Wechsler Memory Scale

The patient refused to do more than a few items of this test. He gave his age as 34 (incorrect), and the year as 1971 or 2, but knew where he was.

Several other tests—Color Form Sorting, Memory Paragraph, Bender, Benton, and Szondi were refused by the patient. For the Bender he said, "You can't do it Mac—I'll bet you don't believe it, it's all ended—It has to end after awhile, Bill—I can't Bill." He seemed to have difficulty in any tests which require symbolic manipulation of materials, i.e., where there weren't models or designs to be copied.

Object Sorting

The patient rejected two items on active sorting, had two somewhat loose groupings, and manifested a tendency to narrowing. Five concepts were essentially abstract in nature, two of them also reflecting functional and concrete thinking. One grouping in passive sorting was rejected, and two elicited syncretistic reasoning. One functional concept was given. The patient was able to offer abstract concepts for the remainder of the groupings, including some of the most difficult ones. Performance on this test would contra-indicate organic involvement, but the inconsistent and erratic function points to a severely pathological process, psychotic in nature.

Rorschach Examination

The large number of responses suggests an over-ideational individual, one who has emphasized intellectualization as a defense. The stereotypy and banality of content, however, indicate an impoverishment of constructive energies in the personality. In spite of the apparent productivity, constriction is a prominent characteristic. The presence of only three popular responses indicates the degree to which the content of the patient's thinking differs from usual modes. There are also signs of gross disturbance in the structural aspect of thinking, including neologisms. Reality testing in general is quite poor, although there is some residual ability to appraise the outside world.

Chronic difficulties in interpersonal relationships are suggested, with little capacity for dealing adequately with emotional stimulation. Inferiority feelings are seen in the presence of homosexual features and paranoid thinking. Compulsive signs are found, and there appears to be a depressive aspect in the personality.

While a schizophrenia is indicated by these test results, the subtype is not clear. Both paranoid and catatonic features are seen, as well as certain aspects of function consistent with simple type. In view of these intermingled aspects, the diagnostic impression is schizophrenic process, unclassified. Lastly, general test performance would contra-indicate the importance of an organic factor.

This report in some ways resembles the previous one, yet it is different. The patient's verbalizations give much more of a feeling that a live person was present. These comments are most colorful, but unfortunately are not linked with conclusions which they might illustrate.

The report is inconsistent with respect to interpreting the data. There are some meaningful conclusions, for example, those about reality testing. But much material is not interpreted. What is the meaning of the discrepancy between current intellectual functioning and estimated optimal functioning, or what is the significance of the observation that the patient experienced difficulty with tests having certain descriptive characteristics, or what is the behavioral significance of the concepts demonstrated on the Object Sorting test (other than the obvious clinical fact that the patient is psychotic)? The patient evidently was confused about his age and orientation for time, giving an incorrect age and incorrectly identifying the year, yet we must read the analysis of other tests to know that he is not "organic." The psychologist felt it important to include some deviant findings, yet not tell their meaning, although loss of orientation in two of the three "spheres" is commonly an organic indicator. Who then shall make interpretations from such inherently rich material?

This report includes much in the way of concepts and jargon which are likely to be unfamiliar to the report reader. The reader is expected especially to know about the Rorschach and the Object Sorting tests, and to appreciate the significance of constriction, of three popular responses (how many should there be then, and what is a popular response anyway?), of loose groupings, and of narrowing. In general the patient is presented as an individual, although a few minor Aunt Fanny comments are to be found. Here note especially references to "inferiority feelings," "compulsive signs," and a "depressive aspect in the personality." These could all be spelled out with profit, as could the information on "homosexual features" if it is of any importance.

Workshop Case 6

The following report, which attempts some segmentalization of personality, also illustrates a number of other principles.

Intelligence, Memory, and Organization of Perception and Thought

The patient is presently functioning toward the lower limits of the Superior range of intelligence, with a full scale WAIS IQ of 120. Qualitative analysis suggests that anxiety, mild negativisms, obsessiveness, and excessive compulsivity may have had the effect of lowering the score somewhat from an optimal measure, which would probably fall higher in the Superior range.

It appears that there are temporary periods of preoccupation that may hinder the "intake of presented material, but the memory function seems to be otherwise intact. There is a tendency for verbal material to be distorted, but this is mitigated somewhat by the patient's capacity for critical self-appraisal. So, while reality-corrupting factors are present, the patient is able to exert some degree of control over them.

Basic perceptual functioning is apparently largely intact—perceived figures are drawn in quite faithful reproduction.

In the sphere of thinking, particularly as reflected in the Object Sorting test, the level is not as abstract as would be expected in an individual of superior intelligence. Groupings are mainly assembled on the basis of functional and concrete concepts. This test further reveals the patient's over-ideational nature, and the severely obsessive-compulsive character of his thinking. The looseness of thought structure which is also observed here assumes more pathological proportions in this configuration. Looseness of psychotic degree is also evident in the Word Association test, where the patient gave distant, highly personalized, clang, and even neologistic responses.

Personality

Analysis of projective material indicates a passive-dependent, insecure individual with marked feelings of rejection, inferiority, and inadequacy, and with a strong felt need to be wanted and cared for. There is also a desire, on the other hand, to be active, assertive, and masterful, with the resultant incongruence contributing to a passive-aggressive conflict.

Hostility and its expression is a problem of magnitude for the patient. He harbors a great deal of such feeling, which is variously directed toward the father figure, toward females (who are regarded as castrating, rejecting agents), and toward himself. The extrapunitive feeling arouses a considerable amount of guilt, anxiety, and fearful apprehension of morbid proportions. The intropunitively directed aggression contributes to a marked depressive feeling-tone as well as other self-preoccupations of a more malignant nature. He pictures himself as being helplessly exposed to, and buffeted by, hostile environmental forces, with consequent feelings of futility. Worse than this, there are indications of feelings of self-disintegration and decay, which smacks of the apathy of the chronic, deteriorated schizophrenic.

It appears, in fact, that the patient is struggling, almost consciously, to achieve an emotional nirvana through schizophrenic apathy, but he has not been at all successful in this attempt. There are persistent signs of high emotional responsivity and lability, inner tension and turmoil, rather intense and apparently chronic anxiety, as well as the aforementioned hostility, guilt, and fearfulness.

All of these factors threaten the integrity of the patient's personality organization, and control over them is attempted by means of diverse defenses. Obsessive-compulsive mechanisms, principally intellectualization, predominate and result in thinking which may be characterized as over-ideational, obsessional, doubt-ridden, and ambivalent. He is extremely attentive to the minutiae in his environment, attempting to figure out the meaning and significance behind the details of events. This, in company with a somewhat suspicious criticalness, lends a strong paranoid flavor to the thought content. There is excessive ambivalence concerning almost anything which the patient considers he wants, but at the same time doesn't want, likes but doesn't like, etc. Other defensive mechanisms which the patient is utilizing include strong inhibitory efforts and repression, which give an hysterical aspect to the personality picture. These, together with observed oral material and negativism, could contribute toward catatonic features in the patient's behavior.

As a result of these various regulatory mechanisms, particularly the intellectual factors, the patient can probably succeed at times in presenting a facade which may make him appear more psychologically intact than he actually is. Large areas of thinking are apparently reality-bound, but this is achieved at the expense of rather severe constriction of personality resources. The patient has retained some ability to appraise his own thinking and behavior in order to keep it consonant to a degree with reality.

That the patient's attempts at control are not adequate is most apparent in the intensity and content of his morbid, autistic preoccupations. There is a marked, malignant self-preoccupation, indicating severe withdrawal—the patient is "all wrapped up" in himself. There is an inordinate preoccupation with his sexuality, which is undifferentiated and chaotic. Homoerotic tendencies are strong, but they are not recognized or welcome—as manifested by the extent to which the patient is absorbed with heterosexual problems. There is evidence, too, of guilt concerning autoerotic behavior. The possibility of perverse sexuality should be considered. Another area of preoccupation is religion, problems of good vs. evil, etc.

The patient's apparent willingness to talk about his problems, particularly in glib psychological terminology, would seem to indicate a high degree of positive introspection and insight. Certain test indices suggest, however, that his verboseness is a means of "covering up," of talking about topics of his own choosing. In more ambiguous, non-conversational situations he is cautious, careful, and evasive, thus enabling himself to avoid traumatic topics. This suggests that introspective capacity is actually somewhat limited and insight restricted.

His attitudes toward parental figures indicate marked residuals of unresolved oedipal problems. The father is the object of strong aggressive feelings, while the patient's attitude toward the mother has more warmth, but is still intensely ambivalent due to her rejecting qualities.

In conclusion, the foregoing description indicates a chronic schizophrenic process in an individual who has, nevertheless, retained some degree of reality contact. The type of defenses predominantly employed—i.e., obsessive-compulsive—suggests that paranoid features should be most prominent. The presence of hysterical mechanisms, plus other test indices, would suggest that catatonic features should also be in evidence.

Intelligence is discussed first. It is not optimal.

In this report the headings announce that certain portions of personality are to be separated and treated apart from the rest of "Personality." The psychologist is not successful here (fortunately), for in discussing intelligence he talks about a number of "personality" features—anxiety, negativisms, obsessiveness, compulsiveness. This is quite proper if there is a rationale for discussing the intellect in this report. The same holds true of the discussion of what the psychologist describes as the memory function. It is only the headings and the averred attempt to think of personality in segments that are blameworthy.

The report is exhaustive, overdetailed—a shotgun report. What else can the patient have wrong with him? A chronic case, he is schizophrenic, apathetic, deteriorated. He is depressed, paranoid, catatonic, hysterical, and obsessive-compulsive. He is oral, and anal also, no doubt, because he is obsessive-compulsive, and he didn't do very well during the oedipal period either. He has homosexual problems, heterosexual problems, autoerotic problems, and maybe some other kinds of sexual problems. He turns aggression outward and inward because he is a hostile person. He also has guilt, anxiety, fearfulness, minor tension and turmoil, outward hyperresponsivity and lability. He feels self-disintegration and decay. He is passive-dependent, has feelings of rejection, inferiority and inadequacy, with a strong need to be wanted and cared for. He hates his father and he hates females (they castrate and reject him). The environment is a hostile place.

What is the focus of all this material? What are the major conclusions? What is the supporting material?

All of the faults written into the report would seem to suggest that the psychologist has a jaundiced view of his patient, but possibly some of this comes from close attention to a pathologically oriented theory. The various fixations, conflicts, and problem areas discussed by Freud are also discussed by the psychologist, the patient appearing to be the vehicle by which knowledge of the theory can be demonstrated. Had Freud lived longer, the report might have been longer. In accentuating the negative, the psychologist watches his patient closely lest he present an unjustifiably favorable image. The patient talks well (though sometimes glibly) and would seem to have much positive introspection and insight. But we mustn't be fooled. He is covering up. He is evasive. Then, too, "large areas of thinking are apparently reality-bound, but this is achieved at the expense of rather severe constriction of personality resources." This patient looks better than he actually is because he presents a facade.

Because theory is a matter of generalities, and because Aunt Fanny typifies the banal generalities of man, this report is very much of the Aunt Fanny type. To be brief, consider traits like orality, anxiety, nonoptimal intellectual functioning, oedipal problems not fully resolved, and an imperfect sexuality. This latter theme is as firmly entrenched in many psychological reports as the IQ emphasis. Psychologists, with the diligence and dedication of Diogenes, would seem to be searching for a person with a solid sex identity, complete acceptance of his (her) sex role, lack of guilt or conflict over sex activities, lack of actual or fantasy indulgence in anything but true mature heterosexuality (this is wholesome and good), lack of id impulses that tend in any direction but the latter, and great enjoyment and fulfillment in coitus. Where might we find such a person?

The report has word jargon and test jargon. Terms like intropunitiveness and extrapunitiveness are not generally used clinical terms; they are associated with a test having low rank order in clinical usage. Nevertheless, the theory talk and the test talk may give the reader the impression that he has been here before.

Workshop Case 7

In the next report, which is shorter and contains fewer comments on pathology, the focus is somewhat clearer. At least it would seem that the patient is an intelligent schizophrenic person who is deeply troubled and has, along with several distressing problems, difficulty in controlling the expression of his feelings.

Intellectual Evaluation

Intellectual functioning is generally in the superior range (IQ 127), with very superior verbal intelligence and excellent memory, psychomotor performance, and motor learning. He shows an unusually low drop on social comprehension, however, which is out of keeping with his general performance.

Personality Organization

Objective personality data disclose a generally deviant personality profile with particular emphasis on "depression" and "psychasthenia" scales. Underlying these surface disorders one notes the presence of malignant mental processes in terms of schizophrenic, bizarre manifestations. Thus "Schizophrenia" and "F" scales also show deviant elevations. Disturbed psychosexual functioning is indicated by the elevated "Femininity" scale. Consistent with this picture of severe schizophrenic pathology, the Rorschach and other projective data show marked inner turmoil, multiple unresolved emotional problems, and loss of control of psychotic proportions. Uncontrolled aggressive themes on the Rorschach are exemplified by his percepts of "pelvic bone removed with blood" and "Fox's face." Also his percents of "colored designs" on plates IX and X indicate reduced emotional control which is compensated by evasive defensiveness.

His thematic associations to the figure drawing suggest considerable concern about problems relating to vocational dependability and perseverence and ability to take care of one's family. His own reported difficulties of this type indicate that he is still ruminating and experiencing loss of self-esteem because of them. His sentence completions disclose other basic personal problems having to do with marital relations, attitudes and feelings about his parents, and general interpersonal relations. There are signs of continued angry depression, intropunitiveness, and reduced self-esteem.

Even though some useful conclusions are presented, the effectiveness of this report is, for several reasons, open to question.

First, there is a lot of test talk. If the reader does not have expert knowledge, or at least a working knowledge of the MMPI, what is being discussed cannot be very meaningful (but it can still be impressive). In connection with this emphasis on test performance, as partially opposed to emphasis on the patient, is the seeming transfer of responsibility for conclusions from the psychologist to his tests. "Objective personality data disclose . . . ," "His thematic associations to the figure drawing suggest . . . ," and "His sentence completions disclose. . . ." The MMPI scale scores apparently give conclusions automatically, and the presence of "schizophrenic, bizarre manifestations" are backed up with mention that " 'Schizophrenia' and 'F' scales also show deviant elevations." With this bit of instruction, other team associates may feel free to reach similar conclusions in the presence of such elevations, or to question a psychologist who does not report such conclusions when there are elevations on these scales. Similarly with the interpretation of the elevated "Femininity" scale. In the discussion of intellectual functioning, there is mention of "an unusually low drop on social comprehension," but this is not interpreted. Presumably, this statement has meaning in the context in which it is mentioned, and the reader will reach the correct conclusion. Finally, in reviewing the test talk we note the use of test content both to exemplify and support conclusions. Is it really apparent that "Fox's face," seen somewhere on the Rorschach, is an uncontrolled aggressive theme? Does the isolated information that the patient saw "colored designs" on plates IX and X necessarily indicate "reduced emotional control which is compensated by evasive defensiveness"? All of these observations raise questions about the responsibility of interpretation and about the impression the psychologist gives to his team associates on his method of work and reaching conclusions.

Workshop Case 8

In a passage taken from a longer report, the opposite of the battery approach is demonstrated; the findings of an individual test are summarized and a diagnostic impression is based on this one test. This is generally hazardous and unwise. In the case from which this excerpt was taken, all of the various diagnostic impressions and other conclusions were integrated in the *summary*.
This procedure may seem objective, but it sometimes forces the psychologist to arrive at far-reaching conclusions from too restricted a sample of behaviors.

WAIS

On this test, this patient attained a full scale IQ of 125, giving him a classification of "Superior" general intelligence. His performance IQ of 128 places him in the "Very Superior" category, and his verbal IQ of 116 in the "Bright Normal" group. This discrepancy of 12 IQ points in favor of performance is considered very significant; this pattern would ordinarily tend to point to psychopathy.

Quantitative discrepancies of the type where easy items are missed and more difficult ones of the same subtest are passed, occurred in the following instances—he misses "theater" (0) and "land in city" (0), but gets "forest" and "child labor" on the comprehension subtest. Qualitative analysis of these and other responses on the comprehension subtest reveal some tendency toward psychopathy (he would leave the theater; his only concern would be to remain calm—he does not care about the others there) and some negativism and inaccessibility (taxes—"They're very necessary"—this is an inadequate answer considering patient's age and educational background).

There are no bizarre responses such as would indicate any pathology of psychotic proportions.

A scatter analysis shows significant negative discrepancy from the mean of the subtest scores for comprehension and digit span. The extremely low digit span performance points to an anxiety laden person; this impression is heightened by the discrepancy between digits forward and backward (5 vs. 3). The digit symbol subtest reveals a pervasive insecurity and some hostility (heavy lines).

Summary of the WAIS

This 31-year-old white male patient is now functioning at a "Superior" level of general intelligence (full scale IQ 125, performance IQ 128, verbal IQ 116). This score is taken to be a fairly reliable estimate, but patient probably has capacity to function on a Very Superior level as evidenced by his performance scores; a great amount of anxiety seems to be depressing his digit span and comprehension performance with a resultant constriction of his verbal ability. There is no indication of any psychosis.

Diagnostic Impression
   Neurotic anxiety with pathological personality trends.

   This psychologist seems to have faith in his readers' intimate familiarity with the test under discussion—with its items, the sort of responses it yields, and something of the scoring system too.

   He also appears to be giving his readers some unfortunate instruction in the interpretation of psychological tests. For example, he interprets a qualitative feature of performance on the Digit Symbol subtest to indicate the presence of Aunt Fanny traits like "pervasive insecurity" and "some hostility." The interpretation of the patient's response to the "theatre" and "child labor" items appears quite bold. Nevertheless, the report writer seems to be building toward the conclusion that this patient is a "psychopath." Progress toward this goal is thwarted, however, when it is noted that the Digit Span score is down—the patient repeated 5 digits forward and 3 backward, a result which could come about through various causes—and by the "pervasive insecurity" already noted from performance on the Digit Symbol test. Hence the WAIS-based diagnostic impression now becomes "Neurotic anxiety with pathological personality trends," an unofficial and ambiguous classification.

   The strong need for a summary statement, even though the text is so brief, is interesting. It might also be noted that the summary contains a new integration of material. The meaning of the discrepancy between verbal and performance IQs was suggested in the text (—with some hedging ". . . would ordinarily tend to point to . . .") as a psychopathic indicator. Now, in the summary, comes a new insight. Anxiety is leading to a "constriction" of "verbal ability," and the patient is not a psychopath after all. The report reader, if he can follow the twisting path of the report, is being asked to contribute to the conclusion-making process, rather than being presented with firm conclusions.

   Notice that the psychologist interprets a verbal IQ that is lower than the performance IQ as a "constriction of his verbal ability." What impression is the report reader supposed to reach? "Verbal," in the WAIS sense, refers to tests in which the stimuli are auditory and the responses are made through speech. It is thus a limited technical term. In the usual connotation, "verbal" has to do with linguistic function, and apparently it was not a difficulty of this sort which resulted in a verbal IQ lower than the performance IQ But even if the test were essentially a measure of verbal ability, a score which is a standard deviation above the mean probably should not be thought of as evidence of "constriction." Thinking in terms of "psychological shorthand" can be a handicap to describing a person in terms of real behavior.

Workshop Case 9

Here is a report evidently written about a man who is caught up in some sort of personal-situational difficulty.

General Behavior

This 29-year-old white male was evidently concerned about being scheduled for testing because he sought out the examiner on the morning of the day appointed for testing, asking for information regarding what was going to take place. He seemed likeable and was quite responsive during this interview, seeming to structure the situation along the lines of a therapeutic interview. The patient presented quite an innocuous "front" with regard to his history, and seems to be an expert in the area of creating an impression other than factual about himself. His testing behavior was equally cooperative and pleasant, although, as will be treated later, a hard core of underlying resistiveness and negativism was suspected. The patient tended to under-respond, in general, on tests involving close, interpersonal exchanges between the examiner and the patient.

Test Results

He achieved a verbal IQ of 107, a performance IQ of 116, and a Full-Scale IQ of 112. The variability in subtest scores was rather marked in certain areas, and may suggest either or both: (1) intense underlying anxiety which the patient controls well superficially; (2) a highly variable negativism. It was noted on the WAIS that after saying he did not know the answer, the patient would give the correct answer if pressed. At any rate, it appears that this patient is somewhat defective in judgment and ability to integrate and utilize the factual elements of his environment. His psychomotor performance was adequate, and the patient demonstrated an unusually good recent memory along with concentration and the ability to detect essential elements of his surroundings. Thus, we find him presently functioning within the Bright Normal range of intelligence, with indications that his original potential was within the Superior range.

Mr. Blank was extremely orderly in his productions and was very exacting in representing himself to others. He was under-productive on some of the projective devices and seemed to be quite fearful of "giving himself away" as regards his inner feelings and impulses. In general, there were suggestions of strong, latent resistiveness and negativism which the patient works hard at concealing, but which may break through in antisocial behavior. There were indications of sexual immaturity—an almost childish conception of the requirements of adult heterosexual relationships. Also, he capitalizes on the nurturant needs of others.

The overall impression here is that of an individual with original character defects who became precipitously involved in marriage and family, and whose general immaturity and inability to bind tension precludes any progress on a short-term basis. He does not appear to be a good prospect for conventional techniques of psychotherapy, and it appears that the greatest help which may be offered him at this time is some type of semi-supervised setting where external limits may be utilized as self-restraints, and where the patient may take a "breather" from reality demands for a person of his age and status.

Summary

This individual is functioning within the Bright Normal range of intelligence. He appears to be generally immature with strong negativistic impulses, inability to tolerate anxiety, and a tendency to act out. He needs to control interpersonal relationships and to manipulate others, mainly through nurturant needs of others.

Several impressions quickly come to mind. There is a lack of meaningful organization and of case-focused conclusions. The responsibility with which a number of interpretations are made is questionable, and support for the major conclusions is not to be found.

Writing a more or less traditional report, the psychologist discusses first "general behavior," and then test results. The latter is not divided by headings, but intelligence is discussed in the first paragraph and the projective test findings in the other. Since intelligence is so heavily emphasized in this report (why?), one may wonder why matters pertaining to the intellect as derived from projective testing, or from other sources, were not included.

Since "General Behavior" is treated apart from the "Test Results," what appears to be a major conclusion in the opinion of the psychologist—the discrepancy between the patient's surface behavior and what is "underlying"—is not presented as a unified contribution. The psychologist is evidently tempted to do so, anticipating the test results in the discussion of clinical behavior, but he is unable to break down tradition. One of the effects is unnecessary repetition, making the report longer than it has to be. Though this is not a long report, it still is too long in terms of the useful content it carries. The major conclusions do not seem to be related meaningfully to the adjustment problem that led the person to seek help; its nature is not made clear by the report.

The psychologist takes cognizance of external events—precipitous involvement in marriage and family. Possibly the tentative statement about the "latent resistiveness and negativism"—the inner side of the patient "which may break through in antisocial behavior"—is the key to the patient's difficulties, but the report reader should not be forced to speculate on a speculation.

It may be the patient's "sexual immaturity" which is the basis of the problem. If so, what does it mean? Is it a matter of the patient's naiveté, of an interpersonal attitude on his part, or of a self-attitude that is related to his seeking of help, and to the implications for treatment and disposition that are offered? The reviewer feels uncomfortable in exploring further the extent to which the report is case-focused without first questioning the psychologist's accuracy of interpretation or of expression.

Evidently the patient did not relate "an almost childish conception" of sex in interview, since there are only "indications" of such. Projective tests, such as the Rorschach and the TAT, can of course give insights into some basic sexual attitudes, but apparently something more conscious, palpable, and clearly relevant is being discussed here. If the "indications" were spelled out in language, such as on a Sentence Completion test or a Word Association test, the data should probably be interpreted in at least a summary conclusion, possibly with some illustrative material. As the statement stands, it raises more questions about the patient than it answers. Out of sincere curiosity, the reviewer raises afresh in this case the question as to what might be the psychologist's conception of mature "adult heterosexual relationships," since in this still under-studied field the authorities sanction a broad range of behaviors. This psychologist most likely tends to ascribe a similar "defect" to other patients.

Apart from the recommendations made, there is no development of conclusions that would seem to have implications for action. The questionable responsibility of a number of the statements would tend to reduce further the value of the general and incomplete interpretations offered. We may, for example, wonder about both the nature and the significance of the patient's capitalizing on the nurturant needs of others. Similar questions are raised about the observation that the patient is "somewhat defective in judgment and ability to integrate and utilize the factual elements of his environment." At one level and in many real life circumstances, this incriminating-sounding statement is true of everyone but me and thee. If it has more serious connotations, the behavior to which reference is made and its implications for the case should be made known. (A little later in the report we learn that the patient has the "ability to detect essential elements of his surroundings." One wonders here about the possibility of mutual contradiction. The separate statements were probably derived from inspection of the responses to different subtests. What is the significance of this alertness to environment? The psychologist has the obligation to integrate related findings, and to resolve what appear to be possible contradictions or inconsistencies.)

Poor organization and the lack of buildup to significant conclusions is exemplified again in an "overall impression" and recommendation in which a trait of possible major implications is brought into the discussion as though incidentally. It is here that we find the patient has an "inability to bind tension." This caused the reviewer to reread the report to discover what point he may have missed. He uncovered, relevant to the point at issue, that the patient's "front" and his testing behavior were "cooperative and pleasant." "although . . . underlying resistiveness and negativism *was suspected* (italics supplied)." The examiner raised the question, from the variability of subtest scores, of "a highly variable negativism," although there was no hint as to how this trait was expressed. In the interview the patient seemed to exercise control through under-response, a technique also utilized in projective testing and apparently on the WAIS too. His productions were *"extremely orderly"* and the patient was *"very exacting* in representing himself to others (italics supplied.)" All of this suggests a good degree of control and an excellent ability to bind tension. The psychologist did interpret "suggestions of strong, latent resistiveness and negativism . . . which *may* break through in antisocial behavior (italics supplied)." This is a flimsy, irresponsible basis for the far-reaching conclusion to which it contributes. Questions also have to be raised about the conclusion that the patient is "generally immature." Earlier we read (whether we were convinced or not) that he was sexually immature. Nevertheless, he seems to show at least some rather mature behaviors in his social bearing and ability to control what are presented as unpleasant inner feelings and impulses. Of course the patient is reported to carry about with him some widely distributed traits of immaturity, such as anxiety, resistiveness, and negativism (the latter two being offered to the reader quite tentatively—except in the summary), but how usefully does this differentiate the patient from the legion of the immature?

This report lacks integration and support for conclusions. It is not case-focused and not adequately differentiating. The responsibility of many of its conclusions is suspect. It is not a useful or convincing report.

Workshop Case 10

In the next report we see, with some "contamination," a test-by-test report. It at least follows the modern trend to integration to the extent of omitting test headings from the paragraphs.

Behavioral Note

Mr. Doe is a rather short, paunchy man of 39. He seemed to be quite comfortable in the testing situation. It appears that his many months at the hospital has acclimated him to an institutionalized setting. He took the tests in a matter of fact manner. He seemed neither negative nor particularly anxious to show his skills. He volunteered little information but did respond to direct questions. There was a tendency to agree with the examiner rather than to express his own opinions. For example, when the examiner said, "that must have been a lonely place to live in," he readily agreed. Since he would not elaborate on his answers, it was difficult to note the logic of his thinking. However, on the basis of his conversations, no delusions or other bizarre type of thinking was evident.

Test Results

Although Mr. Doe scores in the mentally defective range (Full Scale IQ of 65), there is a great deal of evidence that this is not a true measure of his potential. There was a great deal of scatter in his scores on the WAIS, which ranged from 0 to 9. It appears that emotional difficulties lowered his I.Q. scores. For example, on the similarities he insisted on giving me the differences rather than the likenesses. On the comprehension, he would not accept the premises of some of the questions, and so did not give a correct answer. For example, "What does 'Shallow brooks are noisy' mean?" Answer: "I don't think shallow brooks are noisy." Although this may be a defense against admitting certain deficiencies, his constant tendency to use negativistic defenses did in fact interfere with his overall performance. (His Benton performance discloses that he could probably score in the 90's on an IQ test.) This stubbornness or negativism seems to disclose a latent catatonic trend, which, under pressure, would become manifest.

Mr. Doe got a score of 0 on the picture arrangements test. This, together with some of his answers on the Sentence Completion ("I want a girl who knows everything") and Draw-a-Person plus inquiries suggest a rather infantile understanding of social relations. However, his comprehension as well as his high F+% on the Rorschach (83%) seem to indicate that he does know right from wrong.

Mr. Doe's usual method of seeing the relationship between objects is through their functional usage. Thus, under optimal conditions, it is unlikely that he would score higher than the average range. At present, there is a great deal of looseness and some inadequacy in his thinking. It seems that he can function well if he responds to a simple situation. When the problems become more complex, idiosyncratic complexes tend to interfere with his solutions to the problems. For example on the Object Sorting Test, he would put the eraser under the red disc since he felt that it would look neater that way. This tendency to be concerned with neatness seems to reflect an anal fixation. This fixation might also be the source of his stubbornness and trend toward resistiveness. His tendency to overextend a concept and to oversimplify stories (Babcock Memory) seems to denote a latent schizophrenic process. On one occasion, he used a "chaining" process to group some objects. This is usually found with people suffering from a schizophrenic disorder. On the Rorschach, he perceived a given object on the basis of one particular part on two occasions (Confabulation). On one of these occasions, the percept was accurate, on the other the percept was grossly inaccurate. Thus, there appears to be remnants of a schizophrenic process in the present makeup of this man.

As was mentioned above, this patient has extremely good contact with his environment. His F+% was over 80; 7 of his 19 Rorschach responses were popular. Thus, when he makes simple responses to his environment, he is able to respond adequately.

The Rorschach seems to reveal a very sensitive person who is quite anxious. (The only overt evidence of anxiety was his smoking of cigarettes.) He seems to be quite anxious about getting a job and working. However, he seems to fear loneliness ("The poor boy wants people around to talk with"—TAT).

With regard to the fulfillment of his needs, he seems to have been rejected by his mother. (I like my mother "but my father best." "The woman is waiting for the boy to leave.") He seems to feel that girls are more fortunate than boys. (The boy is poor but the girls live in a richy section—TAT). It appears that any sexual deviations on his part would be an attempt to receive love regardless of the source. Although unusual sexual responses were relatively rare, on occasion he showed evidence of possible sexual deviations. "Two of the three stooges talking to each other with no clothes on." "The horse is eating grass and the dog is trying to scare him away." Mr. Doe's differentiation of the sexes seems to be poor; e.g., both the girl and the boy in the DAP are laborers. Thus if he happens to act out in a sexually deviant manner, he might be either active or passive.

Summary

Mr. Doe has an IQ of 65 with a potential of about 90. His intelligence seems to be lowered due to negativism and resistiveness as well as to a rather infantile social orientation. Maternal rejection seems to be responsible for his rather immature psychosexual development. He seems to have reacted to this rejection by being stubborn and egocentric. Sexual deviations

seem to be his way of obtaining the love that he desires. At present, he
seems to be in good contact with his environment. He seems to work well
provided he does simple things that do not tax his abilities. Under pressure,
he will tend to regress to a catatonic schizophrenic adjustment.

Aside from the lack of functional integration in this report, there is cause for
great concern, especially with regard to the responsibility with which the
presented interpretations are made, with the inadequate development
of pertinent conclusions, and with the impression this report might give to others
of how a psychologist goes about his work. The report meanders through the
various tests of the battery, picking up what seems to be interpretable rather than
meaningful. There is also much test talk in this report.

In test-by-test reporting it is sometimes easy to be self-contradictory, or
apparently so. Thus, in the "Behavioral Note" the psychologist reports what is
evidently an important feature of personality, a tendency to be agreeable.
In the next paragraph, however, in focusing on the WAIS, we learn of a high
degree of negativism. Or we read that the patient can function well when
responding to a simple situation and he has "extremely good contact with his
environment." How does this tie in with a tumble of the IQ from an
estimated 90 to 65, hardly a trivial matter? Such results could not be brought
about by "temporary inefficiencies." The "emotional difficulties" that
lowered his scores would probably have to be sufficiently severe to affect
reality perception. (This may be presumed by reading further down about a
Rorschach confabulation that was "grossly inaccurate".) Certainly many of the
items of the WAIS on which the patient did poorly must have been simple.

There are so many questionable and ambiguous statements made that
only a few need be pointed out. The reference to the patient's comprehension
is ambiguous (a score on the Comprehension subtest, or some other
estimate of "comprehension"?), but this in combination with a high F+
percent (83 percent) indicates that the patient knows right from wrong!
How much confidence can we place in a few artificial samples of
behavior? This psychologist has evidently never known any dangerous,
self-righteous paranoids with an F+ percent of 100. The interpretation of
the patient's placement of items on the Object Sorting test in such a way as to
look neat is not only regarded as an anal fixation (!), but this fixation, now that
it is "established," is also seen as the possible source of the patient's
stubbornness and trend toward resistiveness. This is the textbook talking, not
the psychologist. The textbook tells the theory, but the psychologist, too
conveniently, fits the patient into the theoretical mold. On the "Babcock
Memory" the tendency to oversimplify stories is associated with a
latent schizophrenic process (why?). Evidence for sexual deviation is flimsy,
particularly since the nature or sources of the responses are not more
fully identified. We cannot automatically relate the response, "The horse is
eating grass and the dog is trying to scare him away," to any known

sexual deviation (regardless of where and on what test this response occurred). Other readers of the report may also have the same difficulty. Of course one would not want to challenge that if the patient is to "act out in a sexually deviant manner he might be either active or passive."

This report, like several previous ones, assumes without hesitation that the report reader knows a good deal about psychological tests and their scoring. The reader presumably can "follow" some of the conclusions which are supported with "evidence," thus lending an air of pseudovalidity. There is evidently no question that the reader will attach pertinent and significant meaning to the observation that the patient's "usual method of seeing the relationship between objects is through their functional usage."

The term "infantile" is used twice. If the patient is severely fixated or retrogressed it may be appropriate to define such a condition. When the reader sees terms like "childish" and "infantile," unless well-supported by behavioral description, the impression is gained that the psychologist is calling names. We have to question, of course, that the patient's smoking of cigarettes is an overt indication of "anxiety." There would have to be more overt information than this to make us think of anxiety. And we would also be eager to know more about this patient's being anxious—in what way, on what occasions, and how it relates to the patient's psychoeconomics and functioning. Finally, consider the statement in the summary that "Sexual deviations seem to be his way of obtaining the love that he desires." In the body of the report the existence of sexual deviations was proposed only tentatively, as was fitting if indeed there were any need to mention it. So numerous and obvious are the faults and inconsistencies in this report that we see no need to carry this discussion any further.

Workshop Case 11

The final report in this workshop is in some important ways different from those preceding. It is the product of a skilled clinician who is respected by his colleagues for the depth of his insights and the incisiveness and carefulness of his observations. If you challenged any of his conclusions, you would probably find that you are wrong. The report is therefore used as an exhibit with mixed feelings. Yet it is important to this workshop because it is an opportunity to show how the traditional approach can be damaging to a report which is solid in its substance.

Behavioral Observations

This 47-year-old, divorced Congregational minister cooperatively took the regular psychological examination on June 1 and 4. He was a quick-moving, fast talking, alert, over-anxious, over-polite individual whose ashen-hued, lined face and drab black suit draped over a spare, narrow-shouldered frame gave him an air of mild dissipation and slipping gentility. He exuded nervous tension and insecurity in various ways—excessive palmar perspiration, chain smoking, abrupt manner of moving and talking, overreactive smiles and laughter, and an abundance of self-depreciating, self-referential, and rationalizing remarks. His test behavior was one of controlled tension punctuated with flurries of fumbling and overdemonstrative emotional display, exclamations, and rationalizations, giving a cumulative impression of avoidant tendencies and egocentricity, clothed in superficially outgoing manners. At times his anxiety rendered him somewhat suspicious, as when he checked on a couple of Vocabulary items he failed, with the transient, expressed idea that the examiner was "up to some tricks." Annoyance was indirectly expressed through ostensibly facetious remarks, such as "You *would* bring out math again—I despise it," and "you're a hard taskmaster!" when the examiner maintained a nondirective role.

In describing his background, the patient appeared to be glossing over some aspects, particularly his drinking, and tended to point to external circumstances such as his wife's desertion of him and misinterpretations of well-intentioned church members, rather than to internal sources for explanations of his behavior. He inconsistently both denied and admitted excessive drinking at various times during testing. A recurrent theme in his conversation concerned the benevolent support he was receiving from various ecclesiastical friends and authorities, the implication being that his difficulties would soon be smoothed over by his cooperation with their advice.

Intellectual Status

The patient, a college graduate, is operating at the upper limit of the Bright Normal range of intelligence; on the Wechsler Adult Intelligence Scale, he achieves a Full Scale IQ of 119, a Verbal IQ of 122, and a Performance IQ of 114. He is a verbally astute individual whose fluency exceeds and to some extent masks his actual ability to put his intelligence to concrete, practical use. On material requiring manual execution he displays somewhat more inefficiency than he does in more verbal contexts. Inefficiencies of a mild, reversible kind pervade his functioning, however, and are attributable to the vitiating effects of chronic tension upon which are superimposed flurries of anxiety. Thus, he occasionally fails to check his solutions, makes rather inadequate anticipations (particularly in social contexts), and finds it difficult to maintain the orderliness he obviously strives for.

Despite his relatively low tension tolerance, however, his intellectual control is generally in reasonably good shape. Although his ability to make abstract generalizations on a purely verbal level is not quite on a par with what one would expect from his verbal facility, he nevertheless shows good conceptual contact, i.e., normal abstract reasoning, with everyday affairs. He also displays a well developed awareness of appropriate courses of behavior; this knowledge is somewhat superficial, however, and there is a noteworthy paucity of sensitive introspection. Memorial and learning efficiency are essentially intact but he does manifest a confabulatory trend in keeping with the rationalizing tendencies noted above; suggestive of this feature of his thought processes, as well as of dominant oral preoccupation, is his striking addition of new content to a recall item, to wit, "a man cut his hand *on a bottle*." Finally, the patient's perceptual-motor performance suggests the setting in of some degree of debilitation of resources, accompanying chronically pressing conflicts and insecurity

Personality Organization

The patient presents the picture of a chronically insecure, anxious person with marked oral-addictive inclinations related to an almost insatiable need for nurturance. The sources of his insecure and conflict-ridden personality can be traced to a rather unstable childhood existence as a sickly only child, overprotected by his mother and left wanting in masculine companionship from a father whom he saw become a hard-drinking, undependable, unfaithful individual. The patient's TAT stories abound in themes concerning offspring rebelling against parental wishes and standards yet invariably returning dutifully to the safe haven of reconciliation.

The patient apparently has conducted his life on the unconscious premises of personal inferiority and of the constant availability of someone he can lean on to mediate his difficulties for him, a sort of passive mastery stemming from weakness. His religious vocation, of course, has provided considerable, though insufficient compensation for his inner reservations about his adequacy. It is apparent, however, that he retains certain impulsive, hedonistic tendencies not worked through during his rather deprived boyhood, and that these, as well as other conflicts, have been a constant source of maladjustment for him. Like many alcoholically inclined individuals, he seeks dependent relationships while at the same time resenting that type of position, and often manages to alienate his friends, only to seek to regain his dependency by presenting himself for help out of his difficulties. This self-defeating pattern in effect recapitulates the pattern of his childhood. His emphasis on dutifulness, while sincere enough, appears to serve the purpose often of rationalizing a return to a dependent relationship.

The patient exhibits marked inferiority feelings and a derogatory, almost destructive self-concept. To a considerable extent, this low self-esteem had its beginnings in an early acquired sense of physical shortcomings; his handling of Rorschach percepts frequently is clearly symbolic of unconscious castration anxiety. This rather negative and fearful self-concept naturally has been conducive to much social maladaptation and lack of confidence. His social adjustment has also been rendered troublesome by unresolved conflicts concerning aggressive outlets, sexual needs, and guilt feelings. It is apparent that he differentiates poorly between the sexes, is actually confused about his sexual role, has persisting passive-feminine tendencies, and unconsciously regards heterosexual contacts as dangerous (cf. the anxiety over phallic intactness noted above.) Thus he shows a retreat to a relatively bisexual orientation, and there is a possibility that latent homoerotic pressures may precipitate panic in him.

The patient has a rich intellectual appreciation of the demands of convention; his expressed attitudes and fantasy productions are consistently pervaded with moralistic, even pollyannish platitudes. Yet emotionally he lacks a sustained stamina commensurate with his convictions and idealistic goals, which are commendably altruistic indeed – ". . . to serve God and my fellow man." He falls short of self-confrontation and independent assumption of responsibility for his actions by resorting to denial, rationalization, moralistic generalities, and other avoidant maneuvers. His insecurity renders him defensive enough at times to be suspicious, but paranoid ideation is not noted. Hysterical components are suggested by his egocentricity, histrionic flair, moralism, impulsive tendencies, and overdemonstrativeness superimposed upon relatively shallow emotionality.

The patient's insecurity and oral cravings, as reflected in his fluency, his alcoholism, and almost parasitic, compulsive seeking out of others to intercede for him or actually supply his dependent needs, has created considerable impoverishment of personality, including some debilitation of standards, narrowing of interests, and a general habituation to the evasive, avoidant, and rationalizing patterns seen in many alcoholic individuals. He is relatively lacking in constructive introspection and tends to take the easy way out in his thought processes. There is a possibility that he will express open hostility on occasion, although he will generally avoid such occasions as he does emotional involvement in general, failing to see something through to its consequences.

Summary and Conclusions

The patient possesses superior intelligence but currently is functioning somewhat below his optimum. He is a verbally astute individual with somewhat impaired ability to put his intelligence to practical use. His inefficiencies, though rather numerous, are relatively benign and may be attributed to chronic tension. His intellectual control and reality contact are satisfactory. In personality organization, he is a deeply insecure, conflict-ridden, anxious person with marked oral-addictive inclinations related to persisting needs for nurturance and dependency. His inferiority feelings and derogatory self-concept reflect an unhappy childhood which created in him anxieties and uncertainties concerning his physical and social integratedness. Unresolved conflicts appear in the spheres of aggression, sex, and guilt. He shows a rather diffuse, confused sexual identification which could lead to episodes of panic. Emotionally he lacks stamina commensurate with his facile intellectual appreciation of convention and of moral and altruistic convictions—"to serve God and my fellow man." His oral-addictive propensities have impoverished his personality seriously, leading not only to direct satisfaction via liquor but also socially maladjustive patterns of passive mastery in the form of compulsive dependence on intercessors and some habituation to avoidant, rationalizing, and ingratiating attitudes, at the cost of paucity of constructive self-examination.

Psychotherapy should at the outset be attractive to the patient because of the distress of his current difficulties and because he is partial to verbal expression. Emotional insight will undoubtedly, however, proceed slowly; while therapy should be supportive enough to maintain a relationship, care should be taken to exert pressure in the direction of active mastery. As he himself observes, a man needs to exert some initiative in order to benefit from "faith, hope, and trust in God." His religious and humanistic convictions appear sincere and central enough to his life so that it would seem important to help him preserve his religious work and increase the substitutive values therein.

In diagnostic terms, the patient's disturbance can be classified as a severe, chronic anxiety neurosis complicated by alcoholic addiction and passive-dependent character patterns.

The report is of course noteworthy for its length. Overlooking the value of its content for the moment, we must consider the time demands such a full discussion makes on both writer and reader. We know that many readers refuse to wade through a long report, but possibly feelings on this matter might be attenuated when the quality of content is high and the exposition clear. As for the writer, his colleagues indicate that this psychologist works very hard and very long to develop and present his material. Can the process and the report be streamlined without loss?

The quality of writing clearly meets and exceeds the requirements for a utilitarian, ephemeral document having such limited circulation as a psychological report. We may wonder only if it is "too good," in that such writing is necessarily quite demanding of time. Perhaps the matter is largely of academic concern, since most psychologists could not write this way. Some of the expression, particularly the description of the minister in the second sentence of the report, is in the manner of the novelist. Are such fine efforts misplaced in a psychological report? Are they appreciated?

The question is not easily answered and not easily separated from the ambivalence we feel about the report: its high quality, utility, and excellent composition on the one hand, the economic factors on the other. It is obvious that this report enables the reader to "see" the patient and to contemplate the details and subtleties of his existence. Even individual sentences are packed with details (incidentally, though the sentences flow easily, their length and content saturation might elicit criticism). What we have to decide, essentially, is whether all of this is necessary. Let's look at the report again.

Quite evidently this patient is experiencing what, in current terms, may be regarded as "problems in living," with alcoholism a part of the picture. Whether the referral was general or specific, the goal of the psychologist was to explore rather fully the background and concomitants of the difficulty, and to suggest remedial action. At this distance it looks as if the goal was realistic and meaningful. As already suggested in alluding to the length of the report, its detail, and superior composition (all of which are demanding of labor), the question is more of efficiency than of whether the goal was met.

The traditional report is inefficient, according to the viewpoint presented here. Thus many of the words under "Behavioral Observations" are probably not really necessary. Most of the information in the first sentence, for example, is on file and not organic to the mission. One may wonder here about the detailing. Why is it mentioned that the patient is a Congregational minister? Would it make a difference if he were Episcopalian, Baptist, Lutheran, or a non-Protestant clergyman? Or a businessman or a lawyer? If it would this information should certainly be woven into the psychological evaluation. Do we really want to call up stereotypes? Similarly with the masterful description of the patient. Is that which is described any closer to the ensuing personality information than if the patient were in appearance a beefy, ruddy-complexioned teamster type (or stereotype) with fists like hams? In other words, is all this beside the point of coming to grips with the mission; But there really is considerable material of interest in this section, although some of it repeats test-derived conclusions. Space would probably be saved and "tightness" gained if all this were integrated with the remainder of the report. Loose ends would also be eliminated; for example, there is talk of the patient's being suspicious and commenting that the examiner was "up to some tricks." Paranoids sometimes behave this way, and the reader could not be blamed for being alerted to paranoid content to follow, but material of this sort is not forthcoming. Such, in fact, is later ruled out.

The report is pointed and individualized. General terms like "insecurity" and "oral" are defined as they have meaning for the person under discussion. It is integrated, except as the traditional report demands a certain amount of segmentalization. Nevertheless, intelligence is so clearly related to the rest of "personality" that this astute clinician does not divide the two areas as neatly as the headings would seem to demand.

A few other comments should be made. This content-saturated report is possibly overinclusive. In particular, all the discussion of the patient's intelligence is not easily related to the probable mission. There seems to be an attempt to demonstrate hysterical components, although this personality feature does not seem very important as such. The illustrative material about the patient's mentioning that "a man cut his hand *on a bottle*," though perhaps apt, might leave some readers confused; it is not likely that most nonpsychologists would be aware of the memory paragraph which is distorted in this idiosyncratic manner. A TAT theme is also presented in a very suggestive manner, yet falls slightly short of full interpretation. The "Summary and Conclusions" is perhaps a bit surprising, since the body of the report itself has many conclusions. It is really a matter of additional conclusions. Nevertheless, this section is excellent, succinct, and amazingly complete. Might the reader be tempted to respond to this, and bypass the hundreds of preceding words that were selected and arranged over many painstaking hours?

SOME GENERAL CONCLUSIONS FROM THE WORKSHOP

These eleven selections show in context many of the criticisms of psychological reports that were cited in Chapter 2. There was no attempt to find an illustration for every error, but we have seen enough to have faith that the rest exist. We have taken a long look at the field and also noted some practices that we consider "good." The workshop has also demonstrated, without doubt, how much of the total assessment function of the psychologist is available to those who would study it through the psychological report.

We pointed out in the introduction to this workshop that our presentation was to be in the nature of a supervisory conference, but not a full supervisory conference.

In effect, it was an exercise in "blind supervision!" Reports were reviewed without knowledge of missions or of protocols. In most supervisory conferences the clinical behavior and test products are probably reviewed before turning to the report. Yet, as an interesting and probably useful variation, one may start with the written product of the consultation. Why not? Many assets may be identified—and many probable faults or almost certain inaccuracies discovered in a report without examining the data on which it is based. The report reader does the same. Later we may examine whether the conclusions of the report follow from the data.

This workshop shows that there are recurring "errors" in reports by different psychologists; it also demonstrates how some report writers can be original in an unfortunate way. The pitfalls reported in Chapter 2 are real!

Lest we close this section on too tentative a note, this workshop supplements the basic text in compelling at least one far-reaching conclusion. Psychological report writing, if indeed a proper topic for isolated study is far more than a matter of communicating "findings." The brunt of criticism that we make of the above reports is not on composition, though a teacher of English well might be harsher, but on the psychology that trails behind. Rhetoric, although it may be important, is accessory to the mission.

CHAPTER SEVEN

Some Case-Focused Reports: Exemplification of an Approach

Exemplification is integral to the presentation of an approach. First, exemplification makes concrete and sufficiently detailed the necessarily more general exposition of principles. Then it enables the reader to judge for himself the substance and effectiveness of the approach. On the following pages are reports by the author from a hospital setting, reports from a school setting, reports of rehabilitation psychologists, and variously oriented reports from a community mental health clinic.

First presented is a baker's dozen of reports prepared essentially in accordance with the principles of this text. They are production line samples written by the author and are fair game for evaluation in accordance with any point of view, including that developed in this book. Following these are two reports prepared by Dr. Donald N. Bersoff[1] and reproduced with permission.

[1] Case-focused reports 14 and 15 from Bersoff, D.N. *The Psychological Evaluation of Children: A Manual of Report Writing for Psychologists Who Work With Children in an Educational Setting* (Mimeographed), Undated.

They are valued by the author because they effectively illustrate the concept of case-focusing. And finally there is a group of reports prepared in a community mental health clinic[2] and two reports prepared by a counseling psychologist.

These examples are presented to show how a task may be done, and as a source of ideas. They will lose their purpose if others try to make them a mold to shape their own reports. Every writer's product has a personal quality about it. It is usually difficult for one writer to duplicate the style of another, and rarely is it desirable to make the attempt.

CASES AND COMMENTS

Case-focused Report 1

The first report is on a 40-year-old skilled worker of moderate, but comfortable means. He had made three suicidal attempts, the last one resulting in a gunshot wound to the abdomen, being particularly serious. All of the attempts were associated with drink. His psychiatrist referred him to us for an opinion on his readiness for hospital discharge.

Test Battery: Rorschach, TAT, WAIS, Bender, DAP, Sacks Sentence Completions, MMPI

Psychological Evaluation: The most obvious personal and social trait of this patient is a remarkably poor tolerance for frustrating situations—a trait which is directly relatable to his multiple suicidal attempts. This man's need is for large quantities of love and acceptance, and he refuses to stand up to stress. When the going gets rough he will "pick up his marbles and go home." This type of behavior is to be understood as including suicidal attempts.

Mr. M does not want to know the frustration of the real world. He thinks in terms of platitudes and seeks to avoid the unpleasant (even if this means killing himself). For example, he minimizes his suicidal behavior and seems to protest that such is a matter for casualness. He is clearly an alert and perceptive person (his current IQ is 108) but he is reluctant to use his intellectual powers to help him in his adjustments. It is far easier to believe that unpleasantries are always someone else's fault.

This negative social attitude in fact is a rather strong one. An attitude of hostility and impatience is always close to the surface and many life circumstances are sufficiently frustrating to him to cause these feelings to spill out in undercontrolled behavior. This may take the form of verbal aggression or of physical belligerence. As his behavior demonstrates, there is a proneness also to turn this hostility against himself (although there is reason to believe that such behavior is seen by him as self-righteous and as a punishment for others). Alcohol apparently facilitates such a reaction, so we may partially agree with him that it is the liquor which is to blame.

[2] Case-focused reports 16-20 from The Holyoke, Massachusetts, Area Mental Health Center.

There are no indications suggesting any immediate suicidal threat, but there is also no reason to believe that he is inclined to eliminate self-destructive attempts from his behavioral repertoire. There are no particular evidences of depression, clinically or subclinically. Rather this patient is seen as having a probably unmodifiable characterological defect. This in combination with frustration can again lead to the sort of behavior for which he was hospitalized.

Some "full" psychological evaluations result in a report longer than this, some shorter. A report of this length is probably about right for many referrals, though the necessity for wide variability needs to be recognized.

The approach to this case was to tell what sort of person this is, and then to relate these significant aspects of his life pattern to the problem under study. In focusing on the problem this way, much about the man is left out. Much could have been made of his hostility at the level of the id, and we could call him oral if we wished. However, a judgment has to be made on what sort of content to include and what to exclude. This can be done only when the psychologist focuses on his mission and understands, for himself, what is relevant in terms of this requirement.

The attempt was to compose the report in an integrated, easy-flowing manner, a task which becomes increasingly difficult and time-consuming as report length increases. The language is unstilted, and the intention was that the report be comprehensible to all who have need to use it, such as physicians, social workers, nurses, chaplains, and hospital aides. Words like "frustration" need no longer be regarded as technical and hopefully are used in the nontechnical sense in which most report readers probably understand them. There is no shame in using colloquialisms like "pick up his marbles and go home." Those who believe that technical words are economical and convey what cannot be communicated otherwise should be apprised of the economy and forcefulness to be found in informal expression. Such must be used with discretion, however, and never forced or employed for its own sake.

Case-focused Report 2

Following is another report written on a patient being evaluated for his readiness for discharge from a hospital. The history had indicated a long-term psychosis, but the patient had been maintained on an outpatient basis for most of the previous ten years, during part of which time he apparently had schizophrenic symptoms. The staff was interested in his current psychological status, with attention to diagnostic matters as these pertain to discharge readiness.

Test Battery: Rorschach, TAT, WAIS, Bender, MMPI,
Sacks Sentence Completions

Psychological Evaluation: There seems little question about the diagnostic classification of this patient. He has experienced auditory hallucinations for many years, has had what he calls "most fantastic, weird imaginations—

something like in the comic books," and difficulty in meeting his
daily obligations—what he calls an inability to "get started."

In view of this history, the current findings are that he now is showing
a minimal schizophrenic psychosis. He is somewhat "flat," his thinking may
show some blocking, and he does not have an adequate appreciation of
his condition. He also is more guarded and suspicious than an adequately
functioning person should be. A proneness to easily feel threatened
makes him anxious and tense and hampers his ability to relate comfortably
with others.

On the other hand, he does at the present time adhere to the requirements
of reality in most areas of living. His brightness and mental alertness no
doubt are of value in helping him get along. His IQ is 118, though others might
underestimate the quality of his basic intellectual resources.

What we need to be concerned with in this case is essentially the negative
potentialities in the long run, although there is still a slight doubt about
his present ability to adjust to the community. That is, he might find
it quite difficult at times to "get started." This man entertains some very
deep conflicts about his sex identity, about sex activity, and about
women; and an urge to cope with problems through withdrawal, and even
to regress to a primitive level, is strong. His good imagination can become
"overactive" and cause him grief. This can be further unfortunate
socially since he has decided acting-out impulses which might be indulged
when his controls are lowered, as in a definite psychosis or otherwise.
In view of his conflicts over sex and women, particularly as these
have negative connotation, potentiality for destructive acting out in the
marital situation might be a special concern.

The conceptualization of this report follows quite closely the mission with which
the staff charged the psychologist, a mission that coincided with the psychologist's
understanding of the areas in which the patient needed evaluation.

It will be noted that the resultant answer was not in the nature of a definite
"Yes" or "No." The psychologist had a good degree of confidence in the patient's
immediate prospects for an extramural adjustment, but was not entirely certain.
(Our efforts at understanding are of course human—fallible). It is most proper
to tell what we do not know along with what we do know—if the information is
relevant. Giving a conclusion with a qualified level of confidence is to be
distinguished from hedging. The latter is understood, in the strict dictionary
sense, to refer to the presentation of material in such manner as to shield the self
from danger rather than in the interest of justifiably communicating uncertainty.

The report takes into consideration information gained through (not from)
psychological tests and social history. The decision-making problems of the staff
also set goals for the report. Merely contemplating these few facts shows what
a misnomer is the term "psychological testing."

Since the requirement was that the diagnostic status be explored, it is probably
not possible to do without terms like "schizophrenic psychosis." If we establish
a rule about technical terminology, such is the exception that proves the rule.
On the other hand, a term like "auditory hallucinations," though understood by all
personnel on the hospital treatment team, is possibly not necessary.

Conceivably, the report might be read outside the hospital by someone not familiar with its meaning or significance. The IQ of 118 is more assailable, since such information is perhaps misinterpretable even though placed in a meaningful context. Here, in fact, the intellectual level is dealt with descriptively and the IQ is really gratuitous. But in some settings it is an administrative requirement that the psychologist report an IQ. Our intimate association with the IQ is not readily undone, or relaxed, in the eyes of some associates.

Case-focused Report 3

The next report also stemmed from the question of readiness for hospital discharge. The psychologist felt that in rendering an opinion on this matter it would be important to know the diagnosis, the current state of the condition, and something of its history. The need for a differential diagnosis arose during examination, since the diagnosis was felt by the psychologist to have prognostic significance.

Test Battery: Rorschach, MMPI, TAT, WAIS, Sacks Sentence Completions, Bender

Psychological Evaluation: Mr. N makes a favorable appearance. He shows little overtly in the way of psychotic residuals, nothing more than some mild circumstantiality but with the ability spontaneously to return to the goal idea, some loquaciousness at times, and a tendency to laugh uncontrollably. He seems to be a sincere person and capable of entering warm and pleasant relationships. Apparently he is bright and alert, an obtained IQ of 106 clearly being lower than his basic capacity.

Mr. N has a basic psychological problem and a lifelong pattern for coping with this problem that directly forms the background for his condition. His problem is that he has unusually strong needs for love, support, and a sense of personal security, and he is prone to feel, at a deep level but sometimes consciously too, that these needs are thwarted, even that he is being rejected. He attempts to order his life in a manner that ought to cause people to meet his basic needs; for example, he ascribes to quite high standards of morality and conventionality and he (by virtue of unconscious controls) does not permit himself to experience or to act on the negative impulses he frequently feels toward those who (apparently) reject him. This attempt at adjustment is not fully successful and he typically reacts with various degrees of depressed feelings. But he tries to deny these feelings in himself, has developed what he calls a "sense of humor," and sometimes what is essentially a "whistling in the dark" maneuver leads to an elevated mood. He reports that he has always been a moody person and subject to mood swings. In his more severe states he is prone to mood expansion and to ill-reasoned behavior.

Another matter of concern is the thinking pattern of this patient. This area of functioning is still at variance with the usual requirements for effective living. In some situations his mental apparatus can be quite effective, but at other times undependable, evidencing perhaps confusion and misunderstanding, poor attention, and impulsiveness. More serious, there is close to the surface, if not a present fact, a distinct tendency to think in a very disordered fashion that is more in accordance with inner needs than with outer reality. This will remain indefinitely as a threat to his mental well-being.

Psychodiagnostically, there seems little doubt that the patient is largely remitted from a psychotic state of an affective nature. The diagnosis of manic-depressive illness, manic type suggests itself, but the manner in which his thinking can become disordered, apparently not secondarily to mood elevation, suggests at least the possibility of a schizophrenic condition with a formal diagnosis of schizophrenia, schizo-affective type. Probably the correct differential diagnosis could be arrived at only through observing him during an acute phase.

The problem of disposition is a fairly immediate one. Possibly the patient will improve a bit more in the near future, but it may be that he is now close to his usual state. His family could perhaps advise on this. In view of what appears to be a very favorable employment and family outlook the chances for a successful readjustment to the community appear good. He should be psychiatrically maintained, however.

In this report, an external view of the patient as this bears relationship to his psychological status was taken first. It is a surface illustration. Perhaps this is the intended purpose of the "Behavioral Note" in the traditional report. Commonly, however, the difference is that, in the traditional report, it is difficult to present the clinical data at the appropriate level of interpretation and without repetition, and the guide for selection of information is too implicit and too hazy.

There is perhaps some culpability here with regard to language. This report has a rather technical section which talks directly to the psychiatrist in his language. It was felt he must have this diagnostic information. Perhaps we might rationalize by pointing out that such language is not diffused throughout the report and those not concerned with the issue under discussion may detour around it and still make sense of the report. The psychiatric terminology in the first paragraph is probably less defensible. Psychiatric terminology is a little better than psychological terminology, however, because it is more easily understood by the psychiatrist, and perhaps by some of the other team members.

Notice that this patient needs love and support, is insecure, and feels rejected. The use of Aunt Fanny stereotypy would have been easy here. Nevertheless, persons can be presented as individuals even though they have traits of widespread occurrence.

Case-focused Report 4

A psychological evaluation was requested on Mr. O because his need for hospitalization was questioned by his ward physician. The possibility of a deep disturbance was raised, since it was noted that this patient is a professional person, bright and alert, and without much surface evidence of distress or deviancy. He had complained of "nervousness."

Test Battery: Rorschach, TAT, Sacks Sentence Completions,
WAIS, Bender

Psychological Evaluation: The central and prominent theme of this man's life is belligerence and rebelliousness. This negativeness has contributed to turning his marriage into a stormy affair and his job into an arena of bitter dispute. Thus two of the most vital areas of his life, family and career, now are sources of heavy situational stress.

Although Mr. O is capable of dispensing rancor in many directions, the primary focus of discharge is against authority figures. The origin of this attitude seems to be in the early father-son relationship with the father being seen as unreasonable, not understanding, and overdemanding. In response to this situation the patient has become a great self-justifier and links his rebelliousness with a belief of almost pious self-righteousness. This is true even where his rebelliousness takes the form of flouting conventionality.

Mr. O feels very anxious and tense at times, sometimes unsuccessful and unhappy, not only because of the stress at home and work, but because of a basic conflict in his personal needs. Stemming from his early home life is an ambition for achievement and the need to be conforming, but an even deeper need causes him to secretly yearn for passivity and to wish to overthrow the values which are a part of him but which he does not want. Accordingly, merely fulfilling the role of a responsible male member of our society is a primary source of stress for him. If he could resolve the conflict one way or the other he would feel more comfortable.

His oppositional tendencies are a continuing source of guilt for him, and there is reason to suspect that he precipitates conflict with others so that they will retaliate, punish him and thus relieve some of the guilt. If so, this maneuver is not adequately successful for it does not sufficiently relieve deep doubts which he has about his personal adequacy. These are most readily observed in his need to present himself as a superior person.

This same type of compensating maneuver is seen in his marital infidelity. His basic sense of maleness is not strong, and he is unsure of his adequacy here, hence a need to demonstrate that he is a man. Such activity, of course, is also an expression of hostility against his wife and rebellion against his family standards. He probably would not have difficulty in justifying this kind of behavior. Thus, his pervasive negative feelings cause him to feel that others also feel obliquely toward him. He is on the defensive, feels abused, jealous and suspicious. It is very likely that at one level or another he is suspect of his wife's fidelity.

This is an intellectually bright person (his current IQ is 118) and he has a certain amount of appreciation of his difficulties. He recognizes that he is an openly hostile person and that this causes him trouble, but he also believes that he is "right." He therefore is not able to use his intelligence adequately in relating to others. It is easy to visualize his interpersonal conflicts as severe and ugly, since under stress he becomes impulsive, his judgment tends to give way seriously, and he cannot fairly see the other person's point of view.

Psychodiagnostically, this patient has all the earmarks of an anxiety neurosis that is precipitated or aggravated by a known stress. There are important paranoid trends, but the basic respect for reality is good and there are no disturbances of the thought processes. No psychotic process is seen.

The personality conflicts which this person has should be amenable to a degree of resolution through individual insight-giving therapy of a moderately deep level, but his stay at the hospital might not be long enough to permit adequate time to reach this objective. In the short run relief in the form of symptomatic tension reduction might be of value, but his adjustment can be nothing but poor on returning to his home and work environments.

It soon became apparent to the examining psychologist that this patient sought hospitalization in connection with a "personality" problem, and it was necessary to study his social stimulus value, and the underlying conflicts and adjustment processes on which this is based. An overview of the patient's (clinically pertinent) psychological self is therefore given in the first paragraph, the rest being elaboration. A formal diagnosis is part of the process of understanding the patient—that is, recognizing the extent of his anxiety and subjective stress. A diagnosis is also in keeping with the reason for referral since, as noted, the possibility of an underlying psychotic process had been entertained.

There is a fair amount of negative comment made about this patient— negative in the sense that society regards hostility as a bad thing, and much attention is focused on his hostility (more than in an Aunt Fanny shotgun report, when we say the patient is repressed, anxious, conflicted, insecure, hostile, and withdrawn, and we can't be too concerned with the observation that he is hostile). Is this a prosecuting attorney report? The report was prepared with a knowledge of the socially negative nature of this patient's personality, and it was felt that to understand him we must highlight this trait. The psychologist felt the description to be accurate and individualized. There was no hesitancy in talking about an inadequate sense of maleness in the patient, this seeming to be directly pertinent even though prosecuting attorney psychologists commonly impugn the maleness of their clients. The only way we can be sure whether or not a psychologist writes prosecuting attorney briefs, however, is to look at a number of his reports.

Case-focused Report 5

The two paragraphs that follow were written about a patient who found himself in a mental hospital, and, like a number of other patients, didn't feel he belonged there. He had been reporting to a community clinic with a regularity greater than the staff appreciated, complaining of various food aversions and a host of unlikely aches, pains, and other symptoms. Finally, it was suggested to him that he report to the hospital for examination. What ensued, i.e., his admission to the hospital, was not in keeping with his likes and expectations. The ward physician felt only that he had some very general questions, and asked the psychologist for whatever help he might be able to give in the way of a fuller understanding of the patient.

Test Battery: Rorschach, WAIS, Bender, Sacks Sentence Completions

Psychological Evaluation: This man stands out as something a little odd, "different," or eccentric. This is the manner of personal expression of a simple person, psychologically immature in that he limits his interactions with the world to those that are least demanding and most palatable. Grossly then, many facets of his behavior are childish. He remains essentially uninvolved in matters about him. Hence he is naive and ignorant of many things, including how others might react to him. His reasoning and judgment can be quite poor, sometimes impulsive, sometimes very unthinking, and commonly without sufficient self-criticalness. His thinking is concrete and "earthy," which suggests that what is described here as faulty mentation might be essentially tolerable in certain environments (such as in his home town rural setting). In other environments, however, he is readily misunderstood and might misunderstand others. In general, though, he can get along. He tends to be good-natured, somewhat fluid in emotional expression, and commonly a bit underinhibited, but there are probably no genuine disturbances of mood.

This description of Mr. P. is of course suggestive of a prominent hysteroid make-up (his somatic complaints and food aversions *could* be consistent with this observation), but the level of free anxiety and subjective discomfort is not excessive and he does appear capable of extramural adjustment where he can be maintained medically by a psychiatrist or perhaps by a general practitioner.

This report is very short as compared with other reports based on a full battery. There is no need for apology. The intention was to say everything that was known and pertinent about the circumstances of this person's hospitalization, to make a recommendation concerning disposition, if possible, and to follow all of this with a period. A WAIS was part of the battery, but there is no report of IQ, of scatter, or of verbal-performance score differential. Nevertheless, the WAIS definitely contributed to understanding in this case.

The psychologist had to be alert to the presence of possible psychological factors in the patient's complaints. There was suggestion that such exist, and these were communicated as a lead rather than as a diagnostic statement.

Case-focused Report 6

Mr. Q drinks too much. He periodically finds himself hospitalized as a result. The staff has seen other alcoholics, of course, but the question nevertheless arises, "What sort of person is this?" What can we do for him?

Test Battery: Rorschach, MMPI, TAT, WAIS, Sacks
Sentence Completions, Bender

Psychological Evaluation: This man's dominant orientation to life is characterized by a childlike passivity and dependency, with marked inadequacy in coping with the everyday stresses of life.

Mr. Q has never really gotten into the competitive stream of life, but, without full awareness that he is doing so, inwardly wishes to be taken care of. Superficially he subscribes to the belief that a man should be responsible and productive, but his passive needs are stronger and he can readily rationalize his shortcomings. Thus he can work for only a few months at a time, then becomes unhappy and "exhausted" and finds relief in drink. He sees himself as physically weak, not having recovered from illnesses while in service, namely malaria, jungle rash, and prickly heat. Similarly, he would like to get married for the dependency gratification this might offer (his dependency needs are much more insistent than his sexual needs), but has not sought out a mate because a girl friend married another man 20 years ago and he has not yet gotten over it.

Mr. Q's mode of adjustment is fairly adequate except where he is required to come to grips with life physically or mentally, to put out any form of sustained effort. This is so because of his passive needs, but also because of defects in his intellectual functioning. Though of average endowment, he is very naive about life and about himself, and he is unconcerned either with the world of real everyday living or with the poor quality of his own thinking which so easily makes it possible for him to deceive himself. Beyond this, he is remarkably unsure of himself and any external pressures to make him function responsibly would only lead to indecisiveness, tension, and no doubt drinking.

Psychodiagnostically, this patient would appear to be a case of alcoholism in association with a personality disorder. The latter is probably classifiable as Inadequate Personality, but a reliable social history (the patient is not regarded as a reliable source of information about himself), could help to establish whether this is correct. It is not felt that psychotherapy can provide any real benefits, but there is a possibility that he might be helped by associating actively with Alcoholics Anonymous.

The focus is on personality description as this might be explanatory of the behavior that leads to hospitalization. It was not felt that going into the patient's problem of orality, at a psychoanalytic level, would add to this objective. Certainly it did not seem that simply to mention that he is oral would do much for the man or for the staff.

Being unable to state a precise diagnosis is not to be regarded as a deficiency. Frequently other team members contribute to the psychologist's diagnostic impression. It can be unfortunate when the psychologist feels he has to state an impression without qualification. Most people respect honesty, and the psychologist ought not contribute to a false image of omniscience.

Case-focused Report 7

Mr. R had been acting oddly prior to admission to a hospital, and it was obvious that he was psychotic. The team felt, however, a need for a better understanding as to the nature of his condition. Sometimes he "looked pretty good." What is the outlook?

Test Battery: Rorschach, TAT, WAIS, Bender, DAP,
Sacks Sentence Completions

Psychological Evaluation: Mr. R makes a good superficial appearance, acquitting himself well in conversation, showing that he obviously is bright, alert and perceptive (his current IQ, somewhat depressed by his condition, is 116). But it is very easy to penetrate his psychotic thinking which shows that this is a very disturbed person mentally.

Mr. R's psychosis occurs in the context of a person whose most prominent basic traits are passivity and dependency, a high level of conscientiousness and dedication to moral values and principles. Underneath, though, are strong rebellious tendencies. Accordingly his current "wrongdoing," i.e., cohabitation, is felt by him to be extremely sinful and the ensuing impact of guilt is likely an immediate basis for his condition (it might very well develop otherwise too), and contributes to the particular delusions that he entertains. At the same time this patient would be benefited by the mothering care of a succorant woman older than himself. The relationship with his housekeeper is probably not an entirely negative matter psychologically.

Nevertheless, his current personality is of a primitive sort, characteristic of a much earlier period of mental and emotional development. He is, for example, to some extent preoccupied with eliminative processes. He is confused about himself, his experiences having often a feeling of strangeness and unrealness. His ability to discipline his thinking processes is now quite inferior, and he can believe just about anything he has a need to believe. He is comfortably able to overlook reality and to switch from one idea to another, perhaps contradictory, one. He has no awareness that he is ill. To be sure, his hearing of voices confuses him, but he is able to convince himself that there is a scientific explanation, that the phenomenon could be readily explained in terms of the effects of nuclear explosions, persons in outer space, or voices that come from previous generations buried in the earth.

As has already been intimated, his interest in his woman is more on a passive-dependent basis than due to firm heterosexual tensions. As a matter of fact there is suggestion of homoerotic impulses and his lack of integration between the moral principles he entertains and his immediate urges implies that he might live these out. More generally, his fuzzy and fluent thinking, which could be consistent with virtually any need for impulse expression, would seem to make possible various unpredictable and possible socially variant behaviors.

The content of his delusional thinking is most illuminating in pointing out the central role of guilt in his condition, and the extreme nature of the conflict he experiences. This is of cosmic scope and has a basis in concern with morality. The themes he entertains take the form of—and these are only illustrations—good and evil, beauty and ugliness, birth and creation, death and global, violent destruction, God, Devil, heaven, falling from heaven, damnation, salvation, eternal life, resurrection, forces from outer space, and a physical oneness with God. All misfortune is punishment for sin.

Psychologically, this is a classic picture of catatonic schizophrenia. Commonly such conditions remit, but his condition could continue in chronic form. Since his first acute break occurred some years ago, information on the previous course of his condition might be the best predictor of the future. It is possible that his condition may remit sufficiently so that he might continue to function in the presence of continuing delusions and perhaps even hallucinations. Psychologically, his continued association with his housekeeper might be beneficial (if her characteristics are truly as he describes them, and there are no elements in her make-up that could be harmful to him, such as, for example, a tendency to reject him or sexual demands that are at variance with his needs). If he marries his housekeeper, his continued association with her might lead to less of a feeling of sinfulness. One could hardly advise this, however!

This patient could easily have been presented so that he could not be differentiated from many other schizophrenics. One of the reasons for presenting him as an individual was to enable the staff to understand him better and have an understanding of the meaning that some strange ideas have for him.

Case-focused Report 8

Mr. S was on a medical ward. The internist felt there were indications of Wernicke's syndrome. Could the psychologist find information consistent with this impression? What is the outlook?

Test Battery: WAIS, Wechsler Memory Scale I, Bender

Psychological Evaluation: Mr. S gives clear-cut psychological indications of a brain syndrome. These are in the areas of learning and remembering new material (defect of recent memory), a severe concreteness of thinking which would make it most difficult for him to develop or utilize new ideas, and a pronounced difficulty in shifting from one idea or approach to another. His thinking is hazy and confused, partly because of his memory defect that has taken from him the sort of information he usually has available (for example, current events). Sometimes he has a tendency to try to fill in memory gaps in the apparent hope that he might be right (a mild degree of confabulation).

This condition has a severe impact upon the patient's personality. He has always been ambitious and conscientious and his loss causes in him a deep sense of failure and inadequacy. It also gives rise to a level of tension that seems to disorganize him and certainly, as he is at present, to unfit him for gainful activity. (In fact several times during testing when he found the work difficult he complained of a headache that quickly subsided when less difficult matter was presented—a possible illustration of the effects of tension [?]—and what was scheduled as a relatively short testing session was abbreviated because he seemed to become too tense to continue.)

The psychological course will probably follow closely his organic state. If he is suffering an acute state that will remit, he might recover some psychological function on its remission, and repeat psychological examination would be helpful to establish his efficiencies at that time. Should the organic condition not improve appreciably, his ability to adapt to the normal demands of living that characterized his previous existence will be poor and probably insufficient. As already indicated, he is ambitious, conscientious and of good intellectual endowment (WAIS full-scale IQ is 115, verbal IQ is 126, performance IQ is 97, Wechsler Memory Quotient is 92). As seen now, his drop in efficiency, and more seriously, the disorganizing effects of his tensions, are not at all favorable.

The impression was gained with a high degree of certainty that a brain syndrome was present. A psychological examination, of course, could never establish that the patient was in fact suffering with Wernicke's syndrome. Psychological evaluation cannot establish by name specific physiologic or anatomic conditions. By way of further exemplification of this principle, it was most likely that headache was produced in the patient by psychological stress, but it would not be advisable to do more than hint at this. It is just as inexpensive to type a question mark as a period or an exclamation point.

The diagnostic leads (of organicity) emerging from psychological examination were regarded as part of the evaluation goal, but the impact of organicity on functioning was seen as of greater importance. During examination, it became obvious that the personality functioning of the patient was severely impaired and needed to be explored more fully.

Case-focused Report 9

Mr. T has an unsavory police record. In his early forties, he has been arrested 30 times in the past 15 years for drunkenness and brawling. No doubt this figure would be much higher were he not incarcerated so much of the time. He presents an appearance rather contrary to what the layman might expect from one who spends so much time on the other side of the law. He was referred simply for a fuller understanding of his behavior, anything that would contribute to an understanding of why he is as he is.

Test Battery: Rorschach. MMPI, TAT, Bender,
Sacks Sentence Completions

Psychological Evaluation: Mr. T. prefers to believe, and would have others believe, that he has a "nervous" condition which is directly attributable to war service. He does in fact experience anxiety and tension—which is quite evident, for example, in a speech blockage that he refers to as stuttering—and he does have a tendency to feel quite unhappy at times. An examination of his thinking shows blocking of thought that may be seen in temporary defects in memory and temporary confusion in dealing with problems. These too are definite indications of tension, but Mr. T's primary difficulty is one of social maladjustment.

Mr. T is seen as an unusually self-centered person who feels markedly inadequate and insecure in meeting the requirements of living. He really does not try very hard to function up to the usual expectations that people have of others, and he certainly does not put himself out where sustained effort and perseverance are required. Rather, he leans very heavily on others for support to the extent that he has developed some rather effective techniques for getting such help. But this does not solve the basic problems which are responsible for his difficulties. In particular, negative feelings he has toward himself—the feeling that he is an inadequate person—and his need for support by others, as already mentioned, cause him readily to sense that he is being rejected. He reacts to this with markedly hateful feelings. Initially it was his parents who he felt were unreliable, rejecting, and making difficult demands on him, but now he tends to feel this way about people in general. In fact society itself now seems to be treating him as he felt he was treated as a child. This feeling of being "let down" by others and reacting to people with hateful urges is associated with inward feelings of guilt and unhappiness. He feels bitter toward the world, distrustful of people and suspicious of their motives.

Obviously then, this is a person who has never grown up psychologically and one of his major apparent difficulties is in relating to others. This inability to relate to people on a mature plane is seen quite clearly in the sexual area. The patient admits that he does not feel attracted by members of the opposite sex, but he does have need for a woman because of the things she can do for him. This is one of those men who might be regarded as marrying his mother, not a wife.

On the surface one observes a person with what would ordinarily be sufficient mental capacity to function quite effectively (IQ 106), but he has never adequately developed his intellectual resources any more than he has been able to mature psychologically as a person. He has a good understanding of what society expects from people, and he is alert and able to acquit himself well in nonstressful social contacts. But he is not the sort of person who spends much time thinking. He prefers to do things with his body, to move around physically, rather than think. He is an impulsive person whose rash behavior does not permit him to deal constructively with everyday matters. And he has a lack of mental discipline which permits him from time to time to be unrealistic in his thinking, to deal with events as if they were different from what exists in reality. He just chooses not to see the unpleasant truths of his existence. This permits him to deceive himself about his personal motives and behavior, and to some extent probably to deceive others too, at least temporarily.

Socially Mr. T is rather smooth, glib and ingratiating. He says the "right" things, sounding sincere and convincing. He readily volunteers that he has fallen short of even his own aspirations, but this is quickly explained as due to his childhood circumstances. Mr. T is quite proficient in behaving in such a way that others might become sympathetic and lend support. As a matter of fact, in the testing situation before the examiner had an opportunity to understand the patient more objectively, he (the examiner) was moved to ask, more out of personal curiosity than clinical curiosity, how it happens that a person like himself has such an unsavory police record. This surface behavior is regarded as a technique of relating to others, and probably also of exploiting them, but under stress or frustration this gives way and his more basic nature emerges. He is a person who must have things on his own terms. He cannot tolerate strains or tensions very long and he must live out his needs.

Often this takes the form, when he feels abused by others (possibly as a result of misunderstanding others because of his own negative attitudes), of striking back with violence. This tendency, along with his drinking, is probably an unfortunate combination socially.

Psychodiagnostic Impression: Antisocial Personality.

Notice how many traits Mr. T has in common with much of the rest of the population. He is of average intelligence, narcissistic, impulsive, dependent, anxious, depressed, insecure, a "latent homosexual," and hostile. Yet it is possible to understand all of these as they have meaning for the patient in the context of his individuality.

Notice also the participant-observer role of the psychologist. Part of the impression gained of the patient was through the effect he had on the examiner. This is not in keeping with the principles of laboratory work.

Case-focused Report 10

The next report, on a 65-year-old patient, was in response to what was received as a general referral. The patient had made a suicidal attempt some time after a cancerous growth was removed, the outlook for a recurrence being uncertain. The referral was general. Therefore, the psychologist approached the patient's physician for a better idea of the kind of psychological information needed. The physician indicated that he did not regard the patient as suicidal at the time, but wanted to know more about what precipitated the attempt, and what the psychologist thought of the diagnosis (might he have been psychotic or with psychotic tendencies?).

Test Battery: Rorschach, TAT, MMPI, WAIS, Wechsler Memory Scale I, Bender, Benton

Psychological Evaluation: This patient's typical mode of adjustment presents nothing far out of the ordinary. He is seen as a conventional, very compliant individual with high personal standards and group loyalties. He does not always live up to these aspirations, but when he doesn't, he is the worse for his conscience. He is very much concerned with rightness and wrongness and quickly feels guilty when he recognizes that he is wrong. This need to be correct also causes him to be somewhat defensive so that he has difficulties in admitting faults both to himself and to others.

Mr. U is essentially a well-endowed, intellectually capable person. His usual functioning was probably close to the superior level, but quite clearly he has suffered loss in this area (but his current IQ is still 111). He has "slowed down," tends to become confused in new or complex situations, his ability to learn and retain information is mildly impaired, and his reasoning may show some fuzziness. He intuitively senses this decline and is concerned about it— a possible contributing factor to the depression he has suffered. His intellectual difficulty might well be due to organic factors and therefore irreversible.

Currently there is a minor degree of depression that is probably not sufficient to formally classify him as having a significant current depressive neurosis. His belief that his depression was reactive to his awareness of a malignancy is entirely plausible. In addition, he indicates that it is likely that his continuing to

work during the Company strike and the abuse he took from fellow
employees was a factor. This too is likely since he is the sort of person who
would feel strong loyalty to established authority (the company) and would be
deeply conflicted by the role he took during the strike.

Psychodiagnostic Impression: Depressive neurosis (largely in remission),
organicity to be ruled out.

In addition to being concerned with the diagnosis, attention was directed to
the sort of person in whom a pathological reaction occurred (he could have
been described as an "obsessive-compulsive" individual, or at least as
"compulsive"). The highly pertinent situational factors that entered the picture,
definitely not "test findings," were made an essential part of the report.

The evaluation goal did not concern the man's intellectual level or efficiency,
but information of this sort, pertinent to the reason for referral, was discovered on
an intelligence test. Intellectual inefficiencies and possible organicity were
observed. Accordingly, the Wechsler Memory Scale and the Benton Memory test
were added to the original battery, with equivocal results. The information on
intellectual difficulties and possible organicity was then included in the
report, since such content might be related to factors in the patient's readjustment,
his ability to continue with his former employment, or to his prospects for
shifting to a new position.

Case-focused Report 11

Mr. V has been having multiple somatic complaints for which an organic basis
could not be established. The referring physician wanted to know simply what
the psychologist could contribute to the case. It was also a matter of concern
to the staff that he had indicated that his life was not worth living.

Test Battery: Rorschach, MMPI, WAIS, Sacks Sentence Completions, Bender

Psychological Evaluation: This is a grossly maladjusted, thoroughly unhappy
person whose dramatic solution to his difficulties is patently noneffective.
He is very much averse to aggressively interacting with life, seeking instead
comfort and care from others. When these are not directly forthcoming,
his behavior shows a demanding quality on the one hand and an attempt to
extract support through pity on the other. When these fail he is reduced
to a state where it is very difficult for him to function, the presence of this
condition itself being a demand for support.

This patient's solution has an unrealistic air about it, but formally appears
to fall short of a psychosis even though the potentiality for such a solution
may be present. There is an element of social withdrawal accompanied
by sulking and fantasy. Sometimes the latter suggests to him that what he
sees as rejection is cool and deliberate, and a product of the collaboration
of several persons.

Mr. V's condition is not of the nature of malingering. He has little understanding of himself or of his needs; he is in fact especially naive though of better than average intellectual endowment (current IQ: 112). His mode of living emphasizes his passive needs and attempts to gratify them which currently involve the exaggerated display of his helplessness. His lack of success is seen here in a spilling over of his maladjustment—with which he is not at all comfortable—into all areas of living. His family relations of course are very much damaged because his wife cannot "understand" his self-centeredness, and his intellectual efficiency is impaired to the point that his complaints of being unable to concentrate and to remember are true—though he grossly exaggerates them.

That such a person might fantasy suicide as a way out is understandable. Talk of this or the making of suicidal gestures, however, might be used primarily for its dramatic effects. This patient does not appear to ring true as a suicidal risk, but suicidal threats and attempts could be made to extract pity and support.

Psychodiagnostic Impression: Hysterical elements are most prominent here and hypochondriasis is most evident regardless of what is the objective state of his health. Even though some organic difficulty may be discovered, the condition is still compatible with several hysteriform reactions, including conversion.

The approach was first to sketch the highlights of this personality, and then if possible to relate these to the presenting problem. Hysterical features were found to be quite prominent. These could go a long way toward explaining the man's difficulty, but the psychologist cannot establish the basis of a physical complaint. Nevertheless, his comments suggesting the compatibility of the condition with psychological problems can be quite useful to the physician.

On the other hand, the psychologist, whose function includes the prediction of future behavior, can render an opinion on suicidal potentiality. He can be wrong, just as can any clinician, and an error can be far-reaching in its effects. Nevertheless, he has a basis for an opinion and the responsibility for his own conclusions. Were he to provide the referring physician with only the raw data on which an opinion is based, the latter would not be as adequately prepared for reaching an opinion as is the psychologist.

Case-focused Report 12

The next report is on a patient who is most interesting from a clinical point of view. He came to the attention of a psychiatrist after the police arrested him for exposure—a practice that had been going on constantly for some years. In interview with the psychiatrist he also indicated that he had started to choke several girls while having intercourse with them. He was apparently in "good contact" and was referred to the psychologist "for further evaluation." This procedure resulted in what the writer regards as a very long report, though it is no longer than many other reports that choke the file cabinets of clinics.

Test Battery: Rorschach, MMPI, TAT, WAIS, Bender, Projective Sentence Completions

Descriptive Data and Impressions: Mr. W appears more youthful than his age and gives a general appearance of immaturity that is particularly evident when he feels under tension. He seems to be a docile person who relates to the examiner in a passive and compliant manner except when he is reluctant to answer a direct question. At such times he hesitates, evidences tension, especially in the face, arms and hands, emits a somewhat gigglish laugh, and eventually responds. During the first contact he is often remarkably tense, but this decreases appreciably in subsequent interviews. He attributes this change to medication and to the fact that he has related many intimate thoughts to the examiner. Nevertheless, poor control over his behavior is observed in that he sometimes seems to find it necessary to "doodle" in a detached manner, while conversing, to put test materials in his mouth, and to leave his seat and walk about the office. At other times he appears to be quite free of tension. Though he usually has great difficulty in telling of his transgressions and his fantasies, often he relates in a bland manner the most bizarre plans for lurid crimes, highly offensive ideation centering about homicide and virtually unimaginable sadism, accounts of past assaultive behavior and unlawful sex conduct, and grandiose fantasies in which he aspires to destroying the world and being one of the most powerful figures in history.

Psychological Evaluation: The psychological protocol strongly and consistently is indicative of an active schizophrenic psychosis with relatively subtle but practically important paranoid and depressive elements. Superficial encounter with the patient might lead to underestimation of the seriousness of his psychopathology, but a thorough examination reveals severe deviancies, many of which are classically schizophrenic. On the surface he may show himself to be bright, alert, sensitive to others, and quick to understand social situations in which he finds himself. Formal intelligence testing, in fact, classifies him as of better than average cognitive ability— so-called "Bright Normal" intelligence—and is broadly suggestive that under optimal conditions his intellectual functioning could be considered as superior. Nevertheless, formal thought processes are now unsound and reality testing is poor. His reasoning is often primitive, unchecked by logical considerations. His thought content then is frequently bizarre, illogical, and saturated with ideas of magical significance. He misinterprets social stimuli, feeling attacked, "ganged up" upon, and talked about. Sometimes he is concerned with the possible presence of spies.

The question of whether this patient will live out any of his destructive impulses is an urgent one. It is to be noted in this regard that both his unusual ideation and his urges to act out are attended by severe ambivalence and conflict. These factors definitely tend to inhibit criminal conduct, but it appears that he is capable of periodically resolving his conflict and acting out. Thus he points out that concerning the matter of a currently dominant fantasy—committing murder and sadistic torture— " . . . now I don't care— I feel it has to happen anyway." Similar ideation is found in his test productions. It is also noted in the psychological examination that he appears to experience lapses of control or direction over his behavior, during such lapses it being entirely possible that he will follow unchecked his destructive urges.

By way of corroborating this observation, the patient reports that he had an automobile accident several years ago when "I saw the pole but didn't care if I hit it—I don't pay any attention to what I'm doing." Also, in this vein, "sometimes I'll be driving and go around the corner and not want to straighten out—just let the damned thing keep going."

It is instructive to attempt to link the dominant themes in this pathology to the patient's early understanding of reality, it being noted incidentally that the patient reports his first sexual deviancies occurred at the age of 8 or 9 when "sex seemed the main objective—masturbation—running around the woods in the nude," and overt homosexual experiences. Currently the major psychotic ideation centers about (1) mass destruction of the world brought about by the patient and the assumption of massive power brought about by the subjugation to him of the world's peoples, and (2) sexual acting out. The latter includes primarily ideas of killing women, torturing women, and exposing himself to women. All of these main ideas have numerous and changing specific variations. Homosexuality and transvestism (of which he reports one experience) also seem to fit into this complex.

It is the patient's impression that his upbringing was painfully strict and moralistic. The precepts of his church are associated with this upbringing. In the context of a rebellious attitude to such strictness he uses the church and religion as a means to try to keep in check his antisocial impulses. He reports that he prays extensively that he may keep these under control, attends church almost daily, and, in fact, was motivated to seek help by a clergyman who "ordered" him to "tell everything." The patient feels if he ever gives up church and prayer he will be another Hitler or Genghis Khan with the attendant release of sadistic impulses. On the other hand, the precepts of the church are used as a rationalization for justifying his feelings that he should kill women. Feeling that sex outside of marriage is evil, and that women are responsible for sex, he further reasons that the killing of women is therefore good.

The patient's early feelings are that he was rejected and that interpersonal relations were extremely poor. This seems especially true of women, whom he basically fears, although the reason for this is not evident, particularly since the findings are fairly clear that the father figure was experienced as more harsh and aggressive than the mother. Nevertheless, or perhaps because of this, he sought comfort and acceptance by females while at the same time withdrawing and resolving his conflicts in fantasy. The mother is idealized and (currently) divorced from sexuality. The patient knows she is in heaven, at least "she better be." It is also noted that the patient had longed in vain for a sister. It seems he now basically wants love and acceptance from women. He wants girls to hold him, cuddle him, feel sorry for him. His original idea in exposing himself was that the girls would feel sorry for him, that they would "understand." Later that act took on hostile significance for him, and, in general, it appears that his frustrated love promptings have given way to brutal hate. He thinks of women in terms like "dirt," and "bitch," and responds to a Sentence Completion item: "The kind of people I like most—are dead women." But these viciously destructive feelings are also accompanied by guilt and feelings of unworthiness—Sentence Completion item: "I am—a bastard—to say the least."

His orientation may best be described, in most general terms, as "sadomasochistic," and though contrary to his religious precepts, suicide is seen as a possible alternative to killing. Associated with many of his deviant practices are mixtures of ecstatic pleasure and pain. He is subject to the notion, probably usually a distortion, that people are making fun of him. Though this makes him angry enough to kill, he also enjoys it. He reports such dual experiences while exposing himself when he feels his victims are laughing at him.

The basic significance of the female is seen in a return to the womb fantasy that he experiences during intercourse. He wishes the girl to be his mother, "to crawl inside her, to be a baby again." He further indicates he feels this is a way of hiding from the world. In another context he indicates that the only time he feels safe is in church. This is interpreted as meaning safe from himself as well as from others.

Some Samples of Thought Content: Some samples of the patient's ideation are presented by way of making more meaningful the psychological evaluation. It will be noted that some of the statements tend to be contradictory, perhaps illustrating the conflicts and ambivalences he experiences.

"I can't adjust myself to the proper ideas. I feel sex relations are just not right—I have an urge to choke girls—not to kill them but to hurt them—make them scream and writhe. It's wrong but there is a certain enjoyment in it. I just started to choke one girl—we were kissing etc.—I wanted to go the limit but didn't have the strength in my hands—I couldn't get my hands to do what I wanted. The majority of times I get an erection when choking a girl. Sometimes I wish I would kill the girl, be arrested and then I wouldn't have to worry about it any more."

"When these things happen it's almost as if you're drunk. I feel light headed, giddiness, probably from getting so damned excited. Sometimes I masturbate after that and feel all pooped out and tired like I've been working a 24-hour shift."

"If girls didn't exist I wouldn't have sex desires. Maybe the girl represents all girls and that way eliminate 'em. I do it to girls the way they look at me—either they give a dirty look or act like they've had a lot of suffering in their life."

"I daydream of choking 'em—beatin' the heck out of 'em. I usually prefer to do it to girls 13, or 14 or 15—or older ones—35 or more. I want to make them afraid, cringe, beg for mercy."

"The hate starts building up and I try to expose myself. I think I'd rather grab her than expose, but this is the lesser of two evils. I don't really hurt her—I think it horrifies her."

"I prefer to expose myself to girls usually 15 or 16, but the old ones, I'd rather strangle them. I suddenly get the impulse to expose—hits me like a flash. I don't get satisfaction so much from exposure now. I prefer the strangling part."

"Sometimes when I'm hurting a girl I feel I'm hurting her father. Hurting him by hurting her. I think of taking a young girl, killing her, cutting her apart, put her head in a box and send it to her parents."

"I have hating periods, kill people periods. When I get mad I hear a voice yelling 'kill, kill, kill.' "

"When I get depressed I start hating women—just calling 'em 'bitch, bitch'—no reason it would seem."

"They always seem so smug to me—any girl—so superior—better than thou. They get everything in life. A fella has to work for a living—they get everything free."

"When you're going to start killing or start hurting it may as well be wholesale."

"Playing a cat and mouse game with the police appeals to me. I pray every day not to do it, but I feel myself sinking deeper into moods. Now I feel a lot calmer due to going to church."

"Every day I wonder if it'll be the real thing or just fantasy again."

"There's the me that wants to get rid of these thoughts and the me, that's the one I'm afraid of, that I'll do it."

"The last year I've decided it's gonna happen—so let it. I've given into it."

Additional Information: The patient indicates he spends a good deal of time contemplating where he will carry out his crimes. He says he is actively considering an abandoned factory in Midberg, but, then again, this might not be the place. Every time he goes walking he looks for an appropriate spot.

He also reports having selected two tentative victims and that "I'll take hours, beat 'em and torture 'em, just sit and look at 'em." One he identifies as about 17 years of age and as working in the restaurant where he eats. The other he refers to as "Jinx—she's in her twenties—she's from Sweden—beautiful accent on her." On the other hand, he assures the examiner ". . . it's not something I plan—I just see the girl and I say 'that's the girl.' "

Recommendations: Psychological findings do not permit any confident prognostic statements concerning a lasting change in ideation, impulse strength, and impulse control, particularly with regard to the less radical of the current therapeutic modalities. It might be anticipated that hospitalization and treatment will reduce tension and the need for the patient to disclose his ideation or to be entirely truthful about it. Currently he is regarded as very dangerous, particularly in the direction of homicidal and/or sadistic acting out, but suicide is seen as a possible alternative. A psychological reexamination prior to any contemplated discharge action is recommended. It was also noted that he currently does not appear to be capable of operating motor vehicles responsibly, and this factor would also have to be considered should he otherwise appear safe to discharge.

In evaluating the total case, it is to be noted that the patient is sometimes given to the use of alcohol which has an influence both on his ideation and on his impulse control. He therefore might be capable of acting out behavior in the community which he would seem less likely to engage in on the basis of observations within the hospital. Similarly, discontinuance of treatment, for example chemotherapy, on leaving the hospital might result in a decrease of some of the gains achieved during the period of hospitalization.

The length of the report was intentional, for the purpose of achieving effect in two ways. The psychologist had crucial information not available elsewhere, and felt that in addition to presenting "the facts" he had some persuading to do in the interest of meeting his responsibilities to the community and to the patient. This could be effected through the liberal, indeed overliberal, use of persuasive content, especially the lurid quotes of the patient. The length of this report also stands in sharp contrast to the writer's usual reports. The hope was that this contrast would alert the reader that this report is "something special."

Concerning the anatomy of the report, there is a section on "Descriptive Data and Impressions" similar to that found in traditional reports. With the emphasis on persuasion, this section attempts to capture as much as possible of the "flavor" of the patient. Again the reader is being alerted to "something special." He is told at the start that there is something about this patient not to be found elsewhere in the clinical record.

The evaluation starts with a statement of diagnosis, although typically the writer underemphasizes this matter. The concern again is with effect. Whether true or not, a schizophrenic with the tendencies described probably would be regarded as more dangerous than a nonschizophrenic with similar tendencies. To reinforce this, the features of the patient that may contribute to a favorable impression (nurses reported him to be the "nicest" patient—including one nurse about whom he entertained vivid choking fantasies) were contrasted with serious behavior trends that were regarded as more significant. Because it occasionally may be necessary to present a sharply negative picture of a patient—as done here—it is well to avoid developing the prosecuting attorney stereotype with most cases. One can cry "Wolf!" too often.

That this is a very practically oriented report is quite obvious; the psychologist's feeling of responsibility should also be apparent. The report influenced the staff to hospitalize this patient for an extended period of treatment and observation. The story of this patient is continued in the next psychological report.

Case-focused Report 13

After a period of treatment, including individual and group psychotherapy, it was the impression of the staff that the patient seemed more cheerful, less troubled, more spontaneous in his relationship. His therapist indicated that the patient no longer had his earlier preoccupations, and his conversation indicated a more constructive attitude and realistic planning for the future. In particular, his bothersome destructive urges no longer seemed present and he hoped they would not recur. Accordingly, the team asked for a psychological reevaluation per the psychologist's earlier recommendation.

Test Battery: Rorschach, MMPI, TAT, WAIS, Bender, Projective Sentence Completions

Psychological Reevaluation: A comparison of the current psychological evaluation with the patient's original examination on March 1, 19— shows some very real, even dramatic changes that are of significance in view of the previous impression that the patient was a threat to the community. The change is obvious on the surface where he is much less tense than noted previously, and in his concerns as reflected in his conversation. To be sure, he still has severe sex conflicts which augur ill for a favorable adjustment in this area, and he is still troubled by thoughts about sex. But he is not now obsessed by sexual and hateful ideas. There has, in fact, been a sharp general decrease in all of the previously noted areas of psychopathology—paranoid ideation, psychotic thought disorganization, depressive trends and pressures for acting out, as well as in sexual and destructive obsessions. Psychologically he now shows very minimal or residual psychotic involvement in the form of deviances in his thinking—possibly an optimal level of functioning for him. Clinically he might give no specific indications of psychosis other than that he is somewhat "different," tends to be shy and withdrawn, and to show forced emotional expression.

On initial examination the patient evidenced a consciousness overwhelmed by previously unconscious material. He felt involved in a primitive struggle for existence in a world that was populated with hostile and evil persons. This and primitive sexual ideation including maternal incest wishes and conscious return to the womb fantasies existed side by side with hypermoral, hyperreligious strivings and overwhelming raw hatred. His thinking centered about concepts usually not prominent in everyday living—sin, God, heaven, universe, birth, death, love, mass destruction, and grandiose personal power. Such ideation now is almost entirely absent and with this change has come a decrease in turbulence and tenseness, and the reinstitution of effective control over his behavior. He is now much more oriented toward "real" matters and his attitude to others is more benign, cynicism, for example, replacing his attitude of unbridled hatred to women. He does not feel so threatened or afraid of others, that he is being belittled or laughed at, and he does not have—as he once put it—the need to "retaliate."

Recommendations: The patient is not regarded as dangerous *at this time* and the psychological findings are such as to favor ground privileges and a planned return to his community. The future, especially the long-range future, is of course not predictable and a return to a psychotic adjustment and its attendant hazards remains at least a possibility. For the time being it is suggested that it would be well to plan for the patient's return to the community, but with continuing therapy and surveillance. It is also urged that prior to leaving the hospital the patient be referred to the Counseling Psychologist for appraisal and necessary counseling in the vocational and/or educational areas. The patient volunteers the need for such help and it is felt that employment which is sufficiently challenging and satisfying to him might help in the maintenance of a satisfactory adjustment status.

Again responsibility is thrust in the psychologist's lap, and he has to accept it. As with the previous report, the psychological conclusions are his, whether they are right or wrong. Of course, for each consultation on this patient the psychologist availed himself of the opinions of colleagues. Although he has the responsibility for his own report, he can, and sometimes should, get help in reaching decisions.

A report based on a reevaluation should concentrate only on the pertinent topics that need to be compared. Were the psychologist to present his usual report, the possible changes thought to be of interest might easily be lost in what is less pertinent. The case-focused approach is especially important when a report is to be compared with an earlier evaluation. When a report deals in generalities, it is hard to know what is really important, or where its full significance lies. If two reports contain the same generalities, particularly when they are written about the same individual, the problem of comparison becomes difficult indeed.

Case-focused reports 14 and 15 are reproduced with the permission of Dr. Donald N. Bersoff.

Case-focused Report 14

The boy described below was almost 17 years old when he was referred by the school guidance counselor because he was making repeated, almost continual visits to the nurse's office for vague complaints that were never substantiated. The school was interested in knowing how disturbed he was emotionally and what could be done to help him (and most likely, to help the school nurse rid herself of a disturbing child although that was not given as the major reason for referral).

Richard was administered the Wechsler Adult Intelligence Scale, the Minnesota Multiphasic Inventory, and the Rorschach Psychodiagnostic Test. Richard's mother was also seen, with her son, for a brief interview. (In addition, a long telephone conversation was held with the school counselor.)

Richard is an essentially normal boy with little evidence of overt, serious emotional difficulty. He does have a tendency, however, to exaggerate minor problems and embellish their significance. He then proceeds to brood, ruminate, feel all sorts of catastrophic events are about to occur and will consequently react to the perceived problem rather than to the problem as it is in reality. As his major modes of responding to problems in living are to escape rather than confront them, and to act quickly with only moderate forethought rather than to unemotionally weigh alternatives, he wants to find a workable expedient that will aid him in his escape.

He finds school aversive for several reasons: He is compared in his athletic endeavors unfavorably to his more adept brother; he is forced to comply to schedules; he is infinitely more interested in nonacademic activities and school time prevents him from engaging in those activities when he wants to; and finally, because he has little patience to work through or think through a difficult but manageable problem, he must then find a way to escape from this aversive stimulus. This he has done by, initially, finding his parents and the school infirmary vulnerable to somatic complaints. Thus, reinforced by sympathetic understanding and excuses from class, he has found the hypochondriacal route quite appropriate to his ends.

However, this behavior is quite amendable to extinction, both at home and in school. He simply needs to be refused treatment and classroom excuses (after a brief examination in case of genuine physical illness) and his "nurse-seeing" behavior will stop. There is no reason to be inhibited in doing so. As indicated earlier, he is not suffering from any severe emotional illness; he is neither psychotic nor neurotic, and most of his outpourings of grief are a histrionic display, easily eliminated. He is an intelligent boy (Full Scale

IQ Score is 113—"Bright Normal" and better than 80% of the adolescents his age) and he has merely used his intelligence to find a convenient and feasible means for avoiding frustrating and challenging work. He might fuss and fume about this refusal because he does feel victimized and picked on, a sort of hapless victim of adult irrationality, but he also has a deep well of humor and is smart enough to give up when he understands that he cannot avoid limits being set. One final note of caution: he is also bright enough to try something else.

Case-focused Report 15

This boy was referred by the family physician although a copy of the report was sent to his school. He was referred because he exhibited all the behaviors associated with those children typically labeled as "neurologically handicapped," and the doctor wanted to know if there were any psychological indications of brain damage. The boy was in the first grade and about six and one-half years old when seen.

David was administered the Stanford-Binet Intelligence Scale, Children's Apperception Test, Thematic Apperception Test, Bender Motor-Gestalt Test, Rorschach Psychodiagnostic Test and Figure Drawings. Both parents were interviewed and a telephone conversation was held with the doctor.

David is an imaginative, talkative, active boy of high intelligence with no overt evidence of brain injury. His measured intelligence on the Stanford-Binet is 126, which places him in the "Superior" range of intellectual ability, ranking him better than 90% of the children his age. He is able to perform tasks expected of the average seven, eight, nine, and even ten year old. It is not until he is given problems appropriate for an average eleven year old that he shows consistent failure. His vocabulary, the best single indicator of intelligence and academic success, is equivalent to that of a bright eight year old.

His intellectual capacity, however, is not matched by his emotional maturity. When frustrated or overstimulated he is very likely to become hyperactive, impulsive, disorganized, and infantile. He is an intense child whose impishness can easily turn to annoying and seemingly negativistic behavior.

It appears as if general family relationships are good, but he tends to see his mother as more restrictive and punitive than his father. But, while he sees his father as protective and concerned, David is moderately angry about the fact that he is gone a great deal. At one point he responded to a picture of a little boy looking at a violin and said, "The boy isn't very happy. His Daddy won't fix his banjo because he doesn't have time." When the examiner asked what the little boy's father does for a living David responded, "he fixes cars" (his real father's occupation). He also has been affected, more than most children by the birth of his next youngest sibling. The usual feelings of displacement and "being left out in the cold" seem to be heightened in David.

While the syndrome of hyperactivity, impulsivity, low frustration tolerance, and irritability are classically seen in the so-called hyperkinetic child and is usually associated with intracranial damage, demonstrable brain damage does not seem to be the etiological agent in this case. His visual-motor functioning is good and at least average for his age. Any deficiencies are not due to perceptual or motor disturbances but are attributable to his difficulty in sitting still or attending to many stimuli at one time. When stimulation is reduced (for instance, presenting one card at a time to copy on separate pieces of paper rather than having 8 or 9 copied all on one sheet) his performance is more controlled, accurate, and commensurate with his intellectual level. Thus, he cannot be expected, despite his high intelligence, to consistently react and behave like the average six or seven year old. It may be that high expectations both at home and school, demands made that he was physiologically incapable of fulfilling, and attempts at restraint that were doomed to failure, all served to increase his frustration and irritability beyond his control to the point where he has begun to be viewed in such negative terms as destructive, vicious, and uncontrollable.

He is controllable and will respond to discipline if a comprehensive management regimen is begun. His parents could use brief counseling of an educative nature, during which ways of reacting to him and ways of controlling his behavior can be detailed. He can be imaginative, clever, and a highly effective child both at home and school, and proper management and perception of his problem will be helpful in securing this goal.

The language in the fifth paragraph is technical, directed as it is to the referring physician. Dr. Bersoff indicates that he would have written this paragraph differently if the referral had come from a teacher.

Here are additional reports to illustrate the variety of problems and settings to which the concept of case-focusing is applicable.

The following report on a disturbed ten-year-old boy illustrates the importance that cultural factors can have. The impact of family instability and cultural shock on this boy's mental health is great. There is no permanent father in the home, the mother speaks only Spanish, and the next two older brothers are themselves quite disturbed according to reports.

Concern with such factors has become of increasing importance as we work with victims of poverty, inner city people, and, in general, those who are not in the cultural mainstream or whose lot is to be at the bottom of the social totem pole.

The first paragraph gives the child's background and something of importance in his living situation which defines the psychologist's mission: What is the problem or problems, and what can be done to help? The writer speculates early on the possibility of epilepsy, since checking for organicity with psychological instruments and otherwise is defined as part of the mission. "Clinical behavior," treated in the second paragraph, covers only material relevant to presenting a useful picture when integrated with interpretive material. From the paragraph one gets considerable feeling for why the child does poorly in school and presents a number of problem behaviors.

Case-focused Report 16

Jesus was referred for psychological evaluation after a protracted period of acting out at school and at home. He was accompanied to the interview by his mother and a male companion who acted as a translator for Mrs. R. Mrs. R, who speaks no English, related that Jesus has always had difficulty in school, both here and previously in New York, that he frequently gets into fights and has been a difficult child all along. She was obviously out of resources as to how to cope with her son's behavior, and referred to him, in the child's presence, as a "crazy boy." She reported that Jesus has had several head injuries in Puerto Rico when he was much younger. She noted that at times Jesus either plays dead or is in fact unconscious. It was difficult to determine what she meant, acting through an interpreter. However, she revives him from this state by rubbing alcohol over his body. There is at least a possibility that these episodes may be epileptic seizures. In speaking with the school psychologist and reading an extensive behavioral report from the school it is apparent that Jesus' behavior at school is both disruptive and unpredictable.

Jesus achieved a Full Scale IQ of 80 on the WISC. However, I must point out that I feel his intelligence is higher than this, probably in the low normal range. The reason for his poor showing was a general lack of interest. At times Jesus seemed to just lose focus on the material presented to him. At times he would work diligently and productively and at other times he would simply sit and look at the material. Although there were no distinct signs of minimal brain dysfunction, these lapses of attention might be related to petit mal seizures. On the other hand Jesus seems to be at times only marginally oriented in general and this may very well be functional rather than organic. He showed signs of loss of mental control, that is, difficulty in maintaining focus on a test through its completion. He was oriented as to place and person, but not very well oriented as to time. His behavior during the interview was appropriate and he showed no grossly inappropriate affect. He was rather quiet but cooperated in a distant sort of way. It was difficult to elicit spontaneity or laughter from Jesus.

There are findings of impulsivity with but tenuous control over behavior outbursts. There was some tendency to perseverate, that is, to apply a previous answer to a subsequent but different question. Jesus also has a tenuous hold on reality, and there is little doubt that at times he is out of contact with reality. He denies hallucinations or delusions although he is bothered by nightmares.

The following recommendations are in order: (1) an E.E.G. to help rule out the possibility of organic brain involvement; (2) therapy for the entire family and especially for Mrs. R, by a Spanish-speaking mental health worker who understands the social milieu in which this family lives; (3) psychotherapy for Jesus; (4) psychotropic medication should be considered for the purpose of helping Jesus maintain a better grasp on reality and to help him to control his impulsivity.

The diagnostic impression at this time is Schizophrenia, Childhood Type (D.S.M. 295.8). In spite of this diagnosis, I would like to point out that the majority of time Jesus is able to function adequately; it is the exception that mandates the diagnosis.

The following is a progress report written by the psychologist in charge of a remediation program. It is addressed to the parents who may become part of the treatment team, and who have a right to know what is being done for this child and how he is progressing.

Case-focused Report 17

We have worked with Jeff in three areas this year: visual memory, academic subjects, and behavior modification. Jeff's progress has been extremely slow and we feel his attitude has been the chief cause of this.

Jeff has reached a satisfactory level of ability in visual memory. We feel that no further work is required here.

We worked with Jeff in the following academic areas: reading, spelling, math, and library skills. In reading we started with a review of vowel sounds and after becoming sure of these, Jeff worked on blending and syllable division. He was placed in the beginning of the Merrill Reader, Book 2. Gradually his oral reading grew smoother and his comprehension improved. Often Jeff randomly guessed at a word by its context rather than trying to sound it out. Consequently Jeff has moved very slowly through Book 2 and still has not finished it. Another academic area we worked in was spelling. We used the same list which Jeff used in school. He had difficulty in reading the words on the list. We would study as much of the week's words as Jeff could handle. Occasionally he could tackle the whole list and at other times only one or two words. Again, Jeff would prefer to guess rather than make a calculated attempt at the correct answer. In math Jeff would count on his fingers when doing multiplication or addition and subtraction problems. This slowed his responses down considerably. We worked on his remembering the multiplication tables, but Jeff was able to remember only up to the "three times" tables out of order without using his fingers. In the area of library skills we covered alphabetical order along with puzzles involving library vocabulary.

During the year we needed an increasingly more structured behavior modification program for Jeff. Toward the end of the year we gave him chips for: good work, effort, listening to directions, and for the completion of a given task. We took chips away when Jeff was late, wasting time, guessing wildly, and for failure to complete a task. We also gave him time limits for each activity and he received chips when he came within the time limits. Jeff's teacher was able to use a similar approach in the form of a "weekly report." Jeff received checks from his teacher for copying down his assignments, for correct answers, for good behavior, and he received a bonus for a perfect paper. He received minuses for bad behavior. After he accumulated a certain number of checks he was allowed to do a job in the classroom he enjoyed. We found this to be the most effective approach in encouraging Jeff to apply himself more in a learning situation.

Conclusions and Recommendations

Overall Jeff has shown only a small amount of improvement. He no longer requires tutorial assistance for his learning disability. We are concerned over Jeff's being below grade level and avoidance behavior in a learning situation. Outside counseling might help him a great deal. We feel he should continue to seek remediation in school.

It is strongly recommended that a comprehensive behavior modification program be set up at home and at school. We would be happy to work this out with you and the school at your convenience.

Case-focused Report 18

Debbie is a twelve and a half-year-old girl from a broken home (father deserted six years ago and continues to upset the family by calling to complain to Debbie's mother about his present wife). Debbie is thought to be underachieving in school. Her teachers see her as an angry, troubled child. Debbie herself complains that schoolwork overwhelms her, tires her out. The following report seeks to achieve an understanding of Debbie as a basis for taking further action.

Debbie's intellectual status is above average. Her observations are accurate and there is originality of thought. She is an insecure child who has many fears. She fears the loss of her integrity, attack from others, and her own impulses. Debbie has a great need for acceptance and affection, but is inhibited by an overpowering fear of being rejected and hurt. There seems to be hostility directed to the mother. The relationship has not been mutually satisfying, often leaving Debbie frustrated. It is my impression that the mother's inconsistencies in handling the child may be a source of anger. Now she wants her own way and is conflicted about her dependency. Her attitudes to men are also unwholesome. They are seen as weak and mutilated. And she is confused about herself. She feels inadequate, and having a specific learning disability she requires more guidance and love than most children her age. However, not being able successfully to reach out to others has only left her more frustrated. Since Debbie finds it difficult to relate to people and because her own feelings are threatening to her, she withdraws to an immature fantasy world that provides little refuge. Even her fantasy is fearful, involving aggression and fear of being injured emotionally. Debbie is a very unhappy child.

The following two reports were written on the same child. The first is written for the clinic staff as a basis for advising the child's mother and the physician who referred the case. The reason for referral and pertinent history (his restlessness and distractability are considered along with current findings in making a diagnosis) are given, then the findings are disclosed, a diagnosis is made (a diagnosis that has direct implications for treatment), and a conclusion as to what must be done was offered. The scores are important. They are meaningful to those who work with minimal brain dysfunction children. The scores will be available at a later date should the child be retested, hence there is a basis for measuring change.

The letter to the physician spells out the meaning of the scores and completes the picture with a description of his behaviors and the diagnosis. The psychologist has reason to believe that this physician knows little about MBD and its treatment, hence tactfully suggests appropriate medication together with its physiological rationale.

Case-focused Report 19

Re: Henry Dennis

Henry Dennis, aged 9 years, 2 months, was evaluated at the Center.
Presenting problems were impulsivity, social problems, and poor school
functioning. From Henry I understand he was tested at school this past year.
A retest here on part of the WISC revealed Henry to have good average
intelligence. He was noted to have poor attention span, concentration and
memory. He was an extremely restless and distractible child. He has a history
of hearing problems related to a familial pattern.

The Frostig gave the following results:

Eye-hand coordination:	5 yrs - 3
Figure-ground	8 - 3
Form constancy	3 - 0
Position in space	5 - 6
Spatial relations	8 - 3

giving the basis for severe learning disability based on perceptual handicaps.
The Wide Range Achievement Test yielded the following findings:

Reading	Grade 1.9
Spelling	1.6
Arithmetic	2.6

There was no real association between sound and symbol in reading and
spelling. Arithmetic is weaker than the obtained rating. For practical purposes,
Henry has not really mastered the first stage of literacy. Even the personality
test (Rorschach) revealed severe figure-ground problems, inability to cope
with percepts and, in general, the primary finding was that associated with a
minimal brain dysfunction as the core basis of Henry's problems.

Our conclusion was that he will need special help to progress in school as
well as an awareness of these special problems on an emotional level in
order to keep Henry from becoming demoralized and so making worse his social
adjustment. Mrs. Dennis was also referred to her physician for further
consultation.

Case-focused Report 20

Re: Henry Dennis

Dear Dr. Prinz:

You referred Henry Dennis to us last winter for evaluation. Major complaints
were bedwetting, soiling, stealing, impulsivity and "does not listen."
Henry was seen in February and we had a family conference with mother
on April 10. The school's and our testing of Henry revealed him to be of good
average intelligence but with serious physical problems. From our history
the difficulties became remarkable at 3 years when Henry developed high
fevers, then a hearing disability. Concurrently he became over-active, difficult
to manage. Psychological studies here revealed Henry to be indeed a
hyperactive child, easily stimulated and perseverative. Attention span and

concentration were very poor; he was highly distractible by even tiny auditory
and visual stimuli. He seemed to lack the ability to differentiate figure-
ground not only in paper work but in general activity. He had no sense of
body orientation, which presented continuous confusions to him.
Tests revealed him to be four years below his expectancy in perceptual
functioning. School achievement was still at Grade 1 level instead of
Grade 3. The severity of his disabilities suggests a minimal brain dysfunction
which would account for much of his basic difficulties, including the
inefficiency of sphincter functions. Exacerbating these problems has been
very poor parental management, leading to even greater confusion and
disorganization.
   We have found that children such as Henry often benefit markedly from
medication (dexedrine or ritalin) by increasing efficiency of neurological
functioning. Parental guidance was offered by the Center but the mother did
not respond. The school is being alerted to Henry's academic disabilities
and to the need for special tutorial help.

Sincerely Yours,

_____

   The next two reports were written by rehabilitation counselors. They are both
very much action-oriented reports. The first records the problem, the steps
taken, and the tentative solution. A copy was sent to the mental hygiene clinic
that referred the client, and a copy was retained in the files for future reference.
The second report documents the counseling that was done and the implications of
assessment for rehabilitation training. It is beside the point for our purpose that
the counselor's advice may have been less than objective.

Case-focused Report 21

   Jeb was referred by the MHC where he has been under treatment for
depression for the past three months. Progress has been good and early discharge
from treatment is planned. The principal stress appears to have been his job,
which was low paying, unsatisfying, and a dead end. Other problems are denied,
and he reports that his marriage is good.
   The client is a high school graduate who had no aspirations to go on to
college. His premilitary work history consists of after-school clerking
in a neighborhood pharmacy during his junior and senior years. In the service
he did paper work in a base supply unit. He reports that he enjoyed this
work. His rank was E-6.
   Following service Jeb took a job as an inspector in the electronic component
factory where his father is employed. He has worked steadily at this job for
the past five years. In his first contact he indicated that he didn't know what
sort of work he wished to do. He was administered the Strong Vocational
Interest Blank, the MMPI and the Rorschach—primarily to assess the degree
of residual depression—and the WAIS to estimate his educational aptitude.
There is decided interest in the business area and salesmanship. Depression is
currently minimal as judged both clinically and by tests. Intelligence is in
the superior range.
   These results were shared with Jeb who concurred with my conclusions.

He recollected that he had enjoyed his work in the pharmacy while in high school, and also looks back with pleasure on a Junior Achievement project. In two additional sessions he focused on the sales area, with thoughts that he might like eventually to be a sales executive. I suggested that schooling might be desirable if he continues with this goal. He has eligibility under the G.I. Bill. He decided that he would like to enter the Springfield Community College next fall and work for an associate degree in salesmanship. His child will be in first grade then and his wife plans to take a job at that time so he can attend school full time.

In the meantime Jeb would like to gain some experience in the sales field. He feels ready to return to work. With his concurrence I called Ed Whaley at the Severin Company and arranged for Jeb to have an interview. Jeb phoned me this morning and told me that he has been hired to sell a line of automotive supplies.

We have scheduled a follow-up contact for November 5.

Case-focused Report 22

This man has been an active member of my group on the alcoholic ward and I have seen him four times in individual counseling.

From the beginning of individual counseling Gene maintained that he had always wanted to be an undertaker. I have never been a believer in the so-called theory that certain occupations tend to produce or cause a problem with alcoholism. However, the one occupation whose statistics would tend to have some validity to support this relationship is the undertaking profession. This was carefully pointed out to him several times during counseling.

Despite this, he maintained that this is his goal when he leaves the hospital. He further emphasized that at his age (39) this might be the last opportunity for him to ever fulfill his goal. I scheduled him for an interview with Mr. Harold Alston, our consultant from the state rehabilitation commission, concerning the possibilities for financial sponsorship. Mr. Alston was also skeptical and dubious about the practicability of such a rehabilitation objective for an alcoholic. After several interviews Gene maintained his steadfast and apparent sincere motivation to pursue his goal. Mr. Alston would not, at this point, approve enrollment in formal academic training, but did agree to sponsor an apprenticeship with a licensed undertaking firm. Gene, on his own initiative, has already contacted two undertakers who have indicated a willingness to hire him on this basis. Gene has an appointment with Mr. Alston next week concerning the administrative details and contract involved. Gene will contact the firms regarding financial arrangements.

Gene has worked for several undertakers in the past on a part-time basis and seems well versed and oriented as to what we might refer to as the horrors of such a job. He was given the General Aptitude Test Battery while at the hospital. His scores were well above the mean in all categories. He has the capacity to meet the study requirements for the profession he has selected.

CHAPTER EIGHT

Some New Departures in Psychological Report Writing

Changes in psychological report writing have come thick and fast, an aspect of the general ferment in the field. The advance of the behavioral and humanistic philosophies and methods has necessitated the development of a variety of report writing techniques to accommodate their unique perspectives. The availability of computer technology inevitably has led to automated reports—not only for the quantitative MMPI, but also for the complex Rorschach! Attention to economic realities and the need for rapid assessment and delivery of evaluative material has led to the development of quickie reports—not as elegant or comprehensive as the reports of the last chapter, but serviceable.

Looking back over the past several decades, we see much that is new in psychology and allied disciplines. There are new and modified theories, new techniques and new treatments, both psychological and medical, and new technology. We have also been alerted to the impact of cultural factors, particularly the role of deprivation.

While the basic need to understand people, to pinpoint problems, and to develop goals for the client remain, variations in how we intervene in people's lives have come about through necessity. The behavior therapies define for us the sort of pictures we must paint of clients. Working with people in the humanistic-existential dimension requires that we work with another set of concepts. In psychiatric settings, the new drugs that have become available since the 1950s require that there be more emphasis on formal diagnosis than was once justified. How else shall we know when an antidepressant might be helpful, when antipsychotic medication is called for, when an antianxiety agent is indicated, or when lithium carbonate is to be prescribed? This last decision, for example, is complicated because of the toxicity of the drug and the need for continual monitoring. The pharmacological properties of lithium also mandate *not* to prescribe it unless absolutely indicated.

With the widespread availability of computers, it was probably inevitable that the MMPI, an empirical instrument with scores, patterns, and rules for interpretation would lend itself to computer interpretation. Computer interpretation of the Rorschach, an instrument where an intuitive element in interpretation is often stressed, was perhaps less predictable.

BEHAVIORAL REPORTS

The following behavioral reports require little in the way of explanation. They follow behavior theory explicitly. There is a logical juxtaposition of problems and treatments. Behavioral reports are case-focused reports par excellence.

The first report was supplied by Dr. Marvin Goldfried.[1] Note the emphasis on understanding the client, on grasping him as a person, not merely as a skinful of symptoms to be treated.

Sample Intake Report

Name: BRIAN, James (fictitious name)   *Age:* 21   *Sex:* Male
Class: Junior   *Date of interview:* April 12, 19–

Behavior during interview and physical description

James is a long-haired young man, with a budding beard, who appeared for the intake interview with well-coordinated Stony Brook garb: dungarees, wide belt, open shirt, and sandals. He came across as being shy and soft-spoken, with occasional minor speech blocks. Although uneasy during most of the session, he nonetheless spoke freely and candidly.

Presenting problem

A. *Nature of problem:* Anxiety in public speaking situations, and other instances in which he is being evaluated by others.

---

[1] From *Clinical Behavior Therapy,* by Marvin R. Goldfried & Gerald C. Davison. Copyright © 1976 Holt, Rinehart & Winston, Publishers. Reprinted by permission of Holt, Rinehart & Winston, Publishers.

B. *Historical setting events:* James was born in France, and arrived in this country 7 years ago, at which time he experienced both a social and language problem. His social contact had been minimal until the time he entered college, at which time a socially aggressive friend of his helped him to break out of his shell. James describes his father as being an overly-critical and perfectionistic person, who would, on occasion, rip up his homework if it fell short of the mark. The client's mother is pictured as a controlling, overly affectionate person who was always showing concern about his welfare. His younger sister, who has always been a good student, was continually thrown up to James by his parents as being far better than he.

C. *Current situational determinants:* Interaction with his parents, examinations, family gatherings, participation in classes, initial social contacts.

D. *Dimensions of problem:* The client's social and evaluative anxiety are of long-standing, and occur in a wide variety of day-to-day situations.

D. *Consequences of problem:* His chronic level of anxiety has resulted in an ulcer operation at the age of 19. In addition, he has developed a skin rash on his hands and arms, which apparently has resulted from excessive perspiration. He reports that his nervousness at one time caused him to stutter, but this appears to be less of a problem in more recent years. His anxiety in examination situations has typically interfered with his ability to perform well.

Other problems

(A) *Assertiveness:* Although obviously a shy and timid individual, James said that lack of assertiveness is no longer a problem for him. At one time in the past, his friends would take advantage of him, but he claims that this is no longer the case. This should be followed up further, as it is unclear as to what he means by assertiveness.

(B) *Forgetfulness:* The client reports that he frequently misses appointments, misplaces items (e.g., frequently locking himself out of his room, and generally being absent-minded).

Personal Assets:

The client is fairly bright, and comes across as being a warm, friendly, and sensitive individual.

Targets for modification

Anxiety in evaluative situations, possibly unassertiveness, and forgetfulness.

Recommended treatment

It appears that relaxation training would be a good way to begin, especially in light of the client's high level of anxiety. Further assessment is needed to determine whether or not the treatment should move along the lines of systematic desensitization, rational-emotive therapy, and possibly role playing.

Motivation for treatment

High.

Prognosis

Very good.

Priority for treatment

High.

Other comments

On occasion, especially when going out on a date with a new girl, James would take half a sleeping pill to calm himself down. He wants to get away from this, and feels what he needs is to learn to cope with his anxieties by himself. It would appear that he will be very receptive to whatever treatment plan we finally decide on, especially if the emphasis is on self-control of anxiety.

Next is an out-of-context report prepared by Lazarus (1973).[2] In addition to the logic of approach, it is worth noting the various areas of subjective problems— indeed the subjective problems far outnumber the objective ones.

Modality	Problem	Proposed Treatment
Behavior	Inappropriate withdrawal responses	Assertive training
	Frequent crying	Nonreinforcement
	Unkempt appearance	Grooming instructions
	Excessive eating	Low calorie regimen
	Negative self-statements	Positive self-talk assignments
	Poor eye contact	Rehearsal techniques
	Mumbling of words with poor voice projection	Verbal projection exercises
	Avoidance of heterosexual situations	Reeducation and desensitization
Affect	Unable to express overt anger	Role playing
	Frequent anxiety	Relaxation training and reassurance
	Absence of enthusiasm and spontaneous joy	Positive imagery procedures
	Panic attacks (usually precipitated by criticism from authority figures)	Desensitization and assertive training
	Suicidal feelings	Time projection techniques
	Emptiness and aloneness	General relationship building
Sensation	Stomach spasms	Abdominal breathing and relaxing
	Out of touch with most sensual pleasures	Sensate focus method

[2] From "Multimodal Behavior Therapy: Treating the Basic Id" by Arnold A. Lazarus, *Journal of Nervous and Mental Disease*, 1973, *156*, 404-411. ©1973 by The Williams & Wilkins Co., Baltimore, and reproduced by permission of the author and publisher.

	Tension in jaw and neck	Differential relaxation
	Frequent lower back pains	Orthopedic exercises
	Inner tremors	Gendlin's focusing methods
Imagery	Distressing scenes of sister's funeral	Desensitization
	Mother's angry face shouting "You fool!"	Empty chair technique
	Performing fellatio on God	Blow up technique (implosion)
	Recurring dreams about airplane bombings	Eidetic imagery invoking feelings of being safe
Cognition	Irrational self-talk: "I am evil." "I must suffer." "Sex is dirty." "I am inferior."	Deliberate rational disputation and corrective self-talk
	Syllogistic reasoning, overgeneralization	Parsing of irrational sentences
	Sexual misinformation	Sexual education
Interpersonal relationships	Characterized by childlike dependence	Specific self-sufficiency assignments
	Easily exploited/submissive	Assertive training
	Overly suspicious	Exaggerated role taking
	Secondary gains from parental concern	Explain reinforcement principles to parents and try to enlist their help
	Manipulative tendencies	Training in direct and confrontative behaviors

The following two reports were contributed by Dr. Paul Lapuc. They follow the logical approach of Lazarus. Lapuc prepared these initial progress reports, to be updated and revised as treatment is initiated and carried out.

Henry J.   Diagnosis: Schizophrenia, Chronic Undifferentiated Type

This 37-year-old separated male was admitted in an intoxicated state. A review of his history and present condition has delineated several problem areas. These, together with proposed treatment plans, are as follows:

Problem #1: Excessive drinking, blackout spells, and associated physical acting out. Through self-admission and baseline data of a week's duration, it is ascertained that the patient drinks daily between 6 and 18, 12 oz. beers.

Proposed Treatment: A written contractual agreement limiting the number of days he will drink and expected behavior demonstrated upon return to the ward. Violation of contract will lead to restriction in p.j.'s for a period of one week.

Problem #2: Tremors of hand, other unpleasant physiological sensations that disturb him, i.e., the feeling that he can't breathe, headaches, insomnia, tightening sensations in the stomach and other muscular aches.

Proposed Treatment: Relaxation training and biofeedback.

Problem #3: Tearfulness. Occurs whenever he does not get his own way or begins to feel sorry for himself.

Proposed Treatment: Nonreinforcement.

Problem #4: Affective disorders marked by feelings of being ready to explode and then being unable to control his behavior. Feelings of anger. Depression, i.e., entertaining of suicidal thoughts.

Proposed Treatment: Time projection techniques, relaxation and desensitization.

Problem #5: Cognitive disorders marked by thoughts of not being able to do the right thing; inability to accept success; thoughts of letting his family down.

Proposed Treatment: Deliberate rational disputation and corrective self-talk.

Problem #6: Intuitive dysfunctions marked by auditory hallucinations, i.e., hearing father's voice "calling my name" and "I feel that people are out to get me."

Proposed Treatment: Psychodrama and/or role playing involving images of self; rational disputation.

Problem #7: Poor interpersonal relationships marked by dependency upon others to make decisions for him, exploitiveness, submissiveness, and manipulative tendencies.

Proposed Treatment: Specific self-sufficiency assignments; corrective training and training in direct and confrontative behaviors.

William S.   Diagnosis: Manic-Depressive Illness

This 29-year-old man was admitted to this hospital for the fifth time. In previous hospitalizations he has been diagnosed as manic-depressive and he is being maintained on lithium carbonate 0.300 gm. TID. Information gathered by interview with the patient and his wife indicate that he takes his medication faithfully; however, there are sexual problems which have not been resolved. His problems, together with proposed treatment plans, are as follows:

Problem #1: Demandingness and irresponsibility. The patient tends to maximize his own self-gratification needs and becomes agitated when he does not get his own way and immediate gratification. On the other hand, he does not take responsibility for his own actions and operates on the principle "I deserve to be served."

Proposed Treatment: Involvement in a written contractual agreement which spells out what responsibilities he is expected to undertake and the consequences, positive and negative, for either achieving these responsibilities or not achieving them.

Problem #2: Essential hypertension (average BP over one week: 196/130).

Proposed Treatment: Relaxation training and biofeedback training employing syphmostatic feedback.

Problem #3: Impulsiveness. Not only the need to be immediately gratified, but not *stopping and thinking* before talking or acting.

Proposed Treatment: Time-projection techniques.

Problem #4: Sexual incompatibility and inability to satisfy his wife, which leads to arguments and self-incrimination.

Proposed Treatment: Sex therapy utilizing Masters and Johnson technique.

Problem #5: Inability to win arguments, to effectively stand up for his own rights, to make decisions effectively.

Proposed Treatment: Assertion training.

HUMANISTIC REPORTS

The following report was written by Dr. Carl Silver. In the humanistic spectrum, it is illustrative of the *bioenergetic* approach (Carl Silver trained intensively with Alexander Lowen at the Institute for Bioenergetic Analysis.) The report documents the essential findings on the patient that form the basis for the therapeutic approach taken. Interestingly, then, this is a prescriptive approach—as in behavior therapy—in combination with a dynamic construct in a bioenergetic frame of reference. Another unique feature is the extent of teaching in the report. As a general principle such would not sit well with the report reader, but because bioenergetic dynamics and techniques are not yet widely known it is important, particularly for the patient's physician, to know how his patient is being treated and the rationale for the treatment.

Patient, age 51, has been afflicted with essential hypertension for 10 years. His blood pressure over this time has averaged 220/140. He has exhausted all available medical approaches, as evidenced by a lengthy history of treatment with experts in the field.

Drugs had lowered the pressure somewhat, but it remained well above normal, and, as an added problem, one drug in particular apparently rendered the patient impotent. His referral to me seemed a last resort.

Characterologically, the patient presents a picture that I find fairly typical for hypertensives I have seen: He has a high energy body and is extremely well-defended. He cannot say "no" to people. He is always a "nice guy." He always smiles and does his duty uncomplainingly although he is very critical of himself. At the same time he betrays a deep sadness, rage, and loneliness that he cannot reveal. In terms of his pathology, this adds up to a picture consisting of massive negative feelings and energy bottled up behind a mask of smiles and "O.K.-ness." This is very, very deep-seated in him. A good analogy might be that of an inflated balloon. The air pressure from within (the negativity) pushes out, and is resisted by the tough skin of the balloon (the good defenses) resulting in a turgid balloon— a balloon under great pressure. These people can always find logical sounding explanations to justify their self-righteous defenses, such as for example, the need to be responsible for a loved one: plausible, but tricky. They are, indeed, tricky psychologically and usually very bright people who can figure everything out. They also tend to be emotional or high strung as an outlet for some of the tension from the pressure described earlier.

The patient never had a psychotherapeutic experience before and we have done a lot of what might appear to be friendly relating. Our sessions have been warm, relaxed and rather nondirective. The patient views me as a friend in a professional context. We have done only a little bioenergetic work thus far, including lying down on a bed and kicking and going backwards over a special stool while breathing deeply. Since the third week of therapy, the patient reports consistent blood pressure readings of about 160/80, clearly in the normal range, and wants very much for therapy to continue and to deepen. Several behavioral and internal changes have been manifested: He has reestablished intimate contact with his 20-year-old son and has found it moving and fruitful. He has, on his own recognizance, gradually lessened his drug intake, observing a maintaining of blood pressure at 160/80 anyway. He is seriously considering a vacation long denied and is questioning his motives as regards denial in his personal life.

The patient is going through obvious changes, medically (or physically) as well as psychologically. He is getting in touch with his feelings in a setting that encourages this. He is unburdening himself slowly, and starting to say "no." He has apparently needed a warm, nonclinical, trusting environment to do so. Bioenergetics has played a major role diagnostically for the purpose of clearer recognition and understanding of the problems at hand immediately, just based on the physical body of the patient. It has been used effectively though minimally thus far, and will assume a larger role as a technique as the patient unfolds and becomes even more committed to experiencing his deep feelings.

CARL SILVER, Ph.D.
Consultant in BioEnergetic Analysis

The next report, furnished by Dr. Constance T. Fischer, illustrates a bold departure from traditional reporting. It is written from an orientation that conceives of psychology as a specifically human science (Fischer, 1973a), based in part on existential-phenomenological psychology. It eschews *scientistic* (defined in above paper) and medical model constructs (except in direct response to the referral question). The report was specifically developed so that it might be shared with the client (Fischer, 1970) and reflects his participation in the evaluation process (Fischer, 1971). A contextual approach—recognition that "Behaviors occur within particular *contexts*" (Fischer, 1973b)—avoids general statements and stereotypy.

Interestingly, clinical behavior plus liberal test data *are* included but do not merit the criticisms of these type of data made earlier in this book. This is because such material is integrated in the report, presented as particular instances of everyday behaviors.

The narrative is spun out in a disciplined, purposeful manner even while its style is relaxed and unpretentious. The report captures the flavor of the individual as he experiences himself and his world. Note that the unabashed use of *I* and *my* acknowledges the interpersonal character of assessment.

It decidedly has not been modish in psychological reports to include statements such as "I wish now I had also checked my impression. . ." and "For whatever its worth, I might point out a problem *I* might have. . .". Such remarks are intended to emphasize what the report writer regards as the necessarily perspectival, situated, unfinished character of a "finished" report.

Psychological Assessment: DARRELL F. HOLDERIN

Referral: Last January 24-year-old Darrell and his partner were arrested in New Jersey for collecting refunds on department store goods which they simply had picked up from the shelves. They collected $100 to $200 per day in this fashion for several months. Both young men were released on probation in March following a couple months in jail. Mr. and Mrs. Holderin are now seeking psychotherapy for their son in hopes that it will be of personal help to him and will preclude further lawbreaking.

Dr. Thomas Lefrac, the psychiatrist they contacted, has in turn requested a general psychological assessment prior to deciding whether to begin psychotherapy. He is particularly concerned with the possibility of schizoid functioning, especially as it might appear in the Rorschach, and with Darrell's intellectual assets.

Date of assessment: 5-6-74   *Date of report*: 5-12-74

Assessment opportunities: Extended interview, Bender-Gestalt, Wechsler Adult Intelligence Scale (partial), Rorschach, Thematic Apperception Test, human drawings, and mutual discussion of my impressions.

First appearance: Darrell showed up at my office precisely on time. He was dressed in a fashionable doublebreasted suit, wide silk tie, and silk shirt with cufflinks. He carried these well, and indeed struck me as youthfully handsome. After waiting for me to indicate where we were to go, he comfortably explained that he needed change for $10 in order to feed a parking meter. Secretaries, students, and I all scurried around looking for change as he stood by politely and nonchalantly. When he wrote a check for my services, he added the forty cents I had offered him.

Once into my office, Darrell continued to seem at ease. In a casual way he asked permission to smoke, suggested that the window be opened, and took off his jacket. Except when doing pencil work, he seemed bodily relaxed. Later, he smilingly mentioned that his idol is Alexander Mundy of the T.V. program "To Catch a Thief"—boyish in handsome appearance, a lady-killer, mod dresser with expensive entertainment tastes, sports car enthusiast, conman with class, and thief extraordinaire. Darrell remarked both that such aspirations were "unrealistic" *and* that he had thoroughly enjoyed approximating them during his recent misadventure.

Toward the end of our meeting, this suave appearance was thrown into relief as Darrell recounted his favorite horror stories, joked continuously, and drew cartoon figures complete with slapstick captions. He had also earnestly shared his educational ambitions and sought advice from me. Altogether I found him consistently easy to be with and to like—something in the manner of a teacher shaking her head but enjoying a charmingly problematic student.

Darrell as he sees himself: The following is a reconstruction of material that emerged both as Darrell formally presented his situation to me, and as we discussed my impression while going through the tests. Darrell himself is not prone to organize a full account. Also, much of the following material, while not surprising to Darrell, had not been formulated prior to our being together. Finally, all that emerged was in a context of Darrell's wishing to convince me that he has "learned [his] lesson," will "never break the law again," and is sorry that he "distressed [his] parents." In addition, he was under the impression for the first hour that my task was to determine whether he should be placed in a psychiatric hospital (a possibility suggested by his parents, he said).

As mentioned, the Alexander Mundy project is a powerful and often successful one for Darrell. When he has the money, he dresses well and wines and dines well. He even owns a sports car of sorts (a Karman Ghia). And like Mundy, he has only a few male friends, but is highly successful in having his way with women. Although he would "go to pieces" if he saw a girl cry because he had hurt her, he usually lies to get what he wants and sees nothing wrong with doing so. Girls are all phony anyway, except one whom he met since being released from jail. Darrell finds he can't put on airs with her and doesn't want to. She's honest and really likes him. She even invited him to come with her and her parents to Atlantic City—"nobody ever did that for me before!" But he won't get married for at least three years, until he's sure that his criminal conviction (which she doesn't know about yet) would not hurt either of them.

Back to the Mundy style. Even in grade school Darrell was often regarded as some sort of trouble maker who wasn't properly fulfilling his potential. Darrell wouldn't tell much about these years, but he did talk about a haunting memory of a woman principal chastising him about what was going to become of him. He was quite upset when he read a few years ago about her death. But mostly Darrell focuses on his triumphs. For example, he talks his way into job after job easily, and once was able to get an extended leave of absence by making up an intricate tale about having to go to the Mayo Clinic for critical surgery. And, not caring for the "hurry up and wait" routine of military service, and missing his friends and old life, Darrell waited out the requisite six months before applying for a psychiatric discharge that would formally be an honorable discharge. He feels he really put one over on the doctor, who wrote that Darrell was prone to "impulsive outbursts." Darrell acknowledges pride in these behaviors as well as in his recent thievery—if it weren't for his partner, they would never have been caught. But he emphasizes that he doesn't want anyone else to know about his lawbreaking, and he feels it would be stupid to run the risk of again doing something that he might get caught at. He also suspects that what he did was somewhat immature—an abhorrent thought.

Darrell's worries about himself are mostly about circumstances that have happened to him. He resents impressing people as looking only 19 years old, and wishes he could put about fifty pounds on his "slight build." He also wishes his father (a heavy six-footer) would understand him, and not nag him so much, and that his parents would give him more freedom and respect befitting his age. He gave some consideration to what I thought might be worries for him, but apparently had not previously focused on them as such. For example, he fleetingly acknowledged becoming depressed. At such times he hears the principal's words again and again, and sees the day's events replaying. But at these times, he tries to "get [himself] out of the depression" by leaving the house to find someone to do things with—in short, by avoiding reflecting or dwelling in feelings. Indeed, Darrell doesn't think about himself very much at all. Nor does he experience his body very often, except as something on which to show off his clothes, and as sexually excitable. Finally, in response to my puzzlement about his mother's absence in our discussions, Darrell insisted that she's just a good mother. He never mentioned that he had been adopted (neither did I, since I had forgotten that Dr. Lefrac had mentioned this).

His plans are to continue living at home (which he has always done except for eight months in the service and several months prior to being arrested) until he is sure that this time he is leaving his parents with mutual good will. In the meantime he is working for his father in the latter's grocery store. Darrell genuinely admires him for having made a success of the business, but is himself rather bored with it. He earns his father's rebukes for being careless and daydreaming on the job. Nevertheless, following the arrest his father talks with him more, and Darrell is considering going into food promotion work with him. He also wants to go to night school to complete about three more years for a college degree. And he hopes to be a writer, for fun if not for profit.

Darrell through the tests: Darrell plunged right into whatever I asked of him, with the effect of partially masking what I took from his frequent sidewise glances at me as discomfort and uncertainty about his ability. When asked to copy the *Bender* designs, he did so in about half the usual time. He started out carefully counting dots, asking for instructions, and so on, but wound up with the wrong number going in the wrong direction. As he noted my acceptance, he simply frowned at his mistakes and let them go. Not having planned ahead, he also ran out of space. When I mentioned these things to him and asked if they were similar to other events in his life, Darrell readily and amusedly agreed. Examples were getting arrested, not being further ahead in life at his age, and impatience with all his forms of employment (copyboy to clothes salesman).

On the *WAIS* Information section, I noticed Darrell's rapid way of speaking— sort of nonstop, in this case with all kinds of qualifiers, protestations, quick approximations, and requests for feedback. Here, he earned an average score. He acknowledged that this style is typical when a task is not intrinsically interesting and/or when it leaves no room for him to make up his own answers. "I was never any good at math, chemistry, and languages." And sure enough, when asked to repeat a series of digits, Darrell failed to score beyond average; he tried to memorize the digits, but often blurted them out, seemingly hoping that they would fall into place. We agreed that he behaves in a similar fashion while working for his father. Moreover that situation becomes exaggerated when Darrell responds to his father's chidings with even more carelessness.

However, on a subtest asking for reasons behind social practices and interpretations of proverbs, Darrell barely missed a maximum score. Here, he either gave a rote-learned conventional answer or carefully worked out a generalization from his rather striking knowledge of history and from his personal life. Given these variances, Darrell falls in the upper 10-15% of his age group in overall score.

We agreed that his preference for going to school part-time might be a practical one since he has in the past been able to cope with only limited amounts of imposed requirements when the work is not personally interesting. My guess is that he might have some success with writing if he directs his sense of humor, drama, and adventure to science fiction and crime suspense stores. But I really don't have evidence of how creative he might be. At any rate, "verbal facility" and "intelligence" don't seem to be psychotherapeutic issues.

For the most part, Darrell raced through the *Rorschach*, giving rapid responses and elaborations, turning the cards, and stopping abruptly with about three responses to each card. Most of the percepts involved motion, e.g., "scorpions fighting, people dancing at a costume party, men racing to dance with this girl. Keystone cops—'I'm going first; no, I'm going first,' fighting a duel, violent fight, two roadrunners colliding—'beep-beep', atomic bomb explosion, flying dinosaurs." In addition, these percepts were laced with enthusiastic rehashings of T.V. horror stores, movies, and science fiction stories. When I suggested that maybe Darrell is action-oriented, he readily agreed and gave more examples of having acted without thinking. Among these were what he called "instinctive" hitting back when physically pushed around. He denied other combativeness. When I pointed out that much of the Rorschach action seemed to be competitive, he saw no relation to his life, instead asserting that, for example, he doesn't have to compete because he's usually the first choice of the girls he wants. Nevertheless, I have a sense of his struggling in a vague way to be first in order not to be somehow put down— or squashed down.

Much to my surprise, when I reminded him of "cartoon balloons signifying anger," and "dark clouds," as well as some of the above items, Darrell immediately responded to my remark that people who can imagine such things often feel depressed. It was his first and only open acknowledgement that he suffers in any concerned way. It was then he told me about the school principal. In the same vein, although there are some playful responses ("beep-beep," etc.), there are no joyful or aesthetic percepts despite my freewheeling Rorschach style which usually nets a few such items.

Finally, another theme reemerged through the Rorschach, namely the Mundy concern with class and wealth: "movie star—two maitre d's waiting on her at a swanky, stuffy restaurant," and "a very expensive seafood dinner." While Darrell proudly acknowledges his keen interest in the nicer material things in life, he couldn't conceive of having personal desires to be taken care of or some related thing. Nevertheless, here and in other areas I often felt that my words were "missing the boat," but that their direction was true. Darrell, for example, stumbled around but failed to explain why at 24 years he was still living at home despite his professed independence and sexual activities (which, he says incidentally, that he is proud of but doesn't brag about).

Despite the rapidity of his responses, many of them were organized into full stories, again indicating that he can "come through" when given room to personalize the task. Similarly, although his initial responses were sometimes mutually contradictory, Darrell openly played with them until they were resolved.

Moving on to the *TAT* stories, I remarked to Darrell that his stories (again rapidly given) were usually straight adaptations of T.V. stories, novels, and movies. He denied that he watches these much anymore, and couldn't "go" with my observation that there were no real people, no involvements in the present, little interpersonal warmth. But he did reiterate that he has never had many friends and that girls are phony. With that, to the blank card he made up a picture of Annette (his new girl friend, 18 years old) and himself on a picnic in a beautiful meadow, just being alone together listening to music, and looking at the mountains. "Sounds childish, but I enjoy doing it."

Finally, when asked to *draw a person*, Darrell drew modified stick figures. The shapeless woman was wearing a "leopard skin dress—don't want to get in trouble with the censors." She was drawn reaching for the Garden of Eden apple, with cartoon captions, arrows, etc. When I asked Darrell how he would have liked to have drawn the man, he answered "like Alexander Mundy" (of course!), "or a caveman dragging a woman off." It was here that we got into a discussion about Darrell's dissatisfaction with his weight and youthful appearance. I wish now that I had also checked my impression that Darrell's social (including sex) life is lived out in an early adolescent attitude. An example is his joke about not having any nightmares except those in which he missed a date with Raquel Welsh.

Conclusion: In answer to the referral question, there is no evidence of autistic thinking. Although there is a general dysocial picture, it is definitely not of schizoid proportions. Moreover, Darrell has begun to let himself form closer relationships with at least Annette and his father, tentative as these may be. And under nonconfrontational circumstances, such as moments in our assessment session, he has been able to own and explore certain affects. Thus although there were certain similarities to "schizoid functioning." he can be viewed more productively as living an extended adolescence. I suspect that therapy would have to encourage him through some developmental sequences as well as current difficulties. As I see it, he could thus become more intimate with and sensitive to other persons.

He regularly experiences himself as momentarily depressed, but usually resolves this state as well as other problems by leaping into action. Although Darrell is adequately verbal and I.Q.-bright for psychotherapy, he is not a reflective or introspective fellow, which may be a limitation for psychotherapy (?). In addition, he admits that although he wouldn't mind seeing a psychiatrist, it's mostly his parents' idea, and besides he's "sure" he won't get in trouble again.

On the other hand, his jail experience seems to have shaken him into examining his life and being relatively open to new possibilities. A close, extended relationship with an understanding man may be an ideal step in what is probably a critical "make or break" period for Darrell—with his family, with Annette, with parole, a new job, and with his self-evaluation.

For whatever it's worth, I might point out a problem *I* might have in an extended relation with Darrell, a problem which I think he's run into repeatedly. His charm and likeableness are likely to rally people to his side until he lets them down by running off or by not returning their care. Then he is either ignored or nagged, both of which demonstrate to him again that people are phony and there are no close friends. So off he goes to emulate Mundy with little concern for the consequences to others.

Constance T. Fischer, Ph.D.

ENTER THE COMPUTER

In rather few areas of contemporary mass activity can an adequate accounting overlook the role of the computer. In the area of psychological assessment, with the need to quickly produce quantities of data at minimal cost it was inevitable that the computer would be considered, and in the 1960s computer printouts of psychological conclusions became a reality.

The computer lends itself well to data that can be categorized and quantified. The MMPI is an instrument that can readily be adapted to computer analysis. The vast experience had with this instrument and its widespread utilization (Sundberg, 1961) is an added plus. Basic rationale is contained in Meehl's (1954) position on clinical versus statistical prediction. There can be no argument about the superiority of the actuarial over the clinical method for the sort of *predictions* Meehl cites.

Questions are frequently raised, however, over the appropriate weight to be given to prediction in the total clinical scheme of things. Specifically, the MMPI computer report cannot focus on the mission as defined for an individual. It cannot answer ad hoc referral questions that might be raised; however, in some instances conclusions offered automatically (e.g., identifying a suicidal risk) may be right on target. In other instances the psychologist might seek to accommodate printouts to referral questions. It is further noted an MMPI printout, no matter how accurate or useful, is based on but one instrument and hence remains inadequate for those who are committed to the battery approach. Such data may nonetheless contribute to the input and be reflected in the psychological report derived from a battery.

Research to date has encouraged both further studies and applied use of the MMPI printout. Glueck and Reznikoff (undated) describe a study in which psychologists who had administered and interpreted a battery of projective instruments noted areas of agreement and disagreement between their conclusions and printouts. "The psychologists judged the computer interpretations to be consistent with their projective test findings a far greater number of times than would be expected by chance." Higher positive correlations were obtained for conclusions derived from certain scales (e.g., L, Hy) than from others (e.g., Pd, Pt). Disagreement tended to be greater where scale score elevations were of "low and normal" degree. The authors conclude that ". . . computer interpretation of MMPI records yield meaningful psychological information about psychiatric patients with an economy of professional time, and a sharp reduction in cost."

Webb, Miller, and Fowler (1969) asked hundreds of users of a commercial MMPI printout service to rate, on a five-point scale, a report on one of their patients along 16 dimensions, including organization and clarity, validity, and usefulness. Some typically positive statements of results are as follows: "Ninety-five percent of the reports were rated as being well-organized and clear. . . . Eliminating contradictory paragraphs in computer-generated reports is difficult because paragraphs are independently chosen. Particularly is this so when describing persons in conflict, for apparently contradictory paragraphs each accurately portray dimensions of a patient's conflict. In the

present study, the judges indicated that in 85 percent of the reports . . .
no contradictions were present, . . . in 88 percent of the reports the symptoms
reported were accurate; . . . Predictions of response to therapy . . . even with
the obvious problem that various therapy approaches were represented,
were judged correct in 75% of the report; . . . Evaluations were made for
'Barnum' or 'Aunt Fanny' statements in the reports. Less than 9 ₁percent of the
reports were judged to include such trivial information."

Following are four MMPI computer printouts from the laboratory of
Dr. Harold Gilberstadt and made available through his courtesy. One is on a
psychiatric patient and three are on medical patients. These should be regarded
as interim reports. Work is currently underway in a number of directions:
a better coding system is being studied and attention is being given to improving
the item pool and to the method of analysis. Nevertheless, Dr. Gilberstadt
reports a 90 percent "hit rate," that is, user satisfaction as gauged by global
ratings.[3]

Male-age 30-psy

TEST-TAKING ATTITUDE SEEMS TO REVEAL SELF-DEPRECIATION
AND/OR CONFUSED THINKING. HELP-SEEKING. THE PATIENT'S
CURRENT STATE APPEARS TO BE CHARACTERIZED BY NO
SIGNIFICANT DEVIATIONS IN REGARD TO STATES OF RETARDED
DEPRESSION, ANXIETY, AGITATION OR HYPOMANIA.

SINGLE AND PAIR-WISE SCALE ANALYSIS SUGGESTS THE
POSSIBILITY OF THE FOLLOWING TRAITS AND CHARACTERISTICS.
NUMEROUS SOMATIC SYMPTOMS OF A HYPOCHONDRIACAL OR
PSYCHOPHYSIOLOGICAL TYPE. IMMATURE, SELF-CENTERED AND
IMPULSIVE. FAMILY AND SOCIAL MALADJUSTMENTS OF
IMMATURE KINDS. MAY HAVE PSYCHOPATHIC CHARACTER
TRAITS. SUPERFICIALLY SOCIABLE AND OUTGOING.

THE FOLLOWING SHOULD BE LOOKED FOR AMONG TRAIT AND
DIAGNOSTIC ALTERNATIVES. EMOTIONALLY UNSTABLE
PERSONALITY. ALCOHOLISM FREQUENT. HOSTILE. EMOTIONALLY
LABILE PERSONALITY. WIGGINS CONTENT SCALES INDICATE
THAT THE PATIENT'S SELF-REPORT SHOWS THE FOLLOWING
CHARACTERISTICS TO BE PROMINENT—DEPRESSED, WORRYING,
DISTRUSTFUL, DISRESPECT FOR AUTHORITY AND CONVENTIONAL
MORES. PSYCHOPHYSIOLOGICAL OR CNS TYPES OF COMPLAINTS.
EXCITED, RESTLESS, HIGH-STRUNG, CONCERN ABOUT HEALTH
AND/OR GI COMPLAINTS.

IN GENERAL, PROFILE IS A TYPE FREQUENT AMONG PATIENTS

[3] Personal communication.

IN WHOM ALCOHOLISM AND SOMATIZATION ARE PRIMARY
FEATURES.

Male-age 46-med

TEST-TAKING ATTITUDE SEEMS TO REVEAL MARKED
EVASIVENESS. CAUTION SHOULD BE EXERCISED IN EVALUATING
PROFILE. SOME DEFENSIVENESS.
SINGLE AND PAIR-WISE SCALE ANALYSIS SUGGESTS THE
POSSIBILITY OF THE FOLLOWING TRAITS AND CHARACTERISTICS.
NUMEROUS SOMATIC SYMPTOMS OF A HYPOCHONDRIACAL OR
PSYCHOPHYSIOLOGICAL TYPE. DEPRESSION. AUTONOMIC
NERVOUS SYSTEM OVERREACTIVITY. LACK OF STAMINA.
DEPRESSION. LACK OF OPTIMISM. DYSPHORIC, WORRYING,
PESSIMISTIC. BEHAVIORAL CONTROLS MAY BE TENUOUS.
SUPERFICIALLY SOCIABLE AND OUTGOING. THE FOLLOWING
SHOULD BE LOOKED FOR AMONG TRAIT AND DIAGNOSTIC
ALTERNATIVES—DEPRESSION. WIGGINS CONTENT SCALES
INDICATE THAT THE PATIENT'S SELF-REPORT SHOWS
THE FOLLOWING CHARACTERISTICS TO BE PROMINENT—
PSYCHOPHYSIOLOGICAL OR CNS TYPES OF COMPLAINTS.
CONCERN ABOUT HEALTH AND/OR GI COMPLAINTS.
PROFILE IS A TYPE WHICH WHEN OBTAINED FROM MEDICAL
PATIENTS REFERRED FOR CONSULTATION INDICATES A TYPICAL
PROFILE FOR ORGANIC SYNDROMES, INCLUDING C.N.S. TYPES.

Male-age 47-med

TEST-TAKING ATTITUDE SEEMS TO REVEAL SOME
DEFENSIVENESS.
SINGLE AND PAIR-WISE SCALE ANALYSIS SUGGESTS THE
POSSIBILITY OF THE FOLLOWING TRAITS AND CHARACTERISTICS.
EASY FATIGABILITY. MOODY. SOMEWHAT SORROWFUL. UNHAPPY.
MANIFESTS A SAD MOOD. SYMPTOMS RELATED TO ANXIETY,
PROLONGED TENSION, AND WORRY. NO APPARENT ABNORMALITY
IN ENERGY OR ACTIVITY LEVEL. SOMEWHAT SHY AND
INTROSPECTIVE.
PROFILE IS A TYPE WHICH WHEN OBTAINED FROM MEDICAL
PATIENTS REFERRED FOR CONSULTATION INDICATES A LACK OF
PSYCHIATRICALLY SIGNIFICANT PROFILE DEVIATIONS.

Male-age 20-med

TEST-TAKING ATTITUDE SEEMS TO REVEAL SOME DEFENSIVENESS.
SINGLE AND PAIR-WISE SCALE ANALYSIS SUGGESTS THE

POSSIBILITY OF THE FOLLOWING TRAITS AND CHARACTERISTICS.
DEPRESSION. LACK OF OPTIMISM. DYSPHORIC, WORRYING,
PESSIMISTIC, OBSESSIVE TRENDS, SELF-PUNISHING. INTROJECTS
ANGER. ANXIOUS AND DEPRESSED. PROBABLE FEELINGS OF
WORTHLESSNESS AND SINFULNESS. TENSION. PASSIVITY.
INTERESTS IN PASSIVE PURSUITS AND/OR OCCUPATIONS.
SENSITIVE. DEPENDENT. SUBMISSIVE. INSECURE OVER OWN
MASCULINE ROLE. HIGH LEVEL OF AESTHETIC INTERESTS.
BEHAVIORAL CONTROLS MAY BE TENUOUS. SUPERFICIALLY
SOCIABLE AND OUTGOING.
   PROFILE IS A TYPE WHICH WHEN OBTAINED FROM MEDICAL
PATIENTS REFERRED FOR CONSULTATION INDICATES
SOME ELEVATIONS OF ABNORMAL DEGREE AS DESCRIBED ABOVE.

In addition to providing such reports, Gilberstadt's computer also offers
such services as an MMPI profile printout, together with scores, the responses to
all 566 items, raw scores and T scores for special and codebook scales, special
indexes such as the Anxiety Index, Gough's F-K Dissimulation Index, and
the Marks-Seaman Type, plus a list of the Grayson (Critical) Index that may serve
as a basis for interviews with clients or informants and also be used as "stop"
items in screening for serious disorders. The psychologist is thus assisted
in supplementing the basic printout report with data gained from more traditional
clinical-type assessment activities.

Another example, on page 230, is from the Roche Psychiatric Service Institute,
reprinted here with permission of Hoffman- La Roche Inc.

The Piotrowski Automated Rorschach (PAR) was introduced in 1974.
The PAR report is a computerized print-out consisting of 50 to 80
statements. These statements are based on Piotrowski's (1957) system of
perceptanalysis and are worded pretty much as a psychologist would on directly
"reading" a Rorschach, e.g., "quick and decisive," or "tends to view the
world in terms of personal experiences, emotionally self-centered."
The statements are addressed to the usual areas of Rorschach interpretation.

The PAR Center of Hay Associates that provides the computer service
advocates both clinical and administrative applications and notes that "the report
can be modified if desired to reflect the concerns of psychologists and
administrators in nonclinical settings." Thus the report can be used "as is", or
the material translated into the sort of reports presented in Chapter 7.
A psychologist might wish to integrate the printout with other sources of data
and focus the report according to the requirements of a specific mission.

Following, on pp. 231-234, are two PAR printouts, reproduced by
permission of Hay Associates. The first concerns a young criminal who had
accidentally killed three men who wandered into his line of fire during a
shootout with police. He was examined in prison by Dr. Eugene C. Stammeyer.
The second individual was examined by Dr. Piotrowski and the case was
presented in his *Perceptanalysis* (1957, pp. 416-445). The reader might wish
to compare the interpretations made in the book with the computer printout.

ROCHE PSYCHIATRIC SERVICE INSTITUTE

MMPI REPORT

CASE NO: 00000   RPSI NO: 00000
AGE 37 MALE

     THE TEST ITEMS APPEAR TO HAVE BEEN ANSWERED TRUTHFULLY WITH
NO EFFORT TO DENY OR EXAGGERATE.

     THIS PATIENT APPEARS TO BE CURRENTLY DEPRESSED AND ANXIOUS.
HE SHOWS A PATTERN WHICH IS FREQUENT AMONG PSYCHIATRIC PATIENTS.
FEELINGS OF INADEQUACY, SEXUAL CONFLICTS AND RIGIDITY ARE ACCOM-
PANIED BY A LOSS OF EFFICIENCY, INITIATIVE AND SELF CONFIDENCE.
INSOMNIA IS LIKELY, ALONG WITH CHRONIC FATIGUE. HE IS ANXIOUS,
TENSE, AND OVERLY SENSITIVE. SUICIDAL THOUGHTS ARE A POSSIBILITY.
IN THE CLINICAL PICTURE, DEPRESSION PREDOMINATES. PSYCHIATRIC
PATIENTS WITH THIS PATTERN ARE LIKELY TO BE DIAGNOSED AS DEPRESSIVE
REACTION OR ANXIETY REACTION. THE CHARACTERISTICS ARE RESISTANT
TO CHANGE, ALTHOUGH SYMPTOMATIC RELIEF MAY BE OBTAINED WITH BRIEF
TREATMENT.

     HE TENDS TO BE PESSIMISTIC AND COMPLAINING, AND IS LIKELY TO
BE DEFEATIST, CYNICAL, AND UNWILLING TO STICK WITH TREATMENT. HE
MAY NEED FREQUENT REASSURANCE ABOUT HIS MEDICAL CONDITION. DY-
NAMICALLY, HE IS A NARCISSISTIC AND SELF-CENTERED PERSON WHO IS
RIGID IN THOUGHT AND ACTION AND EASILY UPSET IN SOCIAL SITUATIONS.

     REPRESSION AND DENIAL ARE UTILIZED AS A DEFENSE AGAINST AN-
XIETY. IN PERIODS OF HEIGHTENED STRESS HIS ANXIETY IS LIKELY TO BE
EXPRESSED IN SOMATIC SYMPTOMS. HE MAY RESPOND TO SUGGESTION AND
REASSURANCE.

     HE IS A SELF CONTROLLED CAUTIOUS PERSON WHO MAY BE SOMEWHAT
FEMININE IN HIS INTEREST PATTERNS. HE IS IDEALISTIC, SOCIALLY
PERCEPTIVE AND RESPONSIVE. HE SHOWS SOME SELF-AWARENESS, BUT HE
IS SENSITIVE AND PRONE TO WORRY. HE IS VERBALLY FLUENT, PERSUASIVE
AND ABLE TO COMMUNICATE IDEAS CLEARLY.

     THIS PERSON IS HESITANT TO BECOME INVOLVED IN SOCIAL SIT-
UATIONS. HE MAKES AN EFFORT TO CONSCIENTIOUSLY CARRY OUT HIS RE-
SPONSIBILITIES, BUT HE IS RETIRING AND SOMEWHAT WITHDRAWN FROM IN-
TERPERSONAL RELATIONSHIPS.

NOTE: ALTHOUGH NOT A SUBSTITUTE FOR THE CLINICIAN'S PROFESSIONAL
JUDGMENT AND SKILL, THE MMPI CAN BE A USEFUL ADJUNCT IN THE DIAG-
NOSIS AND MANAGEMENT OF EMOTIONAL DISORDERS. THE REPORT IS FOR
PROFESSIONAL USE ONLY AND SHOULD NOT BE SHOWN OR RELEASED TO THE
PATIENT.

0032   QUICK AND DECISIVE.

0080   OCCASIONALLY JUMPS TO UNWARRANTED CONCLUSIONS. ATTEMPTS TO SIZE UP
        SITUATIONS ON INSUFFICIENT EVIDENCE. AT SUCH TIMES DOES NOT THINK
        MATTERS THROUGH CAREFULLY. TRIES TO MAKE REALITY CONFORM WITH
        EXPECTATIONS TO A DEGREE WHICH UNFAVORABLY AFFECTS JUDGMENTS.

0090   SUBJECT IS FREE FROM ANXIETY ALTHOUGH INTELLECTUAL ACHIEVEMENT IS POOR
        ON THE WHOLE AND INTELLECTUAL DISCIPLINE IS LAX. LACK OF ADEQUATE
        SELF-CRITICISM.

0096   SHARES VERY FEW COMMON IDEAS WITH OTHERS.

0148   BECOMES SIGNIFICANTLY MORE ACTIVE, COOPERATIVE, AND PRODUCTIVE WHEN
        SUBJECT FEELS EMOTIONALLY AT HOME.

0197   NORMAL AVERAGE AMOUNT OF INTEREST IN WHAT MAKES OTHERS TICK, IN THEIR
        MOTIVES AND GOALS, AND IN THE POSSIBLE EFFECTS OF THEIR ACTIONS UPON
        OWN LIFE. THIS AMOUNT OF INTEREST IN OTHERS IS NEEDED FOR AN
        EFFECTIVE SOCIAL LIVING WITH OTHERS.

0206   AT TIMES PREFERS TO OBSERVE INTER-HUMAN RELATIONSHIPS FROM A
        POSITION OF SAFE DISTANCE AND THUS INCREASE FEELING OF SECURITY.

0208   MAKES AN EFFORT TO ESTABLISH AND MAINTAIN HARMONIOUS RELATIONS WITH
        OTHERS. AVOIDS CONFLICTS WHICH SUBJECT FEELS ARE UNNECESSARY.

0223   INCLINED TO BE FRANK IN EXPRESSING NEGATIVE ATTITUDES, TRYING TO
        RATIONALIZE THEM AS OBJECTIVE. SPORADICALLY TACTLESS.

0227   FINDS COOPERATION DIFFICULT BECAUSE OF MUCH HOSTILITY AND AGGRESSION
        AND THE CONSTANT NEED TO CONTROL IT WHEN WORKING WITH OTHERS. EASILY
        IRRITATED BY THE AGGRESSIVENESS OF OTHERS.

0229   TENDS TO VIEW THE WORLD IN TERMS OF PERSONAL EXPERIENCES.
        EMOTIONALLY SELF-CENTERED.

0268   DISPLAYS ABOUT AVERAGE EMOTIONAL INTEREST IN OTHERS FOR A PERSON OF
        SUPERIOR INTELLIGENCE.

0283   DISLIKES LOUD AND CRUDE EMOTIONAL EXPRESSIONS.

0288   FEARFUL OF POSSIBLE CONSEQUENCES OF INTENSE EMOTION.

0314   HAS INSUFFICIENT SELF-REGULATING OR AUTOMATIC CONTROL OVER
        MANIFESTATIONS OF EMOTIONS, ESPECIALLY IN STATES OF FATIGUE OR PROLONGED
        EMOTIONAL STIMULATION. MUST RELY HEAVILY ON DELIBERATE AND CONSCIOUS
        SELF-CONTROL.

0315   INSUFFICIENT AND INFERIOR CAPACITY FOR PROLONGED CONSCIOUS CONTROL OVER
        MANIFESTATION OF EMOTION, OVERT ACTION AND THINKING.

0316   INCAPABLE OF MAKING AN ADEQUATE ADJUSTMENT TO REALITY. HANDLES EVERYDAY
        PROBLEMS POORLY. IMPULSIVE.

0322   DOES NOT EXPERIENCE PAINFUL OR DISTURBING ANXIETY. NOT WORRIED. ALERT
        AND EASILY RESPONSIVE. FREE FROM OBSESSIVENESS AND COMPULSIONS.

0327   SPORADICALLY ENGAGES IN SPONTANEOUS PSYCHOLOGICAL SELF-OBSERVATION.

0328   HAS GOOD INSIGHT INTO OWN FEELINGS AND MOTIVES. KNOWS SELF WELL BECAUSE
        OF DEEP-SEATED HABIT OF PSYCHOLOGICAL SELF-OBSERVATION.

0332   BASIC LIFE ROLES ARE SO NUMEROUS THAT IT IS DIFFICULT TO CHARACTERIZE
        SUBJECT. HAS INSIGHT INTO OWN WAYS OF HANDLING OTHERS IN IMPORTANT
        MATTERS. IS AN ACCURATE OBSERVER OF HUMAN INTERRELATIONSHIPS.

0343   SEEKS INDEPENDENCE FROM THE ENVIRONMENT RATHER THAN CONTROL OVER IT.

0397   SENSITIVE TO SPOKEN AND UNSPOKEN CRITICISM. WATCHES OTHERS WITH
        ALERTNESS IN AN ATTEMPT TO DETERMINE WHAT THEY ARE REALLY THINKING AND
        WHAT THE TRUE NATURE OF THEIR RELATIONSHIP IS.

0399   PREOCCUPATION WITH EVALUATIONS BY OTHERS IS SO GREAT THAT IT MAY
        INTERFERE WITH GOOD JUDGEMENT. VERY SENSITIVE AND EASILY HURT EVEN BY
        MILD CRITICISM. SUSPECTS SINCERITY OF OTHERS.

0437   WASTES MUCH TIME AND EMOTIONAL ENERGY IN OBSESSIVE SELF=OBSERVATION.

0466   FROM TIME TO TIME EXHIBITS ASOCIAL. EVEN ANTISOCIAL BEHAVIOR, DESPITE
        AMBIVALENCE ABOUT IT.

0470   FREQUENTLY ASSUMES A DEFENSIVE ATTITUDE EVEN WHEN THERE IS NO ACTUAL
        CHALLENGE. WHEN FREE OF ANXIETY, AND THINGS ARE GOING WELL, IS CALM,
        FRIENDLY, EVEN RELAXED. WHEN ANXIOUS, INTEREST RANGE GREATLY NARROWS,
        STUBBORNNESS AND BELLIGERENCE SUDDENLY INCREASE. MOST ANXIETY STATES
        PASS QUICKLY AS A RESULT OF COUNTERPHOBIC BEHAVIOR.

0473   MORE LIKELY TO BE OVERTLY AGGRESSIVE THAN ANXIOUS. ANXIETY TRIGGERS OFF
        AGGRESSION.

0507   UNDER CONDITIONS OF STRESS OR IN CERTAIN CIRCUMSCRIBED RELATIONSHIPS OR
        AREAS OF LIVING MAY ASSUME A PASSIVE ROLE. ALLOWING SELF TO BE
        MANIPULATED BY WHATEVER INFLUENCES THE ENVIRONMENT PRESENTS.

0532   IN EARLY CHILDHOOD WAS OVER=PROTECTED BY PARENTS, ESPECIALLY MOTHER.
        EXPERIMENTED WITH VARIOUS WAYS OF RELATING TO PARENTS (NOT NECESSARILY
        WITH AWARENESS) IN ORDER TO MINIMIZE CONFLICTS AND ESTABLISH MORE
        SATISFACTORY RELATIONSHIPS. SOUGHT OUT PARENTAL ATTENTION AND
        AFFECTION.

0540   PROBABLY LIVED IN FEAR OF PARENTS IN CHILDHOOD. CARRIED FEAR OF
        AUTHORITIES OVER INTO ADULTHOOD, AT LEAST ON UNCONSCIOUS LEVEL.

0598   AFRAID OF FAILURE IN COMPETITION WITH OTHERS. BELIEVES SUCH FAILURE TO
        BE VERY PROBABLE.

0610   HARBORS EXPECTATION OF DISASTER ALTHOUGH CONTINUES IN PURSUIT OF
        GOALS.

0626   FREQUENT INTERMITTENT DEPRESSIVE MOODS ARE PARTLY WELCOME AND PARTLY
        UNWELCOME. IS STRONGLY INCLINED TO ALLEVIATE ANXIETY THROUGH INCREASE
        IN MOTOR BEHAVIOR. IF OPPOSED WHILE ANXIOUS IS VERY LIKELY TO BECOME
        OPENLY HOSTILE, ESPECIALLY ON THE VERBAL LEVEL. ENERGY INCREASES WITH
        ANXIETY AND SUBJECT FACES CHALLENGES BETTER THAN WHEN IN A RELAXED
        STATE. AVOIDS PAIN LESS THAN MOST PEOPLE AND TAKES SOME PRIDE IN
        CAPACITY TO FACE RISKS AND ENDURE PAIN. COUNTER=PHOBIC. FEELS
        THREATENED BY EXTERNAL DANGERS.

0652   RATHER RESTLESS IN MOTOR BEHAVIOR. MOODS AND EMOTIONS READILY SHOW IN
        OVERT BEHAVIOR. HAS TO BE ON GUARD IN ORDER NOT TO LOSE SELF-CONTROL.

0752   SPORADICALLY MANIFESTS SUPERFICIAL EMOTIONS IN A HYSTEROID MANNER WHICH
        CONTRASTS WITH USUAL, MUCH MORE SPONTANEOUS AND GENUINE EMOTIONAL
        REACTIONS.

0753   NO HYSTERICAL SYMPTOMS.

0831   SCHIZOPHRENIA OR ORGANIC BRAIN DISORDER SHOULD BE CONSIDERED.

0850   SCHIZOPHRENIA.

0863   A SCHIZOPHRENIC WITH FREQUENT STATES OF INTELLECTUAL CONFUSION.

09142   SCHIZOPHRENIA, ACUTE, WITH CONSPICUOUS PARANOID SYSTEMS. THE SUBJECT IS
        LIKELY TO EXPERIENCE HIS PERSONALITY CHANGE AS A PROGRESSION OR
        EXPANSION RATHER THAN AS A REGRESSION. UNUSUAL IDEAS ARE PRODUCED BUT
        THEY ARE BIZARRE AND DERIESTIC. SUBJECT LIVES IN A WORLD OF FANTASY.

0928   IT IS ADVISABLE TO MAKE CONCESSIONS TO THIS SUBJECT, AT FIRST, IN
        ORDER NOT TO AROUSE ANTAGONISM. CAUTIOUSLY AND GRADUALLY ONE CAN MAKE
        CAREFULLY PHRASED SUGGESTIONS ON HOW TO BEHAVE IN A MORE EFFECTIVE
        MANNER. A GOOD THERAPEUTIC RAPPORT MAY BE DIFFICULT. OCCASIONALLY
        REACTS TO DIFFICULTIES OR CHALLENGES WITH A RATHER FORCEFUL THOUGH
        TRANSIENT DECISIVENESS REGARDLESS OF THE DIFFICULTY OF THE PROBLEM AND
        WHETHER OR NOT THE COURSE OF ACTION MAY LEAD TO DISAGREEMENT WITH
        OTHERS.

0004   AT LEAST HIGH AVERAGE INTELLIGENCE.

0025   ENJOYS THE FEELING OF BEING CREATIVE.

0038   MODEL STUDENT TYPE, EAGER TO DO AND KNOW WHAT IS EXPECTED, REGARDLESS
        OF PERSONAL PREFERENCES OR UNDERSTANDING OF PROBLEMS. STRONG TENDENCY TO
        AVOID MAKING STATEMENTS WHICH MIGHT PROMPT OPPOSITION OF OTHERS.
        INTELLECTUALLY A CONFORMIST.

0085   INTELLECTUALLY NAIVE. INADEQUATE ATTENTION IS PAID TO PRACTICAL
        PROBLEMS.

0106   CAPABLE OF A HIGH DEGREE OF INITIATIVE. SELF-RELIANT, ENERGETIC AND
        DARING IN STARTING NEW ACTIVITIES.

0132   EXPENDS A MODERATE AMOUNT OF EFFORT PLANNING FUTURE SUCCESS AND
        RECOGNITION, RELATIVE TO INTELLIGENCE.

0148   BECOMES SIGNIFICANTLY MORE ACTIVE, COOPERATIVE, AND PRODUCTIVE WHEN
        SUBJECT FEELS EMOTIONALLY AT HOME.

0163   UNABLE TO CARRY THROUGH TO A COMPLETION CREATIVE AND DIFFICULT TASKS.
        MAY SHOW A GREAT DEAL OF PROMISE BUT INEVITABLY DISAPPOINTS OTHERS.

0175   HAS NO SINGLE ABSORBING INTEREST AROUND WHICH DRIVE FOR
        AMBITIOUS ACHIEVEMENT COULD BE CENTERED AND ORGANIZED.
        NOT INTERESTED IN COMPETING WITH OTHERS IN ORDER TO
        OCCUPY THE TOP POSITION OF POWER.

0189   NO CONSISTENT GOAL DIRECTION. INTERESTED IN ESTABLISHING SUPERFICIALLY
        PLEASANT SOCIAL RELATIONS. USUALLY AVOIDS APPEARING SERIOUS IN DEALING
        WITH OTHERS IN SIGNIFICANT MATTERS.

0227   FINDS COOPERATION DIFFICULT BECAUSE OF MUCH HOSTILITY AND AGGRESSION
        AND THE CONSTANT NEED TO CONTROL IT WHEN WORKING WITH OTHERS. EASILY
        IRRITATED BY THE AGGRESSIVENESS OF OTHERS.

0229   TENDS TO VIEW THE WORLD IN TERMS OF PERSONAL EXPERIENCES.
        EMOTIONALLY SELF-CENTERED.

0268   DISPLAYS ABOUT AVERAGE EMOTIONAL INTEREST IN OTHERS FOR A PERSON OF
        SUPERIOR INTELLIGENCE.

0327   SPORADICALLY ENGAGES IN SPONTANEOUS PSYCHOLOGICAL SELF-OBSERVATION.

0351   HAS A STRONG TENDENCY TO EXHIBITIONISTIC SELF-ASSERTIVENESS BUT THE AIM
        OF THIS DRIVE IS LIMITED. IT IS PROBABLY INTELLECTUAL AND VERBAL
        RATHER THAN PSYCHO-SEXUAL. SUBJECT IS HESITANT AND FEARFUL ABOUT DIRECT
        EXPRESSION OF EXHIBITIONISM.

0354   SUBJECT IS IN GREAT NEED OF RECOGNITION.

0372   WISHES TO BELONG TO A PRESTIGEFUL GROUP IN ORDER TO MAKE LIFE EASIER AND
        MORE REWARDING. MAKES SOME EFFORT TO IMITATE HIGHER SOCIAL CLASS
        THOUGHT AND BEHAVIOR PATTERNS.

0392   DELIBERATELY CAUTIOUS. DISLIKES BEING EVALUATED.

0394   FREQUENTLY AVOIDS SAYING ANYTHING DEFINITE AND PRECISE. BEATS ABOUT THE
        BUSH. PREFERS STATEMENTS THAT ARE INDETERMINATE AND CAN BE NEITHER
        CONFIRMED NOR CONTRADICTED. AVOIDS CLEAR-CUT COMMITMENTS WHENEVER
        EVASION IS AT ALL POSSIBLE. TRIES TO BE SOCIAL. CONFORMS TO AUTHORITY.

0435   GIVEN TO PSYCHOLOGICAL SELF-OBSERVATION AND DAYDREAMING, FANTASIES
BEING ABLE TO AVOID DECISIONS IN IMPORTANT MATTERS AND DERIVES
SATISFACTION FROM CONSIDERING AND COMPARING MANY ALTERNATIVES FOR
ACTION. HOWEVER, THESE ALTERNATIVES EXIST ONLY IN THE IMAGINATION.

0462   FEELS THAT OWN PERSONALITY HAS NOT CHANGED SINCE CHILDHOOD. IS ALMOST
AS SELF-CONFIDENT AND OPTIMISTIC CONCERNING THE FUTURE AS IN EARLY
CHILDHOOD. HAS ALWAYS BEEN READY TO ASSUME RESPONSIBILITY FOR SELF.
INDEPENDENT IN HANDLING IMPORTANT PERSONAL MATTERS.

0478   PETTY AGGRESSIVENESS MANIFESTED IN WORDS RATHER THAN ACTIONS.
IRRITABLE, A COMPLAINER.

0549   EXPERIENCES ACUTE ANXIETY STATES. SHOWS MARKED VARIATION IN SPEED OF
RESPONSE AND IN INITIATIVE. SOMETIMES BLOCKED, AT OTHER TIMES RESPONDS
WELL AND WITHOUT HESITATION.

0550   SUFFERS FROM VERY ACUTE ANXIETY.

0581   OVERT ACTIVITY IS REDUCED WHEN EMOTIONS ARE AROUSED.

0593   EXPECTS TO SUFFER.

0604   FEARFUL OF BECOMING SERIOUSLY ILL, MENTALLY AND/OR PHYSICALLY, OR OF
DECREASE IN CREATIVE POTENTIAL. FEELS OVER-EXTENDED.

0617   HAS GUILT FEELINGS WITH EXAGGERATED FANTASIES ABOUT POSSIBLE
PUNISHMENT.

0622   FEELS LONELY, SAD, AND ABANDONED. NO PSYCHOMOTOR RETARDATION.

0636   FEELS LONELY AND IMPOSED UPON. SUFFERS WITHOUT HOPE OF ALLEVIATION.
NO PSYCHOMOTOR RETARDATION.

0645   PHYSICALLY ENERGETIC.

0649   LIKES TO BE ACTIVE. DOES NOT TIRE EASILY. MOVES ABOUT QUICKLY.

0666   SEXUAL AS WELL AS OTHER GRATIFICATIONS ARE LOW IN INTENSITY.

0702   HAS A CONFLICT OVER MASTURBATION.

0706   MASOCHISM IS A CONDITION FOR SEXUAL SATISFACTION.

0707   SADOMASOCHISTIC.

0730   COPROPHILIC INTERESTS.

0733   SEXUAL DESIRE IS GREATLY DIMINISHED. FEELS DEPRESSED AND HELPLESS. NO
COMPENSATORY DRIVE TO REVIVE THE SEXUAL URGE.

0747   DECIDEDLY OBSESSIVE - COMPULSIVE.

0748   ATTEMPTS TO RESOLVE OBSESSIVE INDECISIVENESS BY TRYING MANY TENTATIVE
SOLUTIONS HALF-HEARTEDLY, DELAYING DEFINITE DECISIONS FOR LONG TIME.

0768   OCCASIONALLY MAKES IMMATURE AND SELF-CENTERED EMOTIONAL DEMANDS ON
OTHERS, DISREGARDING THE OTHER PERSON'S DESIRES, RIGHTS, COMFORT AND
POSSIBLE REACTIONS.

0771   ULCERS LIKELY.

0915   MARKED PERSONALITY IMPROVEMENT IS VERY IMPROBABLE IN THE NEXT SEVERAL
YEARS. IT IS HARD TO HELP SUBJECT THROUGH PSYCHOTHERAPY.

Still another form of computer printout report is the Thorn Composite Profile, developed by Myron Thorn, CDP, and reprinted (next page) with his permission. It is essentially a counseling tool. Tests can be selected to contribute scores to the profile.

STUDENT I.D.
132642792

THORN COMPOSITE PROFILE FOR SALLY DOE

MAY 4, 1960

Score	Label	Test
91	ARTISTIC INTERESTS	KPR-V
88	EXHIBITIONISM	EPPS
87	FORM PERCEPTION	GATB
87	SPATIAL PERCEPTION	DAT
85	WORKING WITH IDEAS	KPR-P
84	SPATIAL PERCEPTION	GATB
81	CLERICAL PERCEPTION	GATB
78	CLERICAL SPEED	DAT
77	PERSUASIVE INTEREST	KPR-V
76	NEED FOR CHANGE	EPPS
74	DIRECTING OTHERS	KPR-P
73	VERBAL APTITUDE	GATB
73	SPELLING SKILLS	DAT
72	CLERICAL ACCURACY	DAT
72	MOTOR COORDINATION	GATB
72	FINGER DEXTERITY	GATB
70	VERBAL REASONING	DAT
70	ENDURANCE	EPPS
70	HETEROSEXUALITY	EPPS
70	LITERARY INTERESTS	KPR-V
68	ACHIEVEMENT NEEDS	EPPS
67	INTELLIGENCE	GATB
66	MANUAL DEXTERITY	GATB
65	CLERICAL INTEREST	KPR-V
65	AGGRESSION NEEDS	EPPS
64	MECHANICAL APTITUDE	DAT
63	MECHANICAL INTEREST	KPR-V
62	NUMERICAL APTITUDE	GATB
62	NEED TO DOMINATE	EPPS
61	SENTENCE SKILLS	DAT
60	ABSTRACT REASONING	DAT
60	COMPUTING INTEREST	KPR-V
60	MUSICAL INTERESTS	KPR-V
60	CLERICAL INTERESTS	KPR-V
59	NEED FOR ORDER	EPPS
58	NUMERICAL ABILITY	DAT
57	SOCIAL SERV. INT.	KPR-V
53	INTRACEPTION NEEDS	EPPS
53	SUCCORANCE NEEDS	EPPS
50	OUTDOOR INTERESTS	KPR-V

Et cetera. Approximately 10 more scores would appear on the printout.

QUICKIE REPORTS

For the reasons so far advanced, we are very much partial to the sort of case-focused reports presented in Chapter 7. They are regarded also as a good training device, since they require the writer to conceptualize each report in terms of an explicit rationale. However, they share with many other contemporary reports (e.g., those in Chapter 6), the drawback of being more or less time-consuming to prepare.

As an outgrowth of the diagnostic-therapeutic team described in Chapter 1, we have developed the following scheme. The psychologist, together with team colleagues, spends between 45 minutes and an hour (but sometimes less) in analyzing, discussing, and integrating the test protocol and other inputs and in interviewing the patient. Part of the input is from the nursing personnel who spell out the nature of the patient's problem and the questions to be answered. These, though informally stated, are the "reasons for referral." In some instances, there are no clear referral questions and the goal is to create some initial psychological input, to set forth some orienting material to be added to later— perhaps by merely checking the protocol, perhaps through additional testing and/or interviewing. Technical terms and jargon are perhaps more abundant than ordinarily desirable, but they cause no consternation in the immediate team situation where these inputs are used precisely as an ephemeral document, as a contribution primarily to short-term action, but as a record nevertheless. Pertinent data are immediately incorporated in the nursing care plan and in the Problem Check List of the Problem-Oriented Medical Record (POMR) (Weed, 1968, 1969; Enelow & Swisher, 1972; Hurst & Walker, 1972; Ryback, 1974). This system of medical record keeping is now in widespread use and permits the recording of problems to be treated, the action taken (e.g., medication, psychotherapy), and the outcome (e.g., unimproved, improved, in remission, or resolved). Among the reports presented below, the target problems identified range from a general diagnosis (schizophrenia), to a symptom (anxiety, depression, paranoid delusions, drug dependence), to an attitude (nihilistic view of world), to a hypothetical construct (low frustration tolerance).

The written report, organized somewhat less meticulously than the reports in Chapter 7 and perhaps with less grammatical nicety, takes, on the average, but five minutes to put on paper or to dictate—a decided economic plus. Warning: This method is not for beginners.

B. L. W., age 33

The patient has been described as exhibiting elevated behavior, and the diagnosis of manic-depressive psychosis was entertained in the municipal hospital from which he is transferred, but current evidence for such is not forthcoming. He has also been described as delusional, and fitting the category of paranoid schizophrenia. Though this remains a possibility, his talk of the Mafia and the FBI and such appears to be on the order of playful fantasy based on suggestion in the presence of massive repression and denial of reality—usual salient features of his adjustment. The impression is of hysterical personality with episodic periods of hysterical neurosis such as was seen in the brief panic state evidenced at the time of his admission. In multiple respects this is a childlike individual, highly dependent, naive, self-centered, manipulative, exhibitionistic and histrionic, emotionally labile and impulsive with acting-out tendencies, phobic symptomatology, and somatization of anxiety. He does not require hospitalization, but he should be encouraged to establish clinic contacts for long-term guidance and support, including, possibly, vocational guidance and/or placement. Though he impresses clinically as being dull, and he indicates that he dropped out of school in the eighth grade, he is found to be of average intelligence.

Had B. L. W. been stuck with the diagnosis of schizophrenia, paranoid type, he likely would have been prescribed respectable doses of antipsychotic medication and his hospitalization would have been needlessly prolonged. But it soon was clinically confirmed that his playful fantasy was born of suggestion. His future behavior is readily predictable: he won't change much. But the important thing is that we understand the sort of person B. L. W. is. Knowing this, we know that he should have regular outpatient contacts, and we know what sort of supportive techniques to use. Had he been diagnosed as a manic, he likely would have been treated with lithium carbonate, which must be conscientiously monitored lest there be serious toxic effects (Primum, non nocere), and such medication would be beside the point anyway. The physician who treated the patient at a community hospital (where he was under treatment for diabetes) did not consider hysteria, nor did several physicians who had seen him since. The diagnosis of hysteria contributed to a happy outcome, as happy as can be expected for any child who counts his years in the thirties.

D. J. H., age 52

The patient presents a solid picture of hysterical personality disorder. The dominant defenses are denial and repression, with resultant naiveté, poor respect for reality situations, poor judgment, and a variety of socially immature behaviors. He is remarkably self-centered, employing exaggerated histrionic techniques in a continuous attempt to gain support. He is rigid, demanding, and potentially somewhat paranoid in defending what he regards to be his best interests. He thus finds himself involved in frequent interpersonal problems, particularly with those to whom he relates most closely; and low frustration tolerance, exaggerated and labile emotional response, and acting-out tendencies that he regards as "righteous" make for assaultive behaviors. He is preoccupied with sexual fantasy and somatic problems, seeking to live out the sex material in flirtatious behaviors. Marital problems are a source of stress, albeit he contributes to these problems, most recently through his flirtations. The outlook for significant change is not great.

It appears this was hysteria day on the admitting ward. D. J. H. was hospitalized on the "advice" of a judge after he was charged with assault and battery on his wife for the *n*th time during one of their battle royals. There is no "curable" condition, and (barring a minor miracle) only separation of the couple can put a stop to the presenting complaint. This report does not do justice to the polished histrionic behaviors of this man—a veritable Hollywood actor as he plays out the scenes that regularly take place in the home. But what if the report, with the investment of great effort and time, did a superb job of capturing the flavor of this actor, surely one of the most colorful people I have ever met? Would it make any difference at all?

K. C. J., age 49

This is a florid, chronic schizophrenic of the paranoid type, Delusions are unsystematized and involve ideas of influence and persecutory themes, all in a bizarre context. Thought and speech are quite loose, and neologistic expressions are noted. The outlook is guarded.

This man has been as described for a number of years, and the most promising approach would be antipsychotic medication, support, and whatever hospital programs he might fit into. It is well to briefly document the patient's status on admission as a base line against which to evaluate possible changes in the future as these might provide a basis for action. Pages detailing personality and psychopathology could be added, but to what end? Indeed, the comment on outlook is really gratuitous.

B. F. K., age 21

This is a picture of a thoroughgoing "psychopath"—an antisocial personality with a history of disturbance extending far back into childhood. He is essentially an unsocialized individual with a hostile, nihilistic view of the world, capable of dispensing hostility, including assault and physical acts of destruction in many directions. Particularly when under the influence of alcohol and/or drugs is he likely to be destructive, and he may show psychotic-like behaviors. The possibility for any degree of improvement is slim; on the other hand, he could decompensate to psychosis.

Short, if not very sweet. It's telling it like it is. Anyone who believes he has special skills in treating character disorders may volunteer to be this man's therapist. Many nonpsychologists likely would "give up" on such a person, or already have. (Following the patient's discharge, a local district court judge ruling on his most recent transgression selected jail, over the hospital, for him. Perhaps our random selection of cases contains a disproportionate number of "losers"; at any rate this was one person not benefitted by our ministrations. We must remember that though modern treatment helps many, we don't win 'em all.

M. A. B., age 27

There are two opposing sides to this personality: on the one hand there are highly conventional aspirations, on the other, a "psychopathic" side that generally triumphs. This man is remarkably hedonistic (though his marathon sexual expression has recently become "hollow, not worth the effort"), self-indulgent, impulsive, and, in the presence of particularly low tolerance for tensions at the present time, is likely to live out his impulses. He further shows tendencies to schizophrenic behavior that evidently were lived out under LSD, and have at least some potentiality for emerging in stressful situations. He may be diagnosed in terms of his presenting complaint of drug dependence. He might profit from psychotherapy addressed not only to the direction of socialization, but also to deal with problems of hostility and anxiety about sexuality. In addition, there is psychometric evidence for an organic brain syndrome. His WAIS Full Scale I.Q. is 113, his Verbal I.Q. is 121, and his Performance I.Q. is 102. His Wechsler Memory Quotient is 73, with the greatest deficiencies in the areas of logical memory and in making and briefly retaining new visual and verbal associations.

This writer is evidently more hopeful for this than for the previous man, but not very. The prognosis is built into the character structure. Key personality features and problems are identified, though not all in clinical terms. There is, for example, implicit depression in his "hollow" sex experiences. The nature of his sex anxieties is not spelled out, but quickly would become evident to a therapist. He was assessed for a possible organic brain syndrome because of severe, prolonged drug abuse, and the level and quality of his intellectual functioning could be a factor in a rehabilitation program.

A. R., age 59

This patient presents the picture of an introversive, schizoid personality with periodic decompensations to schizophrenia or to alcoholic hallucinosis. He is remarkably undermotivated toward significant life goals, never experiencing much interest in work, in interpersonal relations, or in sex. He requires some sort of supervised existence, a nursing care program, perhaps, or domiciliary type care, but alcohol might well compromise his well-being in such settings.

Another exercise in futility, but at least we know what we're up against, and are warned of what we might expect. But a nonpsychologist likely might have done as well even though the technicalities might have been missed—with no practical loss.

B. A. R., age 30

Though not appearing evidently psychotic, the thrust of clinical impression being predominantly that of depression and discouragement, there nevertheless are indicators of a paranoid schizophrenia. Though autism, ambivalence, and impairment of reality contact are not readily apparent, the following do appear: guardedness, occasional irrelevancy of response to direct questions, and undercriticalness of his intellectual productions. He continues to believe that the sergeants in his unit were involved in a "conspiracy" against him, though his explanation is not convincing, and he continues to lack insight into the reason for any of his hospitalizations, though he does volunteer that he has had "nervous breakdowns" which he remembers as periods of depression.

Particularly at the time of his first hospitalization did he evidently suffer a severe psychosis, for he admits to lengthy periods of amnesia at this time. He is fearful of close relationships, tending to withdraw emotionally and in drink, though the desire for interpersonal contact, particularly heterosexual contact is intense and realized only as a fantasy substitute. He is also fearful of displaying his perceived inadequacies, to become defensive and to project hostility when he feels others threaten him in this regard. He is readily moved to arousal of hostility in the context of poor judgment and acting-out tendencies. Treatment should be symptomatic and supportive.

The diagnosis here is important: there is indicated medication for this condition. Many psychiatrists would consider that to build treatment around antidepressant medication would be ineffective, that the use of antianxiety agents (which would be proper were the person suffering an anxiety neurosis) would probably also be ineffective, and that treatment with chlordiazepoxide (which might be given were he thought to be neurotic) could be counterproductive. Knowing some of this person's cardinal personality features has implications for relating to him.

L. S. M., age 24

Though schizophrenic material definitely seems present, depression seems to be the most compelling issue. This is essentially existential, the patient finding no meaning in life and no goals with which he can identify. He longs for relationship but cannot seem to achieve it. He feels that life is passing him by. An illustrative sentence completion item is: What I want out of life. . . is life. In addition to antipsychotic medication, this patient will require long-term individual and/or group psychotherapy, with much attention given to existential problems.

A long, arduous road ahead, and maybe we can't help the young man to a happy destination, but at least we have some of the makings for a road map. If we travelled only the schizophrenic road we might congratulate ourselves on the remission of schizophrenic symptoms, as such might materialize, but we would only be at a dead end.

PSYCHOLOGICAL REPORTS AS A GROUP PSYCHOTHERAPY TOOL

Noting recent trends toward an egalitarian relationship between therapist and client, Yalom, Brown, and Bloch (1975) describe a new form of psychological report which facilitates the group psychotherapy process. Similar to the manner in which Fischer (1970), Craddick (1972), and Mosak and Gushurst (1972) share psychological data with clients, each report, consisting of a summary of the group meeting, is made available to the client prior to the next meeting. The typical report consists of three to seven pages, double spaced, of narrative and commentary. It requires twenty to forty minutes to dictate and is done immediately following the session. The typed report is then mailed to the clients.

A number of benefits, as perceived either by the therapists or the clients, are described:

1. Revivification of the meeting. A report of the happenings of the meeting refresh the memory and make for continuity between meetings. The next meeting is likely to continue on the theme of the previous one.

2. The participant observer role. In reading the summary report the clients become observers as well as participants in the therapy process. The therapists have an opportunity to repeat interpretations they deem to be important, particularly those that clients may not have adequately attended to because of personal or sociodynamic reasons. Some interpretations are repeated because they are regarded as exceedingly important or exceedingly complex.

3. A second chance. The therapists point out what should have happened in the meeting but didn't, thus encouraging, sometimes goading clients to participate or to follow through.

4. Construction of group norms. The report is used to give structure to the group, a set of rules for the functioning of the group to maximize its effectiveness. Thus, the therapists may focus on the need for here-and-now content, or for the need of the group members to take responsibility for the conduct of the sessions. Certain practices of the group or its members may be questioned, or the members may be criticized.

5. Therapeutic leverage. Important content may be repeated and emphasized. Thus, one client evaded participantion by entertaining the other group members. At one point, however, he remarked, "When you see me smiling like this in the group, it means I'm covering up pain; don't let me keep getting away with it." This crucial statement was tagged for reuse.

6. New contributions. The report provides an opportunity for the therapist to offer new observations, clarifications, or interpretations. It may be that the therapist misses certain insights during the session but arrives at them afterward. Or the timing may not have been right to make comments, or a client for various reasons may have been unreceptive. Or the introduction of cognitive material during a crucial experiential period might have been destructive.

7. Transmission of the therapist's temporal perspective. Typically the therapist has a better temporal perspective than the clients who are involved in the here and now of their own problems. The therapist must therefore become the "group historian, the time-binder." Here is what a therapist wrote into a report about a client who failed to grasp the progress she was making:

"Delores described the despair she had been experiencing. In some ways it sounded almost identical to the kinds of despair Delores described in the group when she first entered—having to do with loneliness, with the feeling that she always had to ask people to be with her and do things with her, that there was no one in the world who cared about her.

However, there is an important difference in her state now and her condition at that time. Several months ago Delores presented these things as though that's the way the world *was*—that there *was* no one in the world for her. This time she has a more realistic view of it. She realizes that this is the way she is thinking right now. She feels discouraged and angry because she knows that there is so much more work to do. She is upset at the fact that her center of self-regard is not inside but still outside of herself, and that she allows others to define her, to tell her whether she is worthwhile rather than having a stable, internal sense of self-worth. In a sense then, at some level, Delores recognizes that she is responsible for her bad feelings about herself, and hence can change these feelings."

8. Therapist self-disclosure. The authors feel strongly that group therapy should be demystified, that their views of the process be disclosed for the purpose of "model setting, deepening the therapist-patient relationship, demonstrating a personal belief in therapy and a trust in the group, and facilitating transference resolution." Faith healing and placebo techniques are shunned as the therapists discuss their "here-and-now feelings in the group— puzzlement, discouragement, pleasure, and annoyance." The following brief excerpt discloses some of the feelings of therapists Dave and Lena:

"Dave and Lena both felt considerable strain in the meeting. We felt caught between our feeling of wanting to continue with Delores, but also being very much aware of Bob's obvious hurting in the meeting. Therefore, even at the risk of Delores's feeling that we were deserting her, we felt strongly about bringing in Bob before the end of the meeting."

9. Filling gaps. The report is helpful to clients and therapists in keeping them informed when meetings are missed because of illness or vacations. It is also the authors' impression that new patients enter the group more smoothly if given reports of the three or four previous meetings.

10. The summary as an event in the group. Individual clients react to the reports in their own idiosyncratic manners. For example, there may be paranoid distortions or feelings of rejection when attention is focused on other members of the group. The feelings aroused by the report may then be dealt with in therapy.

11. Therapist uses. The report facilitates the supervisory process as both supervisor and trainee react to the same material. More important, as in the writing of all psychological reports, the very act of writing can help us to shape and sharpen our conclusions. Writing a report—as opposed to an offhand verbal report—can force us to think more about the case. This is of particularly great importance when the writer is also the therapist.

PSYCHOLOGICAL REPORTS IN JOURNAL ARTICLES

To complete this potpourri, we present a variation of use for the psychological report rather than a new form of reporting.

The presentation of case studies in journals is a time-honored method for illustrating the conclusions of an article and sharing with the reader basic data so that he can follow the arguments. The reader acquires a "feel" for the material. Particularly in psychiatric journals is this practice common.

Psychological reports might effectively be used in this manner, yet such use is decidedly rare. Occasionally a psychologist's conclusions are quoted in an article. Generally, however, psychological data are presented on a group basis in tabular form.

The following two of the writer's reports were presented in a psychiatric journal in an article reporting on the post-surgical adjustment of cancer patients in whom colostomies had been constructed.[4] The group data summarizing the authors' conclusions and clinical case material is presented in the classical way. The psychological reports impart a feel and an understanding for the patients' adjustment that cannot quite be achieved by other means.

Illustrative Rorschach Report—No. 1

In a context of severe intellectual and emotional confusion, we see a conflict centering primarily about a life-death struggle within the self, and about bodily integrity, personality integrity, and self-identity. Things somehow do not seem "right" to him as he turns away from the outside world and focuses on himself, especially on his body and its functions. He feels mutilated, dismembered rather than whole, worthless, and as if he is a lower form of life. Specifically, there is attention directed to alimenation, elimination, the rectum, and other bodily features associated with elimination. There is also concern about sex, but its specific relation to this disordered economy is not certain. All of these difficulties, particularly as they relate to body processes are seen as the result of external assault upon him, as if others have unjustifiably done something to him and damaged him. In fact, in his current state of despair, he tends to see others as at fault and he is critical. In this manner, oppositional tendencies which are now quite strong are pushing for expression and he feels they are justifiable.

This inner state of dysphoric turbulence is seen in a loss of spontaneity, in a marked sense of insecurity, helplessness, and uncertainty, and in social relations which are characterized by tentativeness. He is overcautious. Thus, he is remarkably ineffectual and unadaptable, and unable to come to grips with problems. In novel situations or under pressure, his judgment would not be at all reliable. In a personality not comfortably defended against psychosis, the term "paranoid" intrudes itself. The possibility of further regression with depersonalization, depression, and bodily delusions has to be considered.

Illustrative Rorschach Report—No. 2

This person is existing in the context of a rigid, constricted, narrow, unspontaneous approach to daily events. It is this withdrawal from active interaction with life which may be keeping him on this side of an active psychosis. To demand more of him undoubtedly would precipitate an actual state. His current orientation to life and his very understanding of his existence is through his bodily processes, and his comprehension of threat evidences a severe confusion on a par with the confusion which characterizes his everyday living. He seems to be groping, albeit unconstructively, for some dependable realities in life. In so doing, he constantly gravitates to primitive bodily concerns, to taking in through the mouth, the process of alimentation, elimination, and the nature of anatomical structure. Here anxiety is particularly

[4]Illustrative Rorschach Reports 1 and 2 reprinted by permission from Orbach, Charles E., and Tallent, Norman, Modification of perceived body and body concepts following the construction of a colostomy. *Archives of General Psychiatry*, February 1965, *12*, 126-135. Copyright 1965, American Medical Association.

severe and centers about a deep feeling of bodily loss which leaves him empty, without substance and without life. Sex anxieties have also come to the fore, and he also has concerns about anatomical sex differences which would suggest more the transient mental activity of a boy of 6 rather than a matter of enduring interest in a man of 60. There is the difference, however, that it is internal rather than external anatomy which is sexualized. One gets the feeling that his concern is whether the male or the female is more adequate internally.

References

Abel, G. G., & Blanchard, E. B. The role of fantasy in the treatment of sexual deviation. *Archives of General Psychiatry*, 1974, *30*(4), 467-475.

Affleck, D. C., & Strider, F. D. Contribution of psychological reports to patient management. *Journal of Consulting and Clinical Psychology*, 1971, *37*(2), 177-179.

Alexander, F. The dynamics of psychotherapy in the light of learning theory. *American Journal of Psychiatry*, 1963, *120*, 440-448.

Allen, F. H. *Psychotherapy with children*. New York: Norton, 1942.

Allport, G. *Personality: A psychological interpretation*. New York: Holt, 1937.

American Psychiatric Association. *Diagnostic and statistical manual, mental disorders*. Washington, D.C.: American Psychiatric Association, 1952.

American Psychiatric Association. *Diagnostic and statistical manual, mental disorders*, Second Edition. Washington, D.C.: American Psychiatric Association, 1968.

American Psychiatric Association. *Task Force Report No. 5; Behavior therapy in psychiatry*. Washington, D.C.: American Psychiatric Association, June 1973.

Anonymous. Encounter group change measured by POI and CPS. *Educational and Industrial Testing Service Research and Development*, 1973, *1*(8), 1-4.

Appelbaum, S. A. Science and persuasion in the psychological test report. *Journal of Consulting and Clinical Psychology*, 1970, *35*(3), 349-355.

Auger, T. J. Mental health terminology—A modern tower of babel? *Journal of Community Psychology*, 1974, *2*(2), 113-116.

Berne, E. *Games people play*. New York: Grove Press, 1964.

Bersoff, D. N. *The psychological evaluation of children: A manual of report writing for psychologists who work with children in an educational setting*. (Mimeographed), undated.

Block, J. *The Q-sort method in personality assessment and psychiatric research*. Springfield, Illinois: Charles C Thomas, 1961.

Bonjean, C. M., & Vance, G. G. A short form measure of self-actualization. *Journal of Applied Behavioral Science*, 1968, *4*(3), 299-312.

Breger, L. Psychological testing: treatment and research implications. *Journal of Consulting and Clinical Psychology*, 1968, *32*(2), 178-181.

Brown, E. C. Assessment from a humanistic perspective. *Psychotherapy: Theory, Research and Practice*, 1972, *9*(2), 103-106.

Brown, E. C., & Smith, W. H. Measurement of existential mental health: further exploration. *Journal of Individual Psychology*, 1968, *24*, 71-73.

Bugental, J. F. T. Humanistic psychology: A new break-through. *American Psychologist,* 1963, *18*(9), 563-567.

Bugental, J. F. T. Psychodiagnostics and the quest for certainty. *Psychiatry,* 1964, *27*(1), 73-77.

Carr, A. C. Psychological testing and reporting. *Journal of Projective Techniques and Personality Assessment,* 1968, *32*(6), 513-521.

Carrier, N. A. Need correlates of "gullibility." *Journal of Abnormal and Social Psychology,* 1963, *66*(1), 84-86.

Cautela, J. R. Behavior therapy and the need for behavioral assessment. *Psychotherapy: Theory, Research and Practice,* 1968, *5*(3), 175-179.

Cautela, J. R. & Upper, D. A behavioral coding system. Presidential address presented by Dr. Cautela at Annual Meeting of the Association for the Advancement of Behavior Therapy, Miami, December, 1973.

Cautela, J. R., & Upper, D. Behavioral analysis, assessment, and diagnosis. Proceedings of the Fifth Annual Brockton Symposium on Behavior Therapy, April 22, 1974. Nutley, N.J.: Roche Laboratories, 1974.

Cole, J. K., & Magnussen, M. G. Where the action is. *Journal of Consulting Psychology,* 1966, *30*(6), 539-543.

Conrad, H. S. The validity of personality ratings of preschool children. *Journal of Educational Psychology,* 1932, *23*, 671-680.

Craddick, R. A. Humanistic Assessment: A reply to Brown. *Psychotherapy: Theory, Research and Practice,* 1972, *9*(2), 107-110.

Cuadra, C. A., & Albaugh, W. P. Sources of ambiguity in psychological reports. *Journal of Clinical Psychology,* 1956, *12*, 108-115.

Dailey, C. A. The practical utility of the psychological report. *Journal of Consulting Psychology,* 1953, *17*, 297-302.

Dana, R. H. Eisegesis and assessment. *Journal of Projective Techniques,* 1966, 30(3), 215-222.

Dana, R. H., Hannifin, P., Lancaster, C., Lore, W., & Nelson, D. *Psychological reports and juvenile probation counseling. Journal of Clinical Psychology,* 1963, *19*(3), 352-355.

Davenport, B. F. The semantic validity of TAT interpretation. *Journal of Consulting Psychology,* 1952, *16*, 171-175.

De Courcy, P. The hazard of short-term psychotherapy without assessment: A case history. *Journal of Personality Assessment,* 1971, *35*, 285-288.

Dengrove, E. Practical behavioral diagnosis. In Lazarus, A. A. *Clinical behavior therapy.* New York: Brunner/Mazel, 1972.

Dies, R. R. Personal gullibility or pseudodiagnosis: A further test of the "fallacy of personal validation." *Journal of Clinical Psychology,* 1972, *28*(1), 47-50.

Dmitruk, V. M., Collins, R. W., & Clinger, D. L. The "Barnum effect" and acceptance of negative personal evaluation. *Journal of Consulting and Clinical Psychology,* 1973, *41*(2), 192-194.

Dollin, A., & Reznikoff, M. Diagnostic referral questions in psychological testing. *Psychological Reports,* 1966, *19*, 610.

Eells, J. Therapist views and preferences concerning intake cases. *Journal of Consulting Psychology,* 1964, *28*, 382.

Enelow, A. J., & Swisher, S. N. *Interviewing and patient care.* New York: Oxford University Press, 1972.

English, H. B., & English, A. C. *A comprehensive dictionary of psychological and psychoanalytical terms.* New York: Longmans, Green, and Co., 1958.

Exner, J. E. *The Rorschach systems.* New York: Grune and Stratton, 1969.

Fensterheim, H. The initial interview. In Lazarus, A. A. *Clinical behavior therapy.* New York: Brunner/Mazel, 1972.

Filer, R. N. The clinician's personality and his case reports. *American Psychologist,* 1952, *7,* 336.

Fischer, C. T. The testee as co-evaluator. *Journal of Counseling Psychology,* 1970, *17*(1), 70-76.

Fischer, C. T. Paradigm changes which allow sharing of "results" with the client. Paper presented to the American Psychological Association, September, 1971.

Fischer, C. T. Intelligence Contra IQ: A human science critique and alternative to the natural science approach to man. *Human Development,* 1973, *16,* 8-20.(a)

Fischer, C. T. Contextual approach to assessment. *Community Mental Health Journal,* 1973, *9*(1), 38-45.(b)

Flesch, R. *The art of readable writing.* New York: Harper, 1949.

Flesch, R. *Say what you mean.* New York: Harper & Row, 1972.

Forer, B. R. The fallacy of personal validation: A classical demonstration of gullibility. *Journal of Abnormal and Social Psychology,* 1949, *44,* 118-123.

Foster, A. Writing psychological reports. *Journal of Clinical Psychology,* 1951, *7,* 195.

Garfield, S. L. *Introductory clinical psychology.* New York: Macmillan, 1957.

Garfield, S. L., Heine, R. W., & Leventhal, M. An evaluation of psychological reports in a clinical setting. *Journal of Consulting Psychology,* 1954, *18,* 281-286.

Glueck, B. C., Jr., & Reznikoff, M. Comparison of computer derived personality profile and projective psychological test findings. (Mimeographed), undated.

Goldfried, M. R., & Davison, G. C. *Clinical behavior therapy.* New York: Holt, Rinehart, and Winston, 1976.

Goldfried, M. R., & Pomeranz, D. M. Role of assessment in behavior modification. *Psychological Reports,* 1968, *23,* 75-87.

Goldfried, M. R., & Kent, R. N. Traditional vs. behavioral personality assessment: A comparison of methodological and theoretical assumptions. *Psychological Bulletin,* 1972, *77,* 409-420.

Goodkin, R. Some neglected issues in the literature on behavior therapy. *Psychological Reports,* 1967, *20,* 415-420.

Grayson, H. M., & Tolman, R. S. A semantic study of concepts of clinical psychologists and psychiatrists. *Journal of Abnormal and Social Psychology,* 1950, *45,* 216-231.

Greenspoon, J., & Gersten, C. D. A new look at psychological testing: Psychological testing from the standpoint of a behaviorist. *American Psychologist,* 1967, *22*(10), 848-853.

Hacker, S. L., Gaitz, C. M., & Hacker, B. C. A humanistic view of measuring mental health. *Journal of Humanistic Psychology,* 1972, *12*(1), 94-106.

Hammer, E., & Piotrowski, Z. A. Hostility as a factor in the clinician's personality as it affects his interpretation of projective drawings (H-T-P). *Journal of Projective Techniques,* 1953, *17,* 210-216.

Hammond, K. R., & Allen, J. M. *Writing clinical reports.* Englewood Cliffs, N.J.: Prentice-Hall, 1953.

Hartlage, L., Freeman, W., Horine, L., & Walton, C. Decisional utility of psychological reports. *Journal of Clinical Psychology,* 1968, *24*(4), 481-483.

Headrick, L. B. From Hadlock, W. O. Engineer as author. *RCA Engineer,* August-September, 1956.

Hinkle, J. E., Nelson, S. E., & Miller, D. Psychological test usage by psychologist psychotherapists in private practice. *Psychotherapy: Theory, Research and Practice,* 1968, *5*(4), 210-213.

Holt, R. R. Diagnostic testing: Present status and future prospects. *Journal of Nervous and Mental Disease,* 1967, *144*(6), 444-465.

Holtzman, W. H. Recurring dilemmas in personality assessment. *Journal of Projective Techniques and Personality Assessment,* 1964, *28*(2), 144-150.

Holzberg, J., Allessi, S. L., & Wexler, M. Psychological case reporting at psychiatric staff conferences. *Journal of Consulting Psychology,* 1951, *5,* 425-429.

Hurst, J. W., & Walker, H. K. *The problem-oriented system.* New York: Medcom, 1972.

Johnson, W. The degree of extensional agreement among twenty psychologists in their use of the labels "hypothesis," "theory," and "law." *Iowa Academy of Science,* 1945, *52,* 255-259.

Kelly, E. L. Clinical psychology—1960; a report of survey findings. *Newsletter, Division of Clinical Psychology of the American Psychological Association,* 1961, *14,* 1-11.

Klopfer, W. G. *The psychological report.* New York: Grune and Stratton, 1960.

Klopfer, W. G. The blind leading the blind: psychotherapy without assessment. *Journal of Projective Techniques and Personality Assessment,* 1964, *28*(4), 387-392.

Korner, I. N. Test report evaluation. *Journal of Clinical Psychology,* 1962, *18,* 194-197.

Kotchen, T. Existential mental health: an empirical approach. *Journal of Individual Psychology,* 1960, *16,* 174-181.

Lacey, H. M., & Ross, A. O. Multidisciplinary views on psychological reports in child guidance clinics. *Journal of Clinical Psychology,* 1964, *20*(4), 522-526.

Lachar, D. Accuracy and generalizability of an automated MMPI interpretation system. *Journal of Consulting and Clinical Psychology,* 1974, *42*(2), 267-273.

Lacks, P. B., Horton, M. M., & Owen, J. D. A more meaningful and practical approach to psychological reports. *Journal of Clinical Psychology,* 1969, *25,* 383-386.

Lambley, P. The dangers of therapy without assessment: A case study. *Journal of Personality Assessment,* 1974, *38*(3), 263-265.

Lazarus, A. A. Multimodal behavior therapy: treating the "basic id." *Journal of Nervous and Mental Disease,* 1973, *156,* 404-411.

Manning, E. J. "Personal validation": Replication of Forer's study. *Psychological Reports,* 1968, *23,* 181-182.

Marcuse, F. L. Projection, 1953. *Amrican Psychologist,* 1955, *10,* 43.

Marmor, J. Dynamic psychotherapy and behavior therapy. *Archives of General Psychiatry,* 1971, *24,* 22-28.

Matarazzo, J. D. Postdoctoral residency program in clinical psychology. In Conference Committee. *Preconference materials prepared for the conference on the professional preparation of clinical psychologists,* pp. 71-73. American Psychological Association, Washington, D.C., 1965.

May, R., Angel, E., & Ellenberger, H. F. *Existence.* New York: Basic Books, 1958.

Mayman, M. Style, focus, language, and content of an ideal psychological test report. *Journal of Projective Techniques,* 1959, *23,* 453-458.

Meehl, P. E. *Clinical versus statistical prediction: A theoretical analysis and a review of the evidence.* Minneapolis: University of Minnesota Press, 1954.

Meehl, P. E. Wanted—A good cookbook. *American Psychologist,* 1956, *11,* 263-272.

Meehl, P. E. What can the clinician do well? Paper read at the symposium *Clinical skills revisited,* September 4, 1959, American Psychological Association Convention, Cincinnati, Ohio.

Meehl, P. E. The cognitive activity of the clinician. *American Psychologist,* 1960, *15,* 19-27.

Menninger, W. C. Psychiatry and psychology. *American Journal of Psychiatry,* 1948, *105,* 389-390.

Mintz, J. Survey of student therapists' attitudes toward psychodiagnostic reports. *Journal of Consulting and Clinical Psychology,* 1968, *32*(4), 500.

Mischel, W. *Personality and assessment.* New York: Wiley, 1968.

Moore, C. H., Boblitt, W. E., & Wildman, R. W. Psychiatric impressions of psychological reports. *Journal of Clinical Psychology,* 1968, *24*(3), 373-376.

Mosak, H. H., & Gushurst, R. S. Some therapeutic uses of psychologic testing. *American Journal of Psychotherapy,* 1972, *26*(4), 539-546.

O'Dell, J.W. P. T. Barnum explores the computer. *Journal of Consulting and Clinical Psychology,* 1972, *38*(2), 270-273.

Odom, C. L. A study of the time required to do a Rorschach Examination. *Journal of Projective Techniques,* 1950, *14,* 464-468.

Olive, H. Psychoanalysts' opinions of psychologists' reports: 1952 and 1970. *Journal of Clinical Psychology,* 1972, *28*(1), 50-54.

Orbach, C. E., & Tallent, N. Modification of perceived body and body concepts following the construction of a colostomy. *Archives of General Psychiatry,* 1965, *12,* 126-135.

Oxford English dictionary. Compact edition. Oxford University Press, 1971.

Paul, G. L. Strategy of outcome research in psychotherapy. *Journal of Consulting Psychology,* 1967, *31,* 109-119.

Piotrowski, Z. A. *Perceptanalysis.* New York: Macmillan, 1957.

Rhoads, J. M., & Feather, B. W. The application of psychodynamics to behavior therapy. *American Journal of Psychiatry,* 1974, *13*(1), 17-20.

Ritchie, G. C. The use of hypnosis in a case of exhibitionism. *Psychotherapy: Theory, Research and Practice,* 1968, *5*(1), 40-43.

Robinson, J. T. *Some indications of personality differences among clinical psychologists as revealed in their reports on patients.* Unpublished M.A. thesis, Duke University, 1951.

Robinson, J. T., & Cohen, L. D. Individual bias in psychological reports. *Journal of Clinical Psychology,* 1954, *10,* 333-336.

Rogers, C. R. *Counseling and psychotherapy.* Boston: Houghton-Mifflin, 1942.

Rogers, C. R. *Client-centered therapy*. Boston: Houghton-Mifflin, 1951.

Rosen, M. Alice in Rorschachland. *Journal of Personality Assessment*, 1973, *37*(2), 115-121.

Rosenwald, G. C. Psychodiagnostics and its discontents. *Psychiatry*, 1963, *26*(3), 222-240.

Ryback, R. S. *The problem oriented record in psychiatry and mental health care*. New York: Grune and Stratton, 1974.

Sarbin, T. R., Taft, R., & Bailey, D. E. *Clinical inference and cognitive theory*. New York: Holt, Rinehart & Winston, 1960.

Sargent, H. D. Psychological test reporting. An experiment in technique. *Bulletin of the Menninger Clinic*, 1951, *15*, 175-186.

Schafer, R. *Psychoanalytic interpretation in Rorschach testing*. New York: Grune and Stratton, 1954.

Shoben, E. J., Jr. Psychotherapy as a problem in learning theory. *Psychological Bulletin*, 1949, *46*, 366-392.

Siskind, G. Change of attitude? *The clinical psychologist*, 1967, *20*(4), 158.(a)

Siskind, G. Fifteen years later: a replication of "a semantic study of concepts of clinical psychologists and psychiatrists." *The Journal of Psychology*, 1967, *65*, 3-7.(b)

Sloane, R. B. The converging paths of behavior therapy and psychotherapy. *American Journal of Psychiatry*, 1969, *125*, 877-885.

Smyth, R., & Reznikoff, M. Attitudes of psychiatrists toward the usefulness of psychodiagnostic reports. *Professional Psychology*, 1971, *2*(3), 283-288.

Synder, C. R. Acceptance of personality interpretations as a function of assessment procedures. *Journal of Consulting and Clinical Psychology*, 1974, *42*(1), 150.

Snyder, C. R., & Larson, G. R. A further look at student acceptance of general personality interpretations. *Journal of Consulting and Clinical Psychology*, 1972, *38*(3), 384-388.

Souther, J. W. *Technical report writing*. New York: Wiley, 1957.

Sturm, I. E. Toward a composite psychodiagnostic report outline. *Newsletter for Research in Mental Health and Behavioral Science*, 1974, *16*(3), 6-7.

Sundberg, N. D. The acceptability of "fake" versus "bona fide" personality test interpretations. *Journal of Abnormal and Social Psychology*, 1955, *50*, 145-147.

Sundberg, N. D. The practice of psychological testing in clinical services in the United States. *American Psychologist*, 1961, *16*, 79-83.

Tallent, N. An approach to the improvement of clinical psychological reports. *Journal of Clinical Psychology*, 1956, *12*, 103-109.

Tallent, N. On individualizing the psychologist's clinical evaluation. *Journal of Clinical Psychology*, 1958, *14*, 243-244.

Tallent, N., & Reiss, W. J. Multidisciplinary views on the preparation of written clinical psychological reports: I. Spontaneous suggestions for content. *Journal of Clinical Psychology*, 1959, *15*, 218-221.(a)

Tallent, N., & Reiss, W. J. Multidisciplinary views on the preparation of written clinical psychological reports. II. Acceptability of certain common content variables and styles of expression. *Journal of Clinical Psychology*, 1959, *15*, 273-274.(b)

Tallent, N., & Reiss, W. J. Multidisciplinary views on the preparation of written clinical psychological reports. III. The trouble with psychological reports. *Journal of Clinical Psychology*, 1959, *15*, 444-446.(c)

Tallent, N., & Reiss, W. J. A note on an unusually high rate of returns for a mail questionnaire. *The Public Opinion Quarterly*, Winter 1959-1960, *23*(4), 579-581.

Tallent, N., & Rafi, A. A. National and professional factors in psychological consultation. *British Journal of Social and Clinical Psychology*, 1965, *4*, 149-151.

Tallent, N., Kennedy, G., Szafir, A., & Grolimund, B. An expanded role for psychiatric nursing personnel: Psychological evaluation and interpersonal care. *Journal of Psychiatric Nursing and Mental Health Services*, 1974, *12*(3), 19-23.

Taylor, J. L., & Teicher, A. A clinical approach to reporting psychological test data. *Journal of Clinical Psychology*, 1946, *2*, 323-332.

Thorne, F. C. Clinical judgment: a clinician's viewpoint. *Journal of Clinical Psychology*, 1960, *16*, 128-134.

Thorne, F. C. *Clinical judgment: A study of clinical errors.* Brandon, Vt.: Journal of Clinical Psychology, 1961.

Towbin, A. P. When are cookbooks useful? *American Psychologist*, 1960, *15*, 119-123.

Trehub, A., & Scherer, I. W. Wechsler-Bellevue scatter as an index of schizophrenia. *Journal of Consulting Psychology*, 1958, *22*, 147-149.

Ulrich, R. E., Stachnik, T. J., & Stainton, N. R. Student acceptance of generalized personality interpretations. *Psychological Reports*, 1963, *13*, 831-834.

Vernon, W. H. D. Diagnostic testing and some problems of communication between psychiatrists and clinical psychologists. *Bulletin of the Maritime Psychological Association*, Spring 1955, 12-29.

Webb, J. T., Miller, M. L., & Fowler, R. D., Jr. Validation of a computerized MMPI interpretation system. *Proceedings of the 77th Annual Convention, American Psychological Association*, 1969, 523-524.

Wechsler, D. The psychologist in the psychiatric hospital. *Journal of Consulting Psychology*, 1944, *8*, 281-285.

Weed, L. L. Medical records that guide and teach. *New England Journal of Medicine*, 1968, *278*, 593-599, 652-657.

Weed, L. L. *Medical records, medical education, and patient care: The problem oriented record as a basic tool.* Cleveland: Case Western University Press, 1969.

Weiner, I. B. Does psychodiagnosis have a future? *Journal of Personality Assessment*, 1972, *36*(6), 534-546.

Weitzman, B. Behavior therapy and psychotherapy. *Psychological Review*, 1967, *74*(4), 300-317.

Wertheimer, M. *Productive thinking.* New York: Harper, 1945.

Wesman, A. G. Intelligent testing. *American Psychologist*, 1968, *23*, 267-274.

Wiedemann, C., & Mintz, J. Student therapists' assessment of diagnostic testing. *Journal of Personality Assessment*, 1974, *38*(3), 203-214.

Wiener, D. N., & Raths, O. N. Contributions of the mental hygiene clinic team to clinic decisions. *American Journal of Orthopsychiatry*, 1959, *29*, 350-356.

Wolpe, J. *Psychotherapy by reciprocal inhibition.* Stanford, California: Stanford University Press, 1958.

Yalom, I., Brown, S., & Bloch S. The written summary as a group psychotherapy technique. *Archives of General Psychiatry,* 1975, *32*(5), 605-613.

Yates, A. J. *Behavior therapy.* New York: Wiley, 1970.

Author Index

Abel, G. G., 23
Affleck, D. C., 18
Albaugh, W. P., 31
Alexander, F., 23
Allen, F. H., 19
Allen, J. M., 66, 67, 68, 93
Allessi, S. L., 31
Allport, G. W., 89
Appelbaum, S., 13, 16
Auger, T. J., 31

Bailey, D. E., 91
Berne, E., 153
Bersoff, D. N., 181, 204
Blanchard, E. B., 23
Bloch, S., 240
Block, J., 69
Boblitt, W. E., 30
Bonjean, C. M., 25
Breger, L., 18, 31
Brown, E. C., 24, 25
Brown, S., 240
Bugental, J. F. T., 24

Carr, A. C., 105
Carrier, N. A., 31, 55
Cautela, J. R., 22
Clinger, D. L., 31
Cohen, L. D., 56
Cole, J. K., 18, 31
Collins, R. W., 31
Conrad, H. S., 118
Craddick, R. A., 25, 240
Cuadra, C. A., 31

Dailey, C. A., 18, 31
Dana, R. H., 18, 35
Davenport, R. F., 52, 67
De Courcy, P., 19
Dengrove, E., 21
Dmitruk, V. M., 31
Dollin, A., 16

Enelow, A. J., 236
English, A. C., 57
English, H. B., 57
Exner, J. E., 16

Feather, B. W., 23
Fensterheim, H., 21
Filer, R. N., 56
Fischer, C. T., 25, 220, 240
Flesch, R., 51, 63
Forer, B. R., 31, 55
Foster, A., 31
Fowler, R. D., Jr., 226
Freeman, W., 18, 32

Gaitz, C. M., 24
Garfield, S. L., 31, 92
Gersten, C. D., 20
Gilberstadt, H., 227
Glueck, B. C., Jr., 226
Goldfried, M. R., 22, 23, 214
Goodkin, R., 21
Grayson, H. M., 31, 67, 68, 70
Greenspoon, J., 20
Grolimund, B., 12
Gushurst, R. S., 25, 240

Hacker, B. C., 24
Hacker, S. L., 24
Hammer, E., 56
Hammond, K. R., 66, 67, 68, 93
Hartlage, L., 18, 31
Headrick, L. B., 105
Heine, R. W., 31
Hinkle, J. E., 19
Holt, R. R., 13
Holzberg, J., 31
Holtzman, W. H., 32
Horine, L., 18, 32
Horton, M. M., 105
Hurst, J. W., 236

Johnson, W., 67

Kelly, E. L., 19
Kennedy, G., 12
Kent, R. N., 23
Klopfer, W. G., 15, 19, 54, 56
Korner, I. N., 17
Kotchen, T., 25

Lacey, H. M., 7, 30
Lacks, P. B., 105
Lambley, P., 19
Lapuc, P., 217
Larson, G. R., 31, 55, 66
Lazarus, A. A., 216
Leventhal, M., 31

Magnussen, M. G., 18, 31
Manning, E. J., 31
Marmor, J., 23
Matarazzo, J. D., 13
May, R., 24
Mayman, M., 59
Meehl, P. E., 19, 31, 54, 226
Menninger, W. C., 27
Miller, D., 19
Miller, M. L., 226
Mintz, J., 19
Mischel, W., 23
Moore, C. H., 30
Mosak, H. H., 25, 240

Nelson, S. E., 19

Odom, C. L., 17
Olive, H., 30
Orbach, C. E., 243
Owen, J. D., 105

Paterson, D. G., 54, 55
Paul, G. L., 22
Piotrowski, Z. A., 56, 229
Pomeranz, D. M., 22

Rafi, A. A., 7
Raths, O. N., 90
Reiss, W. J., 7, 28, 30, 34, 49, 61, 66, 72, 93
Reznikoff, M., 16, 30, 31, 226
Rhoads, J. M., 23
Ritchie, G. C., 23
Robinson, J. T., 56
Rogers, C. R., 19, 20, 24
Rosen, M., 31
Rosenwald, G., 13
Ross, A. O., 7, 30
Ryback, R. S., 236

Sacks, J. M., 136
Sarbin, T. R., 91
Sargent, H. W., 66
Schafer, R., 13, 14
Scherer, I. W., 89
Shoben, E. J., Jr., 23
Silver, C., 219
Siskind, G., 29, 31
Sloane, R. B., 23
Smith, W. H., 25
Smyth, R., 30, 31
Snyder, C. R., 31, 55, 66
Souther, J. W., 105, 106
Stachnik, T. J., 31, 55, 66
Stainton, N. R., 31, 55, 66
Strider, F. D., 18
Sturm, I. E., 105
Sundberg, N. D., 31, 52, 53, 55, 226
Swisher, S. N., 236
Szafir, A., 12

Taft, R., 91
Tallent, N., 7, 12, 28, 30, 31, 34, 49, 52, 54, 55, 56, 61, 66, 72, 93, 243
Taylor, J. L., 84
Teicher, A., 84
Thorn, M., 234
Thorne, F. C., 14
Tolman, R. S., 31, 67, 68, 70
Towbin, A. P., 13
Trehub, A., 89

Ulrich, R. E., 31, 55, 66
Upper, D., 22

Vance, G. G., 25
Vernon, W. H. D., 8

Walker, H. K., 236
Walton, C., 18, 32
Webb, J. T., 226
Wechsler, D., 16
Weed, L. L., 236
Weitzman, B., 23
Wertheimer, M., 63
Wexler, M., 31
Wiedemann, C., 19
Wiener, D. N., 90
Wildman, R. W., 30
Wolpe, J., 20

Yalom, I., 240
Yates, A. J., 20

Subject Index

Adjustment variables, 98
Anticipation of questions and future
  needs, 75-76
Arranging findings in a report, 124-129
Assessment:
  in behavior therapy, 20-24
  in humanistic therapy, 19-20, 24-26
  in psychotherapy, 19-26
  products of, 75

Behavioral note, 86-87, 186
Behavioral observations, 86-87
Behavioral reports, 10, 214-219
Behavior therapy, 5, 6
  assessment in, 20-24
  diagnosis in, 21
  and psychoanalysis, similarities, 23
  psychological reports in, 10, 214-219
  psychological tests in, 20-21
Bioenergetic therapy, 5

Caricature in psychological report, 119-120
Case-focusing, concept of, 114-118 ·
Case-focused reports, 10
  differentiation from other reports, 115
  exemplifications, 182-212
Client, as unique individual, 52-56
Clinical behavior, 86-87, 94-95, 186
Clinical decisions, psychological report as
      contribution to, 17-18
Clinical vs. actuarial prediction, 226
Colloquial expression, 183
Communication, criticisms of in psychological
      reports, 41-45, (table) 49
  hedging, 45, (table) 49
  length, 43, (table) 49
  organization, 45, (table) 49
  style, 44-45, (table) 49
  too technical, too complex, 43-44, (table)
      49
  vague, unclear, ambiguous, 42-43, (table)
      49
  word usage, 43, (table) 49
Community psychology, 5
Computer reports, 10, 225-235

Computer reports (Cont.'d)
  and clinical mission, 226
  exemplifications, 227-235
  printout, MMPI, 226-230
  printout, MMPI, "hit rate," 227
  printout, MMPI, value of, 226-227
  printout, Rorschach, 229, 231-234
  printout, Thorn composite profile, 234, 235
  relation to referral questions, 226
Conceptualizing a psychological report,
      118-129
Conceptualizing a psychological report,
      exemplification, 129-143
Consultant role of psychologist, 13-14, 87
Consultation, psychological vs. medical, 59
Content, 74-75
  appropriate emphasis of, 101-103
  clinical behavior, 86-87, 94-95, 186
  criticisms of in psychological reports,
      32-35, (table) 49
    diagnoses, prognoses, recommendations,
      34, (table) 49
    improper emphasis, 33-34, (table) 49
    minor relevance, 35, (table) 49
    omission of essential information 34-35,
      (table) 49
    raw data, 32-33, (table) 49
    unnecessary duplication, 35, (table) 49
  definition and classification, 76-78
  descriptive material, 94-95
  developmental vs. contemporary, 102
  diagnosis, 4, 17, 29, 90, 100
  discussion of aggression, 17
  discussion of anxiety, 17
  discussion of ego defects, 17
  discussion of organic deficit, 17
  discussion of sexuality, 17
  "emotional factors," 89-90
  frequently appropriate, 93-101
  illustrative, 55-60, 77-78
  inappropriate, 101
  "intellectual aspects," 88-89, 95-97
  mission, related to, 82-84
  new integration, 80-82
  nonintellectual factors, 97-99

Content (*Cont. 'd*)
  orienting data, 77
  part processes, 85-86
  "personality," 89-90
  persuasive, 16, 77-78, 201-202
  predictive material, 100
  preliminary part of report, 86-87
  primary, 76-77
  prognosis, 29, 92
  recommendations, 29, 92, 100-101
  relevance of, 82-84
  secondary, 76-77
  selection in terms of relevance, 82-84
  sources of, 78-82
  subconclusions, 78
  summary, 93
  test by test, 85
  "test results," 88
  in "traditional" reports, 84-93
  unconscious vs. conscious, 102-103
  unfamiliar concepts, 71
Contextual approach, 220

Data base, 5
Data:
  interpretation of, 56-60, 107-108
  raw, 32-33, 49, 56-60
Decision making, 4
Defenses, 98
Descriptive material, 94-95
Diagnosis, 4, 17, 29, 90-91, 100
  in behavior therapy, 21
  "blind", 79
  diagnostic-therapeutic team, 12, 236
  medical, 91
  new emphasis on, 214
  value of, 9-10
Dynamics, relation to psychotherapy, 9

"Emotional factors," 89-90
Emphasis, means of supplying, 119-120

"Findings," 88
Flexibility in psychological reporting
  104-106

Group psychotherapy, psychological
  reports in, 240-242

Hedging, 184
Humanistic approach, 5, 10 (*See also*
  Psychological report, humanistic)
Humanistic reports, 219-225
Humanistic therapies, assessment in,
  19-20, 24-26

"Intellectual aspects," 88-89
Intellectual factors, 95-97

Interpersonal perception, 99
Interpersonal relationships, 99
Interpretation:
  case-focused, 115-117
  criticisms of, 35-37, (*table*) 49
    inadequate differentiation, 37, (*table*) 49
    irresponsible interpretation, 35-36,
      (*table*) 49
    overspeculation, 36-37, (*table*) 49
  of data, points of view, 56-60
  weighting, 108
IQ:
  as administrative requirement, 185
  role in reports, 88-89

Journal articles, psychological reports in,
  242-244

Language, in conceptualizing reports, 109

Medical model constructs, 220
Mission, 3-6, 6-7, 29, 75, 90, 107-108
  and computer, 226
MMPI:
  computer printout, "hit rate," 227
  computer printout, value of, 226-227
  computer reports, 226-230
Motivational factors in personality, 98-99

Naturalistic observation, 5
Nonintellectual factors of personality, 97-99

Obsequiousness, 90
Operational approach, 110
Oral report, 11, 66
Organicity, diagnostic information on, 100
Organizing the psychological report, basic
  considerations, 106, 108-112
Orientation of report, 63-64
Orienting data, 77
Outlines (general) for psychological reports,
  105
Outlining a report, exemplification, 120-123

Parsimony in psychological reports, 108-109
Personality
  assets and liabilities, 99
  idiographic approach to, 52
  "Personality," as report content, 89-90
Person-orientation vs. test-orientation, 63-64
Physical complaints, psychologist's
  contribution to diagnosis, 197
Pitfalls in psychological reporting, 30-49
Prediction:
  clinical vs. statistical, 226
  role of, 226
Predictive material, 100
Problem Oriented Medical Record, 12, 236

Prognosis, 29, 100
Psychoanalysis and behavior therapy,
   similarities in, 23
Psychological consultation:
   basic scheme, 106-108
   occasion for, 75
Psychological data, sharing with client,
   25-26, 220, 240-242
Psychological evaluation:
   initiation of, 6
   initiation of, general request for information,
      6-8
   initiation of request form, 9
   initiation of specific request for
      information, 6-8
   manner of requesting, 6
   occasion for, 50-51
Psychological report:
   appropriate emphasis of content in,
      101-103
   basic considerations in organizing, 108-112
   behavioral, 5, 10, 214-219
   caricature in, 119-120
   case-focused, 7, 10, 114-118, 203-204
      differentiation from other reports, 115
      exemplification, 182-212
      training value, 236
   clinical notes as, 11
   computer, 10, 225-235
      and clinical mission, 226
      exemplifications, 227-235
      printout, MMPI, 226-230
      printout, MMPI, "hit rate," 227
      printout, MMPI, value of, 226-227
      printout, Rorschach, 229, 231-234
      printout, Thorn composite profile, 234,
         235
      relation to referral questions, 226
   conceptualizing of, 118-129
      exemplification, 129-143
   content, 74-75
      frequently appropriate, 93-101
      illustrative, 56-60, 77-78
      inappropriate content in, 101
      sources, 78-82
      in "traditional" reports, 84-93
   contribution to nursing care plan, 12, 236
   contribution to Problem Oriented Medical
      Record, 12, 236
   cost of, 17
   criticisms of, (table) 49
   defined, 9-11
   evolution of, 16-26
   flavor of, 60
   flexibility in, 104-106
   functional unities in, 111
   general reports, 7
   in group psychotherapy, 240-242

Psychological report (Cont. 'd)
   human interest in, 62-63
   humanistic, 5, 10, 219-225
   implications of, 50-51
   in journal articles, 242-244
   as laboratory or scientific document, 105
   language in conceptualizing, 109
   lay language in, 69-70
   length of, 72-73
   as listing of problems and solutions, 10
   manner of presenting conclusions, 64-66
   means of supplying emphasis, 119-120
   medical model constructs in, 220
   narrative, 10-11
   operational approach in, 110
   oral, 11, 66
   organization as problem, 106
   orientation of, 63-64
   orientation of team members and content, 83
   outlines for, 105
   parsimony in, 108-109
   persuasiveness in, 16, 77-78, 201-202
   pitfalls in, 30-49
   preliminary part, 86-87
   prescriptive, 10
   quickie reports, 236-240
   rationale, 10
   recommendations in, 29
   as record, 75, 76
   in reevaluated case, 203-204
   in rehabilitation counseling, 211-212
   relevant behavior and, 110
   reporting clinical behavior, 94-95
   reporting descriptive material, 94-95
   reporting diagnosis in, 29
   reporting prognosis in, 29
   responsible interpretation in, 51
   rhetoric, role in, 51
   scientistic constructs in, 220
   segmentalized reporting in, 111-112
   "shotgun reports," 7, 72, 109, 119-120
   as statements or adjectives, 11
   stereotypy in, 90 (See also Stereotypy)
   styles of, 61-63
   subconclusions in, 78
   teaching in, 219
   teaching value, 5
   teaching writing of, 148
   terminology in, 66-71
   "traditional," 10
   unfamiliar concepts in, 71
   usefulness of, 17-26, 27-28, 31-32
      for psychotherapy, 19-26
   written presentation, 66
Psychological science and profession,
      criticisms of, 32, 46-48, (table) 49
   problems of role conduct, 47-48 (table) 49
   problems of science, 46, (table) 49

Psychological testing, as a misnomer, 184
Psychological tests:
  in behavior therapy, 20-21
  function of, 79-80
  in humanistic therapy, 19-20, 24-26
    exemplification, 223-225
  nature of, 14
Psychologist:
  as consultant, 13-14, 87
  as "tester," 13-14
  attitude and orientation, criticisms of,
    37-41, (table) 49
    too authoritative, 39, (table) 49
    exhibitionism, 38-39, (table) 49
    miscellaneous deficiencies, 41, (table) 49
    overabstract, 40-41, (table) 49
    not practical or useful, 38, (table) 49
    test orientation vs. client orientation,
      39-40, (table) 49
    too theoretical, 40 (table) 49
  ethical principles of, 101
  function of, 62
  guidelines to function, 101
  participant-observer role, 195
  personal dynamics of, 14-16
  personality of, 15-16
  responsibility of, 50, 65-66
  role of, 13-14, 16, 82, 87, 195
  setting of evaluation goal, 107
  stimulus value of, 95
  theoretical orientation of, 109-110
  "types" of, 15
Psychopathology, interest in, 97
Psychotherapy:
  behavior, 5, 6 (See also Behavior therapy)
  bioenergetic, 5
  hazards in absence of assessment, 19
  humanistic, 5 (See also Humanistic
    therapies)
  and negative views on assessment, 19, 24-25
  utility of psychological reports in, 19-26

Quickie reports, 236-240

Recommendations, 4, 7, 29, 92, 100-101
Reevaluation of case, and psychological
  report, 203-204
Rehabilitation counseling, psychological
  report in, 211-212
Relevant behavior, defined, 110
Responsibility, 50-73, 104
Rhetoric in psychological report, 51

Rorschach, computer printout, 229,
  231-234

Scientistic constructs, 220
Scores, pertinence of, 209
Screening evaluation, 5, 6
Segmentalized reports, 111-112
Self-concept, 99
Self-image, 99
"Shotgun reports," 7, 72, 109, 119-120
Social and cultural factors, 5, 10, 99, 206,
  213
Speculation, 65
Stereotypy, 90
  Aunt Fanny, 52-54, 115-117, 186
  Barnum effect, 31, 54-55
  contextual approach vs., 220
  Madison Avenue report, 15, 54
  maladjustment bias, 56
  prosecuting attorney brief, 15, 56-57, 188,
    202
  trade-marked report, 15, 55-56
Subconclusions, 78
Suicidal potentiality, prediction of, 197
Summary, 93
Symptoms, target, 5

Teaching psychological report writing, 148
Team, 11-13
  forensic psychiatry, 11
  hierarchical structure, 12
  orientation of members and report content,
    83
  parents role on, 207
  personnel in, 11-12
  psychodiagnostic-therapeutic, 12, 236
  role of members, 12-13
  wagon wheel structure, 12-13
Terminology, 66-71
  psychiatric, 186
  psychological, 66, 186
  technical, 31, 66-71, 184
Test-by-test reporting, 85
"Testing for alternative means of
    management," 8
"Testing for areas," 8
Testing, role of, 5
"Test results," 88
Theoretical constructs, 109-110, 112-113
Thorn composite profile, 234, 235
Thought processes, formal, 97

Underlying psychological processes, 98